D0509840

Volume 2

BiG as LiFE

The Everyday Inclusive Curriculum

by
Stacey York

Cover Illustration by Athena Hampton
Interior Illustrations by Susan Avishai

 **Redleaf Press**

Book design by MacLean & Tuminelly
Interior illustrations by Susan Avishai
Cover illustration by Athena Hampton

Published by: Redleaf Press
                  a division of Resources for Child Caring
                  450 N. Syndicate, Suite 5
                  St. Paul, MN 55104

Distributed by: Gryphon House
                  Mailing Address:
                  P.O. Box 207
                  Beltsville, MD 20704-0207

Library of Congress Cataloging-in-Publication Data

York, Stacey, 1957–
      Big as life : the everyday inclusive curriculum / by Stacey York.
           p.   cm.
      Includes bibliographical references and index.
      ISBN 1-884834-39-6 (v. 1). — ISBN 1-884834-51-5 (v. 2)
      1. Multicultural education—United States—Curricula.   2. Early
childhood education—United States—Curricula.   3. Curriculum
planning—United States.   4. Social values—Study and teaching
(Early childhood)—United States.   5. Early childhood education–
–Activity programs—United States.
LC1099.3.Y67   1998
370.117'0973—dc21   98-17429
                                                         CIP

Information and ideas in previous publications were instrumental to writing this book. The following acknowledges these sources and lists the activities they apply to in *Big As Life*:

Bittinger, Gayle. *Learning and Caring About Our World* (Everett, WA: Totline, 1990): Air Pollution, I Am a Can Crusher. Byrnes, Deborah A. *"Teacher, They Called Me a _____!" Prejudice and Discrimination in the Classroom* (New York: Anti-Defamation League of B'nai B'rith, 1987): Ask First, Color Doesn't Change Anything. Crawford, Susan Hoy. *Beyond Dolls and Guns: 101 Ways to Help Children Avoid Gender Bias* (Portsmouth, NH: Heinemann, 1996): Bugs, Spiders, and Snakes. Curtis, Sandra R. *The Joy of Movement in Early Childhood* (New York: Teachers College, 1982): Egg Roll. Edwards, Carolyn Pope. *Social and Moral Development in Young Children* (New York: Teachers College, 1986): Adult Workers, When I Grow Up. Fralick, Paul. *Make It Multicultural—Musical Activities for Early Childhood Education* (Hamilton, Canada: Mohawk College, 1989): Muffins and More. Green, Moira D. *474 Science Activities for Young Children* (Albany, NY: Delmar, 1996): Feathers, Water, and Oil; Feel the Heat; Heavier, Harder, Faster; What's Serrated? Hall, Nadia Saderman, and Valerie Rhomberg. *The Affective Curriculum Teaching: The Anti-Bias Approach to Young Children* (Toronto: Nelson Canada, 1995): Balance It. Harrison, Marta. *For the Fun of It! Selected Cooperative Games for Children and Adults* (Philadelphia: Philadelphia Yearly Meeting of the Religious Society of Friends Peace Committee, 1975): Musical Hugs. Herr, Judy, and Yvonne Libby. *Creative Resources for the Early Childhood Classroom*, 2nd ed. (Albany, NY: Delmar, 1995): Homemade Toothpaste. The Human Rights for Children Committee. *Human Rights for Children: A Curriculum for Teaching Human Rights to Children Ages 3–12* (Alameda, CA: Hunter, 1992): Not Everyone Gets Enough. Jenkins, Peggy. *The Joyful Child: A Sourcebook of Activities and Ideas for Releasing Children's Natural Joy* (Tucson, AZ: Harbinger, 1989): Peepholes Can't See the Whole Picture, Jar of Pennies. Lewis, Barbara A. *The Kid's Guide to Service Projects* (Minneapolis: Free Spirit, 1995): Children's Television, Homeless Animals, Community Barriers, Coupon Collection. Moll, Patricia Buerke. *Children and Books I: African American Story Books and Activities for All Children* (Tampa: Hampton Mae Institute, 1991): People for Sale. Neuman, Susan B., and Renee P. Panoff. *Exploring Feelings: Activities for Young Children* (Atlanta: Humanics Limited, 1983): Danger! Don't Get Lost! Hot and Cold, Show Those Friendly Feelings, Sometimes We're Disappointed, Take Turns. Nichols, Wendy, and Kim Nichols. *Wonderscience: A Developmentally Appropriate Guide to Hands On Science for Young Children* (Albuquerque: Learning Expo, 1990): Build a Water Fountain, Flying Superheroes and Supersheroes, Plumbing. Oppenheim, Carol. *Science Is Fun! For Families and Classroom Groups* (St. Louis: Cracom, 1993): Earthworms, Food Chains, Pollution Solution, Treasure Boxes. Oehlberg, Barbara. *Making It Better: Activities for Children Living in a Stressful World* (St. Paul: Redleaf, 1996): A Community Called Hope, Dear Hero/Shero, Personal Shield or Armor, Power Hats. Orlick, Terry. *The Cooperative Sports & Games Book* (New York: Pantheon, 1978): Boa Constrictor, Find a Place for Everyone, Pass the Melon, Turtles. Orlick, Terry. *The Second Cooperative Sports & Games Book* (New York: Pantheon, 1982): Birds and Worms, Chopsticks and Bagels, Penny Bucket. Parker, Carol Johnson. "Multicultural Awareness Activities." *Dimensions 10* (1982): What's on the Inside? Peterson, Bob. "Columbus in the Elementary Classroom." *Rethinking Columbus: Teaching About the 500th Anniversary of Columbus's Arrival in America* (Milwaukee: Rethinking Schools, 1991): Indians Are Not Animals. Prutzman, Priscilla, et al. *The Friendly Classroom for a Small Planet* (Gabriola Island, Canada: New Society, 1988): Let's Build a Machine, Let's Draw a Store, What Kind of Store? Ramsey, Patricia G. "Social Studies That Is Multicultural." *Multicultural Education in Early Childhood Classrooms* (Washington, DC: National Education Association of the United States, 1992): How Does It Feel? Rice, Judith Anne. *The Kindness Curriculum: Introducing Young Children to Loving Values* (St. Paul: Redleaf, 1995): Friendship Bracelets. Rogers, Fred. *Mister Rogers' Plan and Play Book* (Pittsburgh: Family Communications, 1983): I Have Permission. Rockwell, Robert E., et al. *Everybody Has a Body* (Beltsville, MD: Gryphon, 1992): There's a Cold Going Around! Slaby, Ronald G., et al. *Early Violence Prevention Tools for Teachers of Young Children* (Washington, D.C.: NAEYC, 1995): Stand Up to Annoying Behavior, Stand Up to Cruelty, Stand Up to Hitting and Kicking, Stand Up to Name-Calling, We Can Trade, Walk Away. Smith, Charles A. *The Peaceful Classroom* (Beltsville, MD: Gryphon, 1993): Cooperative Drawings, Cooperative Skyscrapers, Give Away, I Can't Hear You, Give Kindness Coupons, Not Enough, Red Rover, What's this Feeling? Work Together. Sunal, Cynthia. *Early Childhood Social Studies* (Columbus, OH: Merrill, 1990): Do We Have Enough or Do We Need More? Wade, Rahima Carol. *Joining Hands: From Personal to Planetary Friendship in the Primary Classroom* (Tucson, AZ: Zephyr, 1991): Community Helpers. Williams, Leslie R., and Yvonne DeGaetano. *ALERTA: A Multicultural, Bilingual Approach to Teaching Young Children* (Reading, MA: Addison-Wesley, 1985): Cultural Money Traditions. Williams, Robert A., et al. *Mudpies to Magnets: A Preschool Science Curriculum* (Beltsville, MD: Gryphon, 1987): Are All the Oranges Alike? The Power of a Seed, Shiny Pennies. York, Stacey. *Roots and Wings: Affirming Culture in Early Childhood Programs* (St. Paul: Redleaf Press, 1991): Animal Picture Cards, Breads, Career Workers Picture Cards, Community Picture Cards, Draw Me/Draw You, Five Senses Picture Cards, Food Picture Cards, Friends Picture Cards, Friends Puzzles, Hero and Shero Picture Cards, How Would You Feel If…? Just Like You, Money Picture Cards, Multicultural Feast, My Voice, Pick a Friend, Playing with Clay, Real and Pretend Animals, Try It—You'll Like It! What Would You Do If…?

To all early childhood teachers
whose "good works" make a difference in children's lives each day
and who live without receiving appreciation, adoration,
or a worthy wage.

Contra Costa Child Care Council
1035 Detroit Ave., Ste. 200
Concord, CA 94518

CONTENTS

Acknowledgments

It has taken me almost five years to get *Big As Life* into your hands. The book may bear one name, but many people helped along the way. First and foremost, I want to thank God for the vision, inspiration, and perseverance. This book is not about me.

I'd like to thank Jane Toleno for helping me brainstorm the first drafts of the curriculum webs. Thanks to Eileen Nelson and Redleaf Press for their willingness to publish it. I thank Ruth Fahlman, Ann Griffin, Theresa Lenear, and Fran Mattson for reviewing the first draft. Special thanks to Mary Pat Martin for her careful reading and wonderful suggestions, and to Joan Bibeau for her careful review of the first draft. Her stories and ideas about how she would use *Big As Life* in her classroom were so affirming.

Thanks to Beth Wallace, Rosemary Wallner, and Mary Steiner Whelan, who edited and shaped *Big As Life*. Thanks to Sharon Cronin, Louise Derman-Sparks, Sharon Henry, and Cirecie Olatunji for providing support, encouragement, and the most incredible environment for thinking through anti-bias issues.

I'm always grateful for my women's spirituality group—Ann, Barbara, Denise, Mary Jo, Michele, and Nancy. For eleven years you've given me a safe place to be and grow.

A big hug and kiss to my husband, Dennis, who says my writing *Big As Life* meant him suffering so others could benefit. Thanks to my family, who kept asking, "Aren't you done with that yet?" They showed me that I could live among them *and* write, be it on the floor, couch, or bed. Writing seated cross-legged on the living room floor while hosting a Super Bowl party was my greatest accomplishment.

I couldn't have kept my family happy and finished *Big As Life* without my trusty Macintosh PowerBook, which got hit by lightning and didn't skip a beat. Whoever said soda pop, crumbs, drool, dog hair, wet tennis balls, and computers don't mix?

And finally, an "Atta dog!" to Biko and Dakotah, my two faithful writing companions.

PREFACE

Developing curriculum is a fun and creative process. Like many teachers, I have curriculum materials all over the place. Activity books with dog-eared and high-lighted pages fill my bookshelves. Open any drawer in my home or office and you are likely to find unintelligible notes about curriculum ideas scribbled on scrap paper, napkins, and the back of deposit slips. Down in the basement, banker's boxes full of old curriculum materials fill a storage closet. And of course there are my old reliable and beloved curriculum activity files that I compiled in college.

Even with all of these resources, curriculum planning was often frustrating. I knew I had good ideas, I just couldn't find them. Suddenly I had a compelling feeling to pull together all of my curriculum resources—and the organizing, writing, and rewriting began. Now many of my favorite resources are all in one place. I am excited to share them with you.

I have wanted to write a curriculum book for a long time. *Big As Life* is as much for me as it is for you. I would like to know how you used this book and found it helpful in planning your curriculum. You can write to me in care of the publisher, Redleaf Press. I also encourage you to share your ideas with others. Through sharing ideas, resources, and successes and failures, we can all make our curriculum even better!

When I first completed the unit webs and outlines, I laid them out on the floor. It was amazing to see them all at once. For the first time I knew how possible it is to weave multicultural/anti-bias education into the curriculum. Immediately upon seeing the webs, I knew that this curriculum was very do-able. It's not beyond us. It's within our reach. It just takes some time and energy to think it through. It takes a conscious effort to transform the curriculum from the ground up. The end result is a curriculum that is simple, straightforward, and practical.

At the same moment, I also realized that this was big. I kept telling people, "This is big. This is really big." After all, here were sixteen units that intentionally addressed emotions, social skills, culture, diversity, critical thinking, and social action. In a new and deeper way, I realized how multicultural/anti-bias education could change our lives. I knew with every bone in my body that early childhood educators could make a positive difference.

I relived this experience four years later, when I completed the first draft of the manuscript. It was late at night. Everyone else in my family had gone to bed. I sat staring at this huge stack of over 600 pages. My only thought was, "This is big." I walked around the house in amazement, mumbling to myself, "This is big. This is really big." And then a voice inside me said, "Stacey, *life* is big."

It's true. Life is big. What better gift to give children than to give them life, to give them big lives? Life alone is worthy of being the center of education. A curriculum of life gives each of us a sense of belonging, meaning, fullness, conviction, and commitment. This curriculum invites each of us—children, parents, and teachers—to embrace life.

This curriculum makes me laugh. Whenever I think about it, I smile, shrug my shoulders, and shake my head in amazement. Life is good. Life is to be lived. Life is big. Here before us is a curriculum that's as big as life.

Stacey York
September 1997

INTRODUCTION

Welcome to *Big As Life,* volume 2. The journey continues. As with volume 1, the purpose of this curriculum is to help early childhood teachers integrate multicultural/anti-bias education into the curriculum on a daily basis. *Big As Life* helps you foster the development of the whole child as you and the children explore human diversity in a deeper way. Simply stated, the purpose of this curriculum is

1. To offer a curriculum planning process that incorporates the children's and their families' lives.

2. To offer a curriculum that incorporates multicultural and anti-bias education.

3. To offer a curriculum that fosters the development of the whole child with equal emphasis on self-identity, cognitive, language, physical, creative, emotional, and social development.

4. To offer a curriculum that reflects and honors the lives of children and their families.

The Goals of a Transformative Curriculum

As a teacher, you've developed your own educational philosophy that reflects educational traditions, current theories, and the meaning you give to your professional experience. I, too, have been influenced by others. I first learned about the anti-bias curriculum as a graduate student at Pacific Oaks College. In identifying the nine goals of transformative curriculum that guide *Big As Life*, I have incorporated the four goals of an anti-bias curriculum that were originally put forth in Louise Derman-Sparks' *Anti-Bias Curriculum Tools for Empowering Young Children* and then further refined by Carol Brunson Phillips. These first four goals are

1. To foster each child's construction of a positive, knowledgeable self-identity within a cultural context.

2. To foster each child's comfortable, empathetic interaction with diversity among people.

3. To foster each child's critical thinking about bias.

4. To foster each child's ability to stand up for himself or herself and others in the face of bias.

The remaining five goals of the *Big As Life* curriculum deal with fostering children's development. They are

5. To foster each child's social and emotional development.

6. To foster each child's cognitive development.

7. To foster each child's language development.

8. To foster each child's creative development.

9. To foster each child's physical development.

All nine goals are discussed more fully in part one of the first volume of *Big As Life*. Specific objectives for the goals, which will help to make them more concrete, are found there and also in appendix A of this book.

Elements of a Transformative Curriculum

I've also been greatly influenced by the theories of Paulo Freire, a Brazilian educator. As a result, *Big As Life* represents a *transformative curriculum*. Transformative curriculum goes by many names. Sometimes it's called *liberatory education* or *social reconstructionist education*. These lengthy titles simply refer to the fact that this model of education attempts to foster personal empowerment of students and promote social change. In other words, it seeks to liberate the student and reconstruct society.

Transformative education recognizes that all of us are socialized to take our place in society. Our sense of self is influenced by prevailing social values and our social skills are shaped by social practices. The social realities of sexism, racism, classism, ethnocentrism, and heterosexism shape children's self-identity and the formation of prejudice and discriminatory behavior. Transformative education fosters a positive and knowledgeable self-identity by strengthening children's connections to their families, cultural communities, and geographic communities. Transformative education also prepares children to be active, involved citizens within a democracy by promoting decision making, problem solving, social action, community service, and human rights.

A transformative curriculum contains seven basic elements:

1. The curriculum is *contextually relevant*. It accurately reflects the cultural, social, political, and geographic context of the children and families.

2. The curriculum *accommodates the changing nature of knowledge* and supports children in making meaning out of their lives and the world around them.

3. Adults and children are *co-learners and co-teachers*, investigating the curriculum content together and learning from one another.

4. The curriculum is child-centered, reflecting the children's daily lives, questions, and passions.

5. The curriculum is *inquiry-based*. Children learn to think for themselves through open-ended questioning, problem posing, analyzing, reflecting, and problem solving.

6. The curriculum is *integrated* and addresses all areas of development. Traditional subject areas like reading and math are taught through the exploration of the content, which is the children's lives.

7. The curriculum results in *empowerment through taking reflective action*. Children learn to stand up for themselves and others.

How to Use This Book

Like the first volume of *Big As Life,* this second volume is a multicultural/anti-bias curriculum designed for children ages four through eight. It organizes and presents curriculum content through unit themes. Multicultural/anti-bias education explores humanity in all its forms—it is a curriculum about life. Every unit theme in this book addresses an element of life. Even the unit on animals emphasizes the relationship people have to animals and the importance of respecting, caring for, and protecting animals.

Part I contains nine curriculum units and resources. The units, presented in alphabetical order, include an introductory paragraph, a *web*, a *unit outline*, a list of materials to add to the *classroom interest areas*, and activity ideas for each of the *curriculum areas*.

At the beginning of each unit is a description of how young children might approach the topic. A web and unit outline help you visualize the content and flow. The section entitled "Teaching Through the Interest Areas" suggests materials to add to each interest area to support the curriculum unit. The areas are presented alphabetically: Art, Blocks, Dramatic Play, Literacy, Manipulatives, Music, Science, and Sensory.

"Investigating the Theme," the largest section of each unit, contains activity ideas to support the development of the whole child. Math, critical thinking, and science activities support children's cognitive development. Creative development is addressed by activities that focus on art and music. Also included are activities that focus on emotional, social, and language development. Physical development and health, safety, and nutrition activities can also be found within this section.

"Affirming Ourselves and One Another" contains activities that focus on cultural identity, diversity, bias and stereotypes, human rights, social action, and community service.

"Opening the Door" is the final activities section of each unit. In this section, suggestions to support parent involvement, parent education, classroom visitors, and field trips encourage parent and community involvement.

"Classroom Resources" contains a list of commercial resources that support the unit, including visual displays, children's books, videos, music, computer software, organizations, and teaching kits. At the beginning of each unit you will find a materials list for each classroom interest area. You will find more information, including company information and print materials, in the "Resources and References" section at the back of the book.

Like the units in the first volume, the units in this volume deal with familiar topics of interest to young children. The material in volume 2 can be thought of as following up the units in volume 1—the units in this book, are more complex and take the content further. For example, the "Community" theme in volume 2 is a logical extension of the unit on "Our Class" in volume 1. The topics in "Heroes and Sheroes," "Money," and "Work" are new to this book. Child development literature tells us that four to seven year olds begin to form ideas and attitudes about real and pretend, right and wrong, money, and work. But I've never seen popular early childhood curriculum address these issues.

Big As Life also gives you the tools to design your own curriculum. It's important that you aren't limited to the curriculum units presented in the two volumes. The units I've prepared may not be appropriate for the children, families, and communities with which you work. The best curriculum comes from the interests, experiences, and concerns of children, families, and teachers. You may be interested in exploring a topic that's not included in *Big As Life,* or you may want to move more slowly and focus on a more narrow topic (instead of a unit on foods, for example, you might want to do a unit on fruit, or even apples). Part 2, "Designing Your Own Transformative Curriculum," takes you through the nine steps I use to plan curriculum. The appendices include a complete list of curriculum goals and objectives, a blank web form, a blank curriculum planning form, and a blank lesson plan form.

As you use these curriculum units, please remember they are written from my perspective. I am a European American woman who lives in a Midwestern suburb. There may be goals, objectives, activities, or suggested materials that do not reflect you and your children. They may even conflict with the values and beliefs of your families. Please use *Big As Life* as a guide. Create curriculum that centers around your children, families, and community.

Also, recognize that *Big As Life* is a curriculum in process. I've been involved in the multicultural/anti-bias education movement for the past ten years. We're still in the early stages of transforming early childhood education curriculum from the ground up so that it reflects and honors all human life. This is an example of writing curriculum to share with others as soon as it's conceived. So let me know what works and what doesn't; you can write to me in care of the publishers. I'd love to hear your ideas for improving the curriculum.

For More Information

This introduction contains a brief summary of transformative curriculums. Please refer to volume 1 of *Big As Life* for a more complete explanation. The following resources will also provide you with additional information about transformative curriculums.

Arnold, Rick, and Bev Burke. *A Popular Education Handbook* (Toronto: CUSO/Ontario Institute for Studies in Education, 1983).

Bredekamp, Sue, and Teresa Rosegrant, eds. *Reaching Potentials: Appropriate Curriculum and Assessment for Young Children, Volume 1*, (Washington, DC: NAEYC, 1992).

Derman-Sparks, Louise, and the ABC Task Force. *Anti-Bias Curriculum: Tools for Empowering Young Children* (Washington, DC: NAEYC, 1989).

Freire, Paulo. *Education for Critical Consciousness* (New York: Continuum, 1973).

Freire, Paulo, and Ira Shor. *A Pedagogy for Liberation* (South Hadley: Bergin and Garvey, 1987).

Freire, Paulo. *Pedagogy of the Oppressed* (New York: Continuum, 1970).

———. *The Politics of Education* (South Hadley: Bergin and Garvey, 1985).

Horton, Miles, and Paulo Freire. *We Make the Road by Walking* (Philadelphia: Temple University Press, 1990).

Shor, Ira. *Critical Teaching and Everyday Life*. 2nd ed. (Chicago: University of Chicago Press, 1987).

Shor, Ira, ed. *Freire for the Classroom* (Portsmouth, NH: Boynton/Cook, 1987).

PART 1

The Curriculum Units

Animals

Animals fascinate many children. Animal movements and noises capture children's attention. Often their first experience with animals comes through a family or neighbor's pet animal. Most children today are also introduced to additional types of animals through television, children's books, and occasional trips to a zoo or a relative's farm. A unit on animals gives children a chance to explore their favorite animals, find out about unfamiliar animals, and learn how to interact with and care for animals.

Animals

TABLE OF CONTENTS

ANIMALS

 Look for this symbol
to find activities you
can use for circle time.

Web

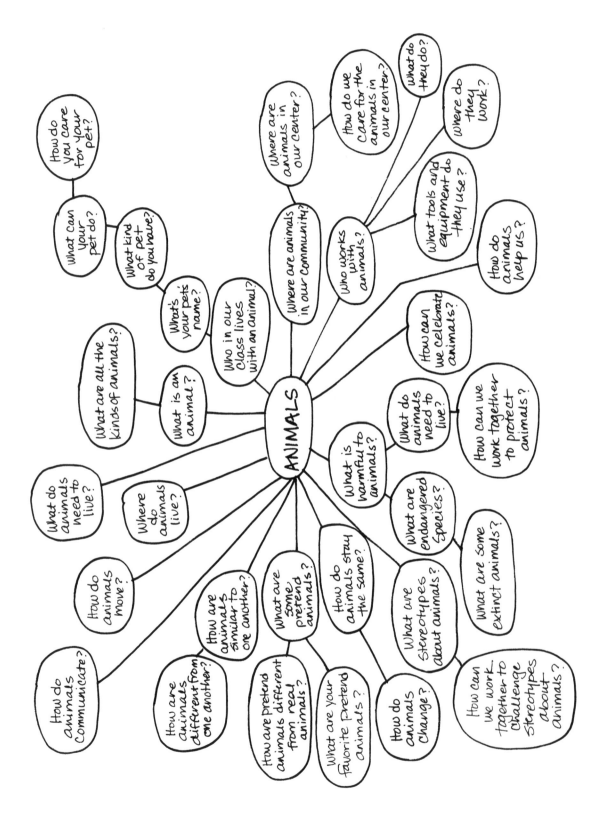

OUTLINE

I. Who in our class lives with an animal?
   A. What's your pet's name?
   B. What kind of pet do you have?
   C. What can your pet do?
   D. How do you care for your pet?
II. Where are animals in our community?
   A. Where are animals in our center?
   B. How do we care for the animals in our center?
III. Who works with animals?
   A. What do they do?
   B. Where do they work?
   C. What tools and equipment do they use?
IV. How do animals help us?
V. What is an animal?
   A. What do animals need to live?
   B. Where do animals live?
   C. How do animals move?
   D. How do animals communicate?
VI. What are all the kinds of animals?
   A. How are animals similar to one another?
   B. How are animals different from one another?
   C. How do animals stay the same?
   D. How do animals change?
VII. What are some pretend animals?
   A. What are your favorite pretend animals?
   B. How are pretend animals different from real animals?
VIII. What are stereotypes about animals?
IX. What is harmful to animals?
   A. What are some endangered animals?
   B. What are some extinct animals?
   C. What do animals need to live?
   D. How can we work together to protect animals?
X. How can we celebrate animals?

MATERIALS LIST

ART

skin-colored paints, crayons, markers, and construction paper

animal-colored art materials (for example, Animal Activity Kit and Animal Colors Felt, *Environments*; Animal Skins Craft Paper, *Kaplan*)

butcher paper roll

animal magazines (for example, *Audubon, Natural History, Ranger Rick, National Geographic*)

animal cookie cutters

animal-shaped sponges (for example, Animal Sponge Painters and Easy-Grip Animal Sponge Painters, *Lakeshore*; Animal Tracks Sponges, Forest Life Sponges, Pond Life Sponges, Sea Life Sponges, *Environments*)

BLOCKS

a variety of multicultural people figures, including figures of people with disabilities

animal play figures (for example, Big Cat Families, Buffalo Herd, Forest Animals, Frogs and Tortoises, Green Snake, Pandas and Tigers, Polar Animals, Savanna Animals Set, Sea Creatures, Whales and Babies, World Wildlife, *Environments*)

animal block sets (for example, Big Bruiser Deluxe Farm Set, *Beckley-Cardy*; Playmobil Animal Shelter, Playmobil Zoo, *Constructive Playthings*; Sea Life Aquarium, *Primary Educator*; Wooden Zoo Fences Set, *Environments*)

berry baskets for fences and zoo cages

scraps of paper and crayons or markers for making signs

carpet squares, branches, twigs, and pine needles

DRAMATIC PLAY

stuffed animals

veterinarian costumes (for example, Play Vet, *Constructive Playthings*, *Lakeshore*)

veterinarian's office: sign, hours of operation, table, chairs, medical supplies, pet care brochures, file folders, notepads, pencils

pet store: empty cages, empty pet food containers, pet toys, pet beds, pet food dishes, pet care books and magazines, cash register, pretend money, receipt pads, pencils, sign

LARGE MOTOR

materials that encourage children to move like animals (for example, *Animal Walks* and *Walk Like The Animals* cassette and guide, *Kimbo Educational*)

LITERACY

children's books: fiction, nonfiction, and bilingual books about animals (see resource list at the end of the unit)

cassette player and theme-related storybook cassettes

animal flannel board sets (for example, Animal Life Cycles Flannel Board Set, Endangered and Threatened Animals of North America Flannel Board Set, *Edvantage*; Animals of the World Flannel Board Set, *The Story Teller*; Sea Life Flannel Board Unit, Wild Animals Flannel Board Concept Kits, *Lakeshore*)

animal puppets (for example, Animal Puppets, *Environments*, *Sandy and Son*)

animal alphabets (for example, Animal Alphabet Photography, *Beckley-Cardy*)

MANIPULATIVES

animal puzzles (for example, Animals Giant Floor Puzzles, *Beckley-Cardy*; A World of Animals Puzzle, Killer Whales Puzzle, Environmental Awareness Jumbo Floor Puzzles, Ocean Life Puzzle, *Edvantage*; Baby Animals Puzzle, Sea Life Puzzle, Birds Floor Puzzle, Dogs Floor Puzzle, Ten Little Ducks Floor Puzzle, *Sandy and Son*; Cow Puzzle, Dolphin Family Puzzles, *Environments*; Animal Parents and Babies Puzzles, *Beckley-Cardy, Edvantage, Lakeshore*; Animal Puzzles, *Beckley-Cardy, Edvantage*; Endangered Animals Jumbo Floor Puzzle, *Edvantage, Lakeshore, Sandy and Son*)

animal board, card, matching, and lotto games (for example, Animal Match-Ups, Insects and Spiders, Sea Life, Wild Animals, Pets Theme Boxes, *Lakeshore*; Go-Go Giraffe Game, Ocean Pick Up Pairs, Wild Life Bingo, *Sandy and Son*; Jumbo Animal Dominoes, Zoo Domino, *Constructive Playthings*; Look Before You Leap Game, *Childswork/Childsplay*; Smithsonian Insect Lotto, *Edvantage*; Baby Animal Lotto, Ocean Lotto Game, *Edvantage, Sandy and Son*)

animal sorting sets (for example, Sea Sort, Farm Animals Sorting Shapes, Wild Animals Sorting Shapes, *Constructive Playthings, Lakeshore, Nasco*; Fun with Numbers Learning Pond, *Lakeshore*)

other animal manipulatives (for example, Build-a-Bug, Lacing and Tracing Animals, *Constructive Playthings*; Linking Elephants, *ABC School Supply*; Problem Solving Pocket Chart Kit, *Lakeshore*)

SCIENCE

fish tank, small animal for a classroom pet, ant or worm farm (for example, Giant Ant Farm or Ladybug Farm, *Lakeshore*)

magnifiers (for example, Bug Viewers, *Edvantage*)

pictures of animals

molds of animal footprints (for example, Animal Mold Model Unit, *Nasco*)

animal skins

animal bones or antlers

growth charts illustrated with animals (for example, Endangered Animal Growth Chart, *Kaplan*)

reference books

collections of different types of animal food and bedding

collections of animals (for example, Insect Collection, Sea Life Collection and Cards, Whales and Poster, *Constructive Playthings*; Animals and Their Environments Discovery Sets, *Lakeshore*)

SENSORY

dirt, sand, or potting soil

twigs, evergreen stems, rocks, and pebbles

small plastic animals

pine shavings, animal food pellets, or birdseed

Teaching Through the Interest Areas

Art

Add animal magazines, animal cookie cutters, clay or playdough, and animal-shaped sponges to the art area.

Blocks

Encourage zoo play by adding zoo animals, fencing, berry baskets, scrap paper, and crayons to the block area.

Set out rubber, plastic, wood, cloth, and carved-bone animals representing jungle, tropical forest, desert, and sea life to encourage animal-related play.

Set out twigs, carpet squares, branches, pine needles, and small animal figures to encourage children to make homes for the animals.

Dramatic Play

Turn the dramatic play corner into a veterinarian's office. Add sign, hours of operation, a table, chairs, stuffed animals, medical supplies, pet care brochures, file folders, notepads, and pencils.

Set up a pet store. Add stuffed animals, empty cages, empty pet food containers, pet toys, pet beds, pet food dishes, pet care books and magazines, a cash register, pretend money, receipt pads, pencils, and a sign. Use unit blocks to make cages, or make a circle with a piece of yarn for each animal.

Literacy

Set out a collection of fiction, nonfiction, and bilingual animal books. Include a tape player and animal-related storybook cassettes, animal flannel board sets, animal puppets, and materials for making journals and books.

Manipulatives

Add puzzles, lotto games, matching games, and sorting games that deal with animals to the manipulative area.

Music

Set out cassette tapes of animal songs and sounds and music that includes animal sounds.

Science

Add fish or a small animal to the classroom. Set out pictures of animals, molds of animal footprints, animal skins, animal bones or antlers, reference books, and collections of different types of animal food and bedding.

Sensory

Create different animal habitats in the sensory table using 1 to 2 inches of dirt, sand, or potting soil and small plastic animals. Add twigs, evergreen stems, rocks, and pebbles as additional props.

For a different sensory experience, put pine shavings (a bedding material used in cages), animal food pellets, or birdseed in the sensory table.

ACTIVITIES:
INVESTIGATING THE THEME

Creative Development

Animal Collages. Make a collage by cutting out magazine pictures of animals and gluing them onto construction paper.

Animal Masks. Set out a variety of collage materials and encourage children to make an animal mask. Include paper sacks, paper plates, construction paper scraps, tissue paper, feathers, buttons, felt tip markers, crayons, scissors, hole punch, glue, and string.

Birdseed Mobiles. Squeeze out a squiggly design of glue onto waxed paper. Sprinkle birdseed over the glue. Let the design dry overnight. The next day, carefully peel away the waxed paper. Tie string to the design and hang it from the ceiling.

Carving. Tell the children that some people enjoy carving things out of stone. Some Inuit sculptors pick out a stone and sit with it. They spend time with the stone and get to know it. They listen to the stone, and when they know the stone well, they find the shape or animal that the stone wants to become. And they begin carving the stone into that shape. Show the children pictures of Inuit people carving stone and pictures of their artwork. Give each child a piece of sandstone. Encourage them to carry the stone with them all morning. Tell them that after lunch they can carve their stone into any shape they want. Encourage them to listen to their stone. Maybe it will tell them what shape it wants to become.

Fish in the Sea. Encourage children to draw and cut out all kinds of different fish. Glue the fish to blue construction paper. Lay a piece of tissue paper over the picture. Paint the tissue with a thin layer of watered down glue.

Handprint Animals. Encourage children to dip the palms of their hands into a pan of paint to make a handprint. Let the handprints dry. Then challenge the children to see if they can turn their handprints into pictures of animals.

Stuffed Animals. Set out the easels. Encourage children to paint a picture of their favorite animal. Let the picture dry. Put a second sheet of easel paper behind the first sheet and cut out the animal pictures. Staple the two forms together around the edges, leaving a wide enough opening so that you can stuff the animal picture with crumpled newspaper. Once the animal is stuffed, staple the rest of the edge closed.

Wildlife Artists. Take watercolors, brushes, and art paper along on a field trip to the zoo. Invite children to pretend to be wildlife artists. Ask them to watch an animal very closely and then see if they can paint a picture of it.

Critical Thinking

Animal Friends. Facilitate a discussion about animals. Ask the children the following questions:

> How do you make friends with an animal?
>
> How does an animal make friends with us?
>
> How can we care for animals?
>
> How can we keep animals safe?
>
> What happens to animals when people are mean to them?
>
> How does an animal act if people have been mean to it?
>
> What if you were an animal and people hit and kicked you, or didn't feed you, or kept you locked up—how would you feel? How would you act?
>
> How do you know when you are ready to get a pet?

Pets and Wild Animals. Encourage children to think about the differences between pets and wild animals. Start a discussion by asking the following questions:

> What is a pet animal like?
>
> What is a wild animal like?
>
> How can you tell the difference between a pet animal and a wild animal?
>
> What makes a pet animal a pet?
>
> What makes an animal wild?

Emotional Development

Animal Feelings. Ask the children how they are feeling. Then ask them to think of an animal that reminds them of how they are feeling. Model describing your feelings this way for the children ("I'm feeling tired like a dog" or "I'm feeling happy like a bird"), and then invite them to do the same. You could also set out a variety of animal puppets and children could pick the puppet that best matches how they are feeling.

The Animal I Am. Ask children to identify themselves as an animal. Ask open-ended questions like, "If you could be any kind of animal, what kind of animal would you be? Why would you like to be that kind of animal? What do you like about that animal?"

How Do You Feel About Animals? Show the children photographs of people interacting with different animals. One picture might be of a person petting a dog, holding a snake, or milking a cow. With each photograph, ask the children to describe what is happening in the pictures. Then ask, "How does the person in the picture feel? How would you feel if you were in that situation?"

Pretend Animals. Introduce the concept of pretend animals. For instance, bring examples of cartoon animals, stuffed animals, animal puppets, and plastic animal figures to group time to show the children. Invite children to bring a stuffed animal to school for a day. Ask them the following questions:

> Who sleeps with a stuffed animal?
>
> Why do some children sleep with a stuffed animal?
>
> Who carries a stuffed animal around with them?
>
> Why do some children carry a stuffed animal with them?

Health, Safety, and Nutrition

Don't Get Bitten. Young children who have little or no experience with animals don't know how to approach and touch animals. Behaviors that set children up to get bitten include screaming, flailing arms, jumping up and down, grabbing, and pulling the animal's ears, nose, tail, and fur. These behaviors scare and hurt animals. Teach children how to approach, handle, and pet animals so that they won't get bitten. Also teach them what to do if they are afraid of an animal.

Tell the children to stand still with their hands at their sides and let the animal come to them. Suggest slowly putting out a hand and letting the animal smell the back of it. The children could gently stroke the animal's back and talk to the animal using their soft voices. You may want to have the children role-play this process—let one child be the dog, rabbit, cat, or guinea pig while the rest of the children practice approaching gently.

Teach children that if they are scared of an animal or they don't like it touching them, they can tell it "No" or "Off" using their strong indoor voices. If it's a small animal, they can ask the teacher or another adult to take it from them, or walk away.

You may want to follow up this activity with a visit from a pet so children have a chance to practice these skills.

Language Development

Home Language. *Introduce the children to the words for different animals in American Sign Language and the children's home languages.*

Animal Picture Cards. Use a commercial set of animal pictures or make your own by cutting out large magazine pictures of animals and gluing them onto construction paper. Hold up one picture at a time. Ask open-ended questions like the following:

Who can tell me about this picture?

What do you see?

What kind of animal is it?

What sound does this animal make?

Where does this animal live?

What else can you tell me about this animal?

Animal Picture Stories. Sit down with a small group of children and some animal pictures. Show the children one picture at a time. Ask the children what they see in the pictures. Encourage the children to make up a story about the animals in the pictures. If possible, write down the children's stories. Older children could write their own stories and read them to one another.

Animal Sounds. Listen to a cassette tape of animal sounds and try to name the animal by the sound that it makes. Invite children to make the sound of each animal.

My Pet Animal Book. Encourage children to dictate and illustrate a story about their pet animals or animals they would like to have as pets. Ask the following questions:

What kind of pet do you have?

What is your pet's name?

What does your pet eat?

How much does your pet eat?

How do you care for your pet?

What tools, equipment, and toys does your pet need?

Name That Animal. Collect pictures of a variety of animals and bring them to circle time. Hide the pictures from the children's view. Give the children clues about the animals in the pictures. Describe its color, shape, size, the sound it makes, and where it lives. Let the children guess after each clue. When a child guesses the correct animal, give him or her the picture to hold while you continue to play the game. You could also use pretend animals for this activity instead of pictures.

Not Say a Single Word. Here's a fun poem about animals that can help children transition from activity to quiet at circle time.

> We'll hop, hop, hop like a bunny
> And run, run, run like a dog;
> We'll walk, walk, walk like an elephant,
> And jump, jump, jump like a frog,
> We'll swim, swim, swim like a goldfish,
> And fly, fly, fly like a bird;
> We'll sit right down and fold our hands,
> And not say a single word!

(*Finger Frolics*, Liz Cromwell and Dixie Hibner. Livonia, MI: Partner Press, 1976; p. 57. Used with permission.)

Math

Animals and Cages. Set out small plastic animals and an equal number of small plastic berry baskets. Invite the children to use the baskets as cages and pair one animal with each. For older children, make a written label for each of the cages and encourage them to put each animal in the cage with the appropriate label.

Animal Match. Make four or more sets of animal matching cards. Find duplicate photos in magazines, use a color photocopier to make duplicates, or trace animal stencils. Place the cards in a basket and encourage children to find the matching sets.

Animal Shapes. Set out a variety of paper geometric shapes, glue, and construction paper. Invite children to see if they can make animals by arranging the shapes on the construction paper.

Animal Sort. Collect a variety of animal pictures or small, realistic plastic animals. Place the animals or pictures in a basket. Set out the basket along with a sorting tray. Invite the children to classify the animals any way they like.

How Big? As you learn about different animals, find out the height and length of baby and adult animals that the children are interested in. Use a tape measure or some other measuring tool to mark the size of the animals on the floor or wall. You can also compare the children's height to the animals' height.

In My Estimation. Show the children a play barn from the block area, or make a barn out of a shoe box. Ask the children how many animals they think will fit into the barn. Write down each child's estimate. Let them see how many toy animals they can fit into the barn. Compare the children's estimates with the actual number. Whose estimate was closest?

Who's Behind the Door? Glue full-size pictures of individual animals to a piece of 8- by 11-inch construction paper. Cut a small door in the middle of a manila file folder. Place the animal picture inside the folder. Ask the children to keep the folder closed and open the door. Can they guess what kind of animal it is by looking at the part of the animal that shows through the door? Invite the children to open the folder to check their answers. Replace the picture with another of a different animal and repeat the activity.

BIG AS LIFE

Music

Six Little Ducks. This popular children's song can easily be extended. Foster creativity and imagination by inviting the children to insert other animals and animal sounds.

Tune: *Bell Bottom Trousers*

Six little ducks that I once knew
fat ones, skinny ones, short ones too
But the one little duck with the feathers on his back
He led the others with a quack, quack, quack
quack, quack, quack, quack, quack, quack,
He led the others with a quack, quack, quack
Down to the river they would go
wibble, wobble, wibble, wobble to and fro
But the one little duck with the feathers on his back
He led the others with a quack, quack, quack
quack, quack, quack, quack, quack, quack,
He led the others with a quack, quack, quack

Zoo Animals. Adapt this song by inserting the names of other zoo animals, such as the monkey, elephant, giraffe, lion, turtle, bear, and snake.

Tune: *The Muffin Man*

Do you know the kangaroo
The kangaroo, the kangaroo?
Oh, do you know the kangaroo
That lives in the zoo?

(*Creative Resources for the Early Childhood Classroom*, second edition, Judy Herr and Libby Yvonne. Albany, NY: Delmar Publishers, 1995; p. 607. Used with permission.)

Physical Development

Be an Animal. Divide the class into small groups of three or four. Invite each group to decide what animal they want to be. Then challenge them to work together to use their bodies to make that animal. Ask the children, "Can the animal move? Can it lie down? Can it curl up or stretch? Can it roll over?"

Birds and Worms. Invite the children to sit around a parachute. One child, the "worm," gets under the parachute and crawls around. Another child, the "bird," gets on top of the parachute and crawls around trying to catch the worm. The rest of the children and adults raise and lower the chute to keep the worm hidden from the bird. The game ends when the worm is caught. Select another two children and repeat the game. Continue until each child has had a turn.

Boa Constrictor. Invite children to move like snakes across the floor. Then invite children to pair up to make a two-person snake by lying on their stomachs on the floor and holding onto the ankles of the person lying in front of them. Encourage

them to slink and slither like a snake across the floor. Older children can work together to make three-, four-, or five-person snakes. You could also challenge children to try to make their snake roll over on its back or curl up and go to sleep.

Butterflies. You might want to read *The Very Hungry Caterpillar* to the children before doing this activity. Invite the children to move their bodies like a caterpillar that grows and changes and turns into a butterfly. Ask them if they can move their bodies like a caterpillar crawling, eating leaves, making a cocoon, and hanging very still from a branch inside the cocoon. Then ask the children if they can move their bodies like a butterfly emerging from a cocoon, drying its wings, and flying.

Elephant March. Invite children to sit in a circle on the floor. Walk around the circle singing the elephant song. Pick one child to join you while you continue singing the song and marching around the circle. That child then picks another child to join you. Continue until all of the children are holding hands, marching around the classroom.

> One elephant went out to play on a spider's web one day.
> I had such enormous fun, I called on another elephant to come.
> *(Shout)* Hey elephant!
> Two elephants went out to play on a spider's web one day.
> We had such enormous fun, we called on another elephant to come.
> *(Shout)* Hey elephant!

Turtles. For this activity you will need a blanket or quilt for every four to seven children. Ask the children to form a small group and get on their hands and knees, all facing the same direction. Drape the blanket over them like a turtle's shell. Challenge them to move in one direction. If they move in all different directions, they will lose or drop their shell. If the children enjoy this activity, get some cardboard and let the children paint the cardboard to resemble a turtle shell.

Science

Animal Life Cycles. Exploring the life cycle of animals helps children recognize ways in which animals stay the same and ways in which they change. Make or purchase a set of animal life cycle sequence cards. Try to have at least three pictures of each animal's life stages. You might include a dog, cat, horse, cow, butterfly, bird, whale, lion, and bear.

Bones. Save the bones when you cook meat like chicken, turkey, or beef. Ask parents to save theirs as well. If there is still meat on the bones, boil them in water. Wash the bones and set them on the counter to dry. Place the dry bones on a tray in the science area. Invite children to sort the bones. You might also include a picture and label for each of the animals and the children can try to match the bone to the animal it came from.

Endangered Animals. Introduce children to the fact that some animals are endangered. They are having a hard time staying alive. Animals become endangered when people destroy or change the places where animals live or when too many of them are killed for food or for other reasons. The changes in their habitat make it hard for the animals to have babies and raise their families. If all of the animals of one type die, they become extinct. Start a picture file or a classroom book of endangered animals. Ask children to look for information about endangered animals in books, magazines, and on television.

Feathers, Water, and Oil. Help children recognize that some feathers are water-resistant and other feathers dry after becoming wet, but when bird feathers get oil on them, the feathers can't dry and the birds get sick or die. Set out a variety of feathers, small dishes of water, small dishes of oil, eyedroppers, and magnifying glasses. Ask the children, "What do you think will happen if a bird is out in the rain? What do you think will happen if we drop water on some bird feathers?" Invite children to use the eyedroppers to drip water onto the feathers. Some of the feathers will resist the water and the water will bead up. Other types of feathers will get wet and then dry over time. Tell the children that sometimes there are oil spills. Ask the children what they think will happen if oil gets on bird feathers. Invite the children to drip oil onto the feathers and observe what happens. Show children pictures of oil spills and animals affected by oil spills.

Feed the Birds. Tie a string around the top of a pinecone. Stuff the pinecone with a mixture of cornmeal and peanut butter, and then roll the bird feeder in birdseed. Hang the feeder from a tree branch outside the classroom at least 6 inches from the trunk so squirrels won't get it. Make a chart to record the different types of birds that use the feeder. Set out reference books to help children learn about the habits of the local birds.

Observing Animals. Children can learn a lot about animals by watching them in their natural habitat. Ask the children, "Where could we watch animals in nature? What would we need to do to watch animals? What would we need to watch animals?" This discussion might lead to a trip to a nature center or hanging a bird feeder outside the classroom window.

Paw Prints. Make plaster molds of an animal's paw prints. Fill a plastic dish tub with wet sand. Press the animal's paw in the sand. Fill the print with plaster and let it harden (about 10 minutes). The children can compare the plaster mold with the animal's real paw.

Social Development

Animals Help Us. Learn about how animals help us. Help children explore which animals give us food, which animals give us clothes and shoes, and which animals help people with disabilities. Also explore which animals help protect us and which animals entertain us.

Be Kind to Animals. Bring a stuffed animal like a dog, cat, or rabbit to circle time and show the children how to hold it carefully and gently. Pass the stuffed animal around the circle from child to child and ask each child to hold and pet the stuffed animal using their gentle touch.

Be Kind to Pets. Help children think about how to be kind to animals. Facilitate a conversation with the class about how to treat animals. Ask questions like the following:

> Who has a pet?
>
> How do you take care of your pet?
>
> What does a pet need to be healthy?
>
> What are gentle ways of handling a pet?
>
> What are kind ways of touching a pet?
>
> What are kind ways of talking to a pet?

Classroom Pet. Having a pet teaches children about interdependence, responsibility, caring for others, and gentleness. Learn about animals that make good classroom pets. As a group, decide what type of animal to get as a pet. Identify all of the things the animal will need. Learn about what type of care it will need. Take a trip to a local pet store or humane society and select a pet for the classroom. Carefully teach the children how to care for the pet. Vote on a name for the pet. Rotate the responsibility for feeding the pet among the children.

Pet Care. Offer to take care of someone's pet rodent or fish for a few weeks. With the children, read books about the care of the pet. Make a chart listing all the tasks involved in caring for the animal, and then set up a system for sharing the caretaking tasks.

Stand Up to Cruelty. Help children develop assertiveness in the face of cruelty to animals. Use a doll or puppet and a stuffed animal to role-play the experience of being cruel to an animal. Ask the children, "How do you think the animal feels? What can we say to the puppet who is being cruel to the animals?" Discuss the children's answers. Tell the children that standing up for yourself and others is a way to respond that is strong and doesn't hurt anyone. You have to stand tall and proud, look at the other person, speak in your strong voice, and speak your truth (what you know, what you feel, and what you need). Model standing up for yourself and others with the puppet. Reenact the cruelty incident and have the children stand tall, look at the puppet who was being cruel, and say in a strong voice, "Stop hurting the animal."

ACTIVITIES: AFFIRMING OURSELVES AND ONE ANOTHER

Human Rights

People have the right to have their cultural relationships with animals respected. Some Native American tribes have the right to hunt or fish at certain times or in the certain ways that have been used from the time when they were the only people on the land that became the United States and Canada. Some people don't kill animals for food because of religious or cultural reasons, and so they don't eat meat at all. Some people only eat meat from certain kinds of animals or meat that has been prepared in certain ways. Some people use animals for transportation, to make clothing, or to help them raise food for their families and community. Some people have pets, and some people don't think it's okay to have pets.

BARRIER: It's easy for us to think that there's only one right way to treat animals. American culture is not set up to be friendly to people who don't eat meat or only eat kosher meat—it can be very hard to find the kind of food that people are used to or need to eat.

Animals have the right to be treated well and with respect by people, whether they are pets, wild animals, working animals, or animals that are raised for food.

BARRIER: In order to make more money, many companies that raise animals for food don't treat the animals very well. Sometimes pets are neglected. Sometimes the places where wild animals need to live (the wilderness, the rain forest, the ocean) are destroyed by companies who want to make money from the land or from the trees. There are getting to be so many people on the earth that there isn't as much room for the animals.

DISCUSSION QUESTIONS: Help children think about the many kinds of relationships people can have with different kinds of animals and the many ways that people can be respectful of animals. You could ask them questions like, "What do you think wild animals need to live and be healthy? Are there stereotypes about some wild animals that encourage people to treat them badly? Why do you think wild animals don't get what they need? What can we do to change that? What do you think animals that are raised for food need to live and be healthy? Why do you think they don't get what they need? How can we change that?"

Cultural Identity

Animal Folktales. Select and read a variety of animal folktales and legends from the cultures represented in your class. You may want to include folktales with an animal as a trickster character or books that include animals that are sacred or very important to the cultures represented in your class. Help children recognize that often animal folktales use animals from the region where the folktale originated. Invite the children to identify all of the animals in the stories, or act out the stories. Ask the children, "Why do stories use animals as characters?"

Cultures and Animals. Different cultures use different animals for food and clothes. Different cultures represent different animals in their art and dance. Help children explore the role of animals in the cultures represented in your classroom. For example, use animal-related folktales or artwork from the cultures represented in your classroom. Often the animals represented in these stories and artwork are native to the local region.

Diversity

Alike and Different Animals. Explore the ways in which animals are similar and different from one another. For instance, the same animal (a horse, for example) may eat different kinds of food (hay and grain), have several different body parts (legs, head, neck, withers) or different coverings on parts of its body (hair, hooves), move in different ways (walk, trot, gallop), make different sounds (whinny, neigh), and have different colors on its body. Different animals (horses and cows, for example) may eat the same food (hay), have similar body parts (legs, head) or body covering (hair, hooves), move in similar ways (walk), have similar sounds, or have the same body color.

Animal Sorts. Make an animal sorting game. Cut out pictures and photographs of animals. Glue them to index cards. Write the name of the animal on the back. Show the children the pictures and see if they can identify all the animals. Next, ask the children to sort the animal pictures by type. You could use the following categories: pet, farm, zoo, forest, pond, ocean, rain forest, African Savannah, desert, Arctic, Antarctic. Try starting with a few simple categories, and gradually introduce others. You could make a mat for each of the animal types and the children could put the picture on the correct mat.

Male and Female Animals. Give children a chance to explore the different coloring, markings, sizes, and roles of male and female animals. You could collect pictures or small plastic models of the male and female animals of different species. Use trips to the zoo or nature center and reference books to help children learn about the similarities and differences between male and female animals.

Bias and Stereotypes

Animal Stereotypes. Identify stereotypes children may have about animals. For instance, children may believe that all dogs and bugs bite, all rodents are dirty, and all snakes are slimy. In Minnesota there has been a widespread campaign to educate children and adults about the timber wolf because there is a widespread stereotype that wolves are mean and will attack people. Hands-on experience and simple, accurate information about these animals can help reduce children's fears that result from misinformation.

Bugs, Spiders, and Snakes. Often we tend to assume that all bugs, spiders, and snakes are males. How often have you said, "Get him, get him!" when you see a spider crawling up the wall? Or "What's he doing?" when you see a snake or other animal? Introduce children to the practice of calling bugs and animals "it" when they can't be sure of its gender.

Indians Are Not Animals. A common source of misinformation about and disrespect to Native Americans is children's books in which the cartoon animal characters dress up or pretend to be "Indians." Introduce the concept of stereotypes, false ideas about a whole group of people. There are stereotypes about how people look, think, talk, act, dress, eat, and live. Tell children that there are stereotypes that make Native Americans seem weird, old fashioned, and more like animals than people. These stereotypes make Native Americans mad and sad. Show children the books *Clifford's Halloween,* by Norman Bridwell, and *Alligators All Around,* by Maurice Sendak. Both of these books have animals dressing up like Indians. Ask children to find the stereotypic pictures. Compare those books to a photographic book of contemporary Native Americans like *Native Americans: 500 Years After* by Michael Dorris. Note: Children need to have been exposed to lots of realistic and current pictures of Native Americans prior to presenting this activity.

Real and Pretend Animals. Make a sorting game to help children begin to tell the difference between real images of animals and pretend images that are unfair (stereotypic). Label one side of a manila file folder "Real" and the other side "Pretend." Gather a variety of photographs and pictures of animals—some that are realistic and some that are not realistic, such as a drawing of a cartoon bear wearing an Indian headdress. Talk about how the stereotypes make fun of people and hurt people's feelings. Invite the children to sort the pictures using the file folder.

The Ugly Duckling. Use the classic children's book *The Ugly Duckling* by Hans Christian Andersen to introduce children to the biased behaviors of rejecting and excluding someone because they look different. Read the book and then ask the children questions like these:

> Why didn't the other ducks like the ugly duckling?
>
> How did he feel?

Was that fair?

What could the ducks have done instead?

What lesson can we learn from this story?

Community Service

Sponsor an Animal. As a class or school, sponsor an endangered animal or an animal at your local zoo.

Social Action Suggestions

Animal Clinic. As a class, work with your local veterinarian to sponsor a low-cost animal clinic.

Homeless Animals. Start an information campaign to educate others about the numbers and needs of abandoned and homeless animals in your community.

Pet Adoption. Work with the local humane society to sponsor a pet adoption day.

ACTIVITIES: OPENING THE DOOR

Classroom Visitors

Invite a person who uses a dog guide to come to the classroom and talk with the children about how the dog helps him and appropriate ways of interacting with a dog guide.

Invite someone from the humane society, Department of Natural Resources, or an animal rights group to talk about what animals in your region need to be safe, what hurts them, and what children can do to help animals be healthy and safe.

Invite a veterinarian to talk about animal care and keeping pets healthy.

Field Trips

Visit a local pet shop, veterinarian clinic, or zoo.

Parent Involvement

Ask parents to bring family pets to school.

Parent Education

Invite a representative from the local humane society to lead a workshop on how to pick a family pet or how to teach your children to behave around cats and dogs.

Ask parents to share animal folktales, songs, or dances from their home culture. Invite parents to share animal-related interests, such as raising and breeding animals, hunting, or fishing.

CLASSROOM RESOURCES

Children's Books

About Birds: A Guide For Children, Cathryn Sill (Atlanta: Peachtree, 1997).

Alligators All Around, Maurice Sendak (New York: Harper, 1962)

Animal Faces, Akira Satoh and Kyoko Toda (Brooklyn, NY: Kane/Miller, 1996).

Animal Tracks, Arthur Dorros (New York: Scholastic, 1991).

Animalia, Graeme Base (New York: Abrams, 1987).

Animals Born Alive And Well, Ruth Heller (New York: Putnam, 1982).

The Animal's Lullaby, Tom Paxton (New York: Morrow, 1993).

Antartida, Helen Cowcher (New York: Farrar, 1993).

Aye-Ayes, Bears, And Condors: An ABC Of Endangered Animals And Their Babies, Neecy Twinem (New York: Freeman, 1994).

The Baby Zoo, Bruce McMillan (New York: Scholastic, 1995).

Biggest, Strongest, Fastest, Steve Jenkins (New York: Ticknor, 1995).

Bugs, Nancy Winslow Parker and Joan Richards Wright (New York: Morrow, 1988).

Chibi: A True Story From Japan, Barbara Brenner and Julia Takaya (New York: Clarion, 1996).

Chickens Aren't The Only Ones, Ruth Heller (New York: Putnam, 1981).

Clifford's Halloween, Norman Bridwell (New York: Four Winds, 1967).

David McPhail's Animals A To Z, David McPhail (New York: Scholastic, 1993).

The Day The Goose Got Loose, Reeve Lindbergh (New York: Puffin, 1995).

Dogs Don't Wear Sneakers, Laura Numeroff (New York: Simon, 1993).

Endangered Animals, Faith McNulty (New York: Scholastic, 1996).

Faithful Elephants: The True Story Of Animals, People, And War, Yukio Tsuchiya (Boston: Houghton, 1997).

Feathers And Fools, Mem Fox (San Diego: Harcourt, 1996).

Going On A Whale Watch, Bruce McMillan (New York: Scholastic, 1992).

The Great White Owl Of Sissinghurst, Dawn Langley Simmons (New York: McElderry, 1993).

Hanna's Cold Winter, Trish Marx (Minneapolis: Carolrhoda, 1993).

Have You Seen Birds? Joanne Oppenheim (New York: Scholastic, 1988).

How Smudge Came, Nan Gregory (New York: Walker, 1997).

Island Baby, Holly Keller (New York: Morrow, 1995).

Leave That Cricket Be, Barbara Ann Porte (New York: Greenwillow, 1993).

Little Elephant, Tana Hoban and Miela Ford (New York: Greenwillow, 1994).

My Buddy, Audrey Osofsky (Boston: Holt, 1994).

Naptime, Laptime, Eileen Spinelli (New York: Scholastic, 1995).

No Dodos: A Counting Book Of Endangered Animals, Amanda Wallwork (New York: Scholastic, 1993).

On My Horse, Eloise Greenfield (New York: Harper, 1995).

A Place For Grace, Jean Davies Okimoto (Seattle: Sasquatch, 1996).

A Possible Tree, Josephine Haskell Aldridge (New York: Simon, 1993).

Rain Forest Babies, Kathy Darling (New York: Walker, 1997).

Story Of A Dolphin, Katherine Orr (Minneapolis: Lerner, 1995).

Subway Sparrow, Leyla Torres (New York: Farrar, 1993).

Tabby: A Story In Pictures, Aliki (New York: Harper, 1995).

Tracks In The Wild, Betsy Bowen (Boston: Little Brown, 1993).

The Ugly Duckling, Hans Christian Andersen (Mahwah, NJ: Troll, 1989).

Under Your Feet, Joanne Ryder (New York: Simon, 1990).

The Very Hungry Caterpillar, Eric Carle (New York: Putnam, 1984).

Music

Grammer, Red. *Teaching Peace* (Smilin' Atcha, 1986).

"Barnyard Boogie"

Hartmann, Jack. *Make A Friend, Be A Friend* (Educational Activities, 1990).

"Let's Take Care of All the Animals"

"Sherlock The Pup"

———. *One Voice For Children* (Educational Activities, 1993).

"Swim To The Top"

Music For Little People. *Fiesta Musical,* with Emilio Delgado (Music for Little People, 1994).

"Los Pollitos"

Orozco, Jose Luis. *Animales Y Movimiento* (Educational Record Center, 1992).

Pirtle, Sarah. *Two Hands Hold The Earth* (Gentle Wind, 1984).

"Pelorus Jack"

"Wish I Was A Whale"

Raffi. *Rise And Shine* (Troubadour, 1982).

"He's Got The Whole World"

Rogers, Sally. *What Can One Little Person Do?* (Round River, 1992).

"Migratin'"

"Where Do The Animals Put All Their Trash?"

Whales And Dolphins (Environments).

What's In The Sea? (Kimbo Educational).

Visual Displays

Beckley-Cardy
Endangered Wildlife Poster

Lakeshore
Animal Alphabet Pictures

Knowledge Unlimited
Marine Life Posters
North American Animals Posters

Northern Sun Merchandising
Making A Difference Poster

Sandy and Son
Farm Animals Poster
Freshwater Fish Poster
Insects Poster
The Living Sea Poster
Marine Fish Poster
Whales and Dolphins Poster
Zoo Animals Poster

Syracuse Cultural Workers
Fragile Kingdom Poster

Videos

Animal Alphabet, by National Geographic (Educational Record Center, 1993).

At the Zoo (Constructive Playthings, 1985).

Bugs Don't Bug Us! (Bo Peep Productions, 1991).

Carnival of Animals (Educational Record Center, 1973).

Eyewitness Amazing Animals Video Series (Education Record Center, 1996).

Eyewitness Natural World Video Series (Education Record Center, 1996).

Geokids Video Series, by National Geographic (Educational Record Center, 1994).

Gift of the Whales (Lakeshore, 1989).

Meet Your Animal Friends (Constructive Playthings, 1983).

See How They Grow Video Series (Educational Record Center, 1996).

Zora the Guide Dog (Education Activities).

Computer Software

A World of Animals CD-ROM, Beckley-Cardy

Animals and How They Grow CD-ROM, Beckley-Cardy

Kid's Zoo CD-ROM, Beckley-Cardy

Teaching Kits

All About Animals Resource Chest, Lakeshore

Insects and Spiders Resource Chest, Lakeshore

Sea Life Resource Chest, Lakeshore

Graeme, Jocelyn, and Ruth Fahlman. *Hand In Hand: Multicultural Experiences For Young Children* (Reading, MA: Addison-Wesley, 1990).

Additional Resources

AKC Children's Education Materials
American Kennel Club
5580 Centerview Drive, Suite 200
Raleigh, NC 27606-3390
(919) 233-9767
Materials to help you teach children about dogs and responsibility, including teaching kits, videos, posters, and newsletters for grades K–3.

American Society for the Prevention of Cruelty to Animals (ASPCA)
Education Department
424 East 92nd Street
New York, NY 10128-6804
(212) 876-7700
The ASPCA offers books, videos, kid's publications, teacher's newsletters, dog bite prevention activity sheets, resource kits, and Spanish language materials.

Insect Lore
P.O. Box 1535
Shafter, CA 93263
(800) Live Bug
A mail order catalog of science-related teaching materials offering books, science kits, puppets, and more.

World Wildlife Fund
1250 24th Street NW
Washington, DC 20037
Provides information on preserving endangered animals.

COMMUNITY

"There's a city bus!" "We go to that store." "Me too. I been there before." "Do you know the park? You know, the one with the slides?" As children grow, their world of people, places, and things expands. Today many young children are out and about in their communities. They go to child care, school, stores, and restaurants, and they accompany their parents on a variety of errands in and around the community.

Preschool children often take an interest in the people and places around them. Each child will be fascinated by a different aspect of community. Some will identify with the people, others with the large equipment and vehicles, and still others will have their favorite places.

A unit on community builds on children's knowledge of and interest in their community to create and foster a sense of belonging and interdependence. It can also introduce different children's communities to each other and uncover aspects of your community that may be hidden to some or all of the children.

UNIT 2:

COMMUNITY

Look for this symbol
to find activities you
can use for circle time.

WEB

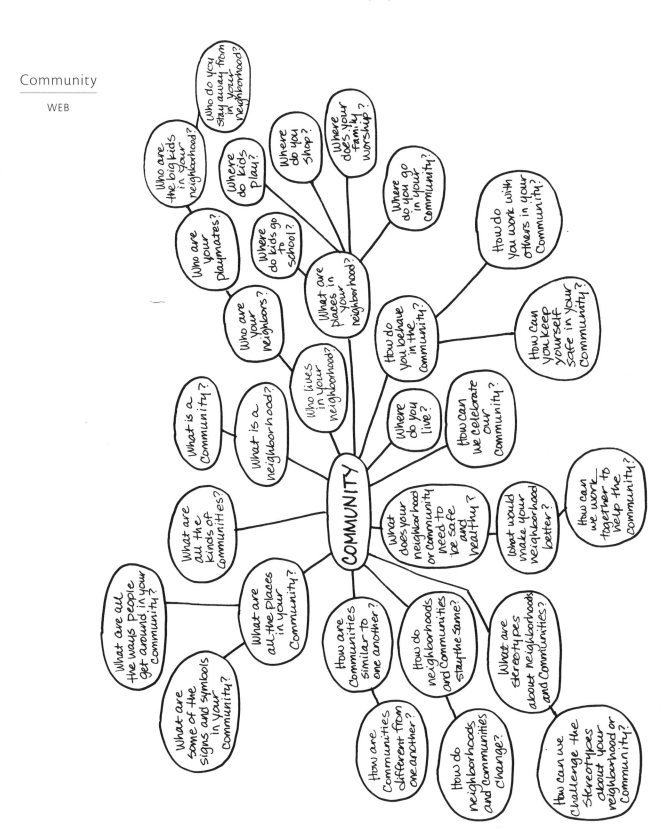

OUTLINE

I. Where do you live?
   A. Who lives in your neighborhood?
   B. Who are your neighbors?
   C. Who are your playmates?
   D. Who are the big kids in your neighborhood?
   E. Who do you stay away from in your neighborhood?

II. What are places in your neighborhood?
   A. Where do kids go to school?
   B. Where do kids play?
   C. Where do you shop?
   D. Where does your family worship?
   E. Where do you go in your community?

III. How do you behave in the community?
   A. How do you work with others in your community?
   B. How can you keep yourself safe in your community?

IV. What is a neighborhood?
   A. What is a community?
   B. What are all the kinds of communities?
   C. What are all the places in your community?
      1. What are some of the signs and symbols in your community?
      2. What are all the ways people get around in your community?
   D. How are communities similar to one another?
   E. How are communities different from one another?
   F. How do neighborhoods and communities stay the same?
   G. How do neighborhoods and communities change?

V. What are stereotypes about neighborhoods and communities?

VI. How can we challenge the stereotypes about our neighborhood or community?

VII. What does your neighborhood or community need to be safe and healthy?
   A. What would make your neighborhood better?
   B. How can we work together to help the community?

VIII. How can we celebrate our community?

Materials List

ART

skin-colored paints, crayons, markers, construction paper

butcher paper roll

newspapers, news magazines, and community newspapers in the different languages of the community

small cars to paint with

boxes for making buildings

sidewalk chalk (for example, Sidewalk Chalk Sticks, *Constructive Playthings*)

design paper (for example, Building Design Paper, *Kaplan*)

BLOCKS

a variety of multicultural people figures, including figures of people with disabilities

figures of community workers (for example, Community Career Figures and Community Workers Bendables, *Constructive Playthings*; Inclusive Play People, *Educational Equity Concepts*; Our Helpers Play People, *Nasco*)

block vehicle sets (for example, Classic Train Set, Real-Action Construction Fleet, *Lakeshore*; Flexi Preschool Transportation Set, *Sandy and Son*; Wooden Community Vehicles, Jumbo Tuf Crane, Dump, and Bulldozer, Over-the-Road Set, *Constructive Playthings*; Super Railway, *Beckley-Cardy*)

roadway mats (for example, Continental Road Plan Playmat, *Environments*)

traffic signs (for example, Block Play Traffic Signs, *Constructive Playthings*, *Environments*, *Lakeshore*, *Nasco*)

block play sets about transportation (for example, Community Service Aids, *Nasco*; Firefighter Play Set, International Airport, Mack Construction Set, Police Set, Skyscrapers, *Beckley-Cardy*; Full Service Garage, Jumbo Jet Activity Set, *Constructive Playthings*)

DRAMATIC PLAY

community worker costumes and accessories (for example, Career Hat Collection, Careers Costume Set, *Lakeshore*; Construction Engineer Costume, Firefighter's Uniform, Mail Carrier Costume, Medical Cart, Medical Kit, Medical Team Costume, Police Officer's Uniform, *Constructive Playthings*)

preschooler dolls (for example, Multi-Ethnic School Dolls, *Lakeshore*)

community signs (for example, Emerging Literacy Community Signs Kit, *Lakeshore*)

poster board, notepads, markers, and pencils for making signs and writing tickets

puppet stage and a variety of people puppets, including community helper puppets

large hollow blocks or milk crates

steering wheel, bus driver's hat, ticket puncher, tickets

LARGE MOTOR

games that are often played in city parks and on sidewalks (Giant Hopscotch Carpet, Jump Rope Set, Mini-Basketball Portable Hoop with Backboard, *Lakeshore*)

equipment to support the community theme (for example, Mailbox, *Beckley-Cardy*; Traffic Cones, *Environments*; Sidewalk Chalk Sticks, Tricycle Traffic Signs, *Constructive Playthings*; Big Loader Sand Truck, Big Dump Sand Truck, *Lakeshore*; Gas Pump, *Beckley-Cardy*, *Edvantage*; Traffic Signs, *Beckley-Cardy*, *Edvantage*, *Environments*)

LITERACY

children's books: fiction, nonfiction, and bilingual books about community (see resource list at the end of the unit)

cassette player and theme-related storybook cassettes

flannel board sets (for example, Make Your Own Community Flannel Board Set, *Edvantage*; We Dress for Work Flannel Board Concept Kits, *Lakeshore*)

community worker puppets and dolls (for example, Machine Washable Career Puppets, *Edvantage*, *Lakeshore*; Career Character Dress-Up Dolls, *Lakeshore*)

MANIPULATIVES

multicultural puzzles about community (for example, City Giant Floor Puzzle, Vehicles Stand-Up Puzzles, *Constructive Playthings*, *Sandy and Son*; City See Inside Puzzle, Community Puzzles, *Sandy and Son*; Non-Sexist Multi-Ethnic Career Puzzles, Safety Signs Knob Inlay Puzzle, *Constructive Playthings*, *Lakeshore*)

board, card, matching, and lotto games about community (for example, Mapping the Town Game, *Lakeshore*; My Home and Places Board Game, *Animal Town*; Our Town Game, *Beckley-Cardy*; Signs and Symbols Flash Cards, *Childswork/Childsplay*)

building sets (for example, Brio-Mec Building System, *Beckley-Cardy*; Pipe Builder, *Lakeshore*)

community counters (for example, Vehicle Counters, *Environments*)

community theme boxes (for example, Community and Careers Theme Box, *Lakeshore*)

SCIENCE

aquarium, terrarium, or vivarium

inclined planes, pulleys, and other physics props

hand-held magnifiers

SENSORY

sand or dirt

small cars, trucks, and building materials

dish tubs, water, and small plastic or wooden boats

Teaching Through the Interest Areas

Art

Set out newspapers, news magazines, community magazines, small cars to paint with, and boxes for making buildings.

Blocks

Encourage children to build a city or skyscrapers with the unit blocks.

Add figures of community workers and small toy vehicles (buses, planes, trains, barges, cars) to encourage community-related play.

Draw roads by laying out rows of masking tape on the floor in the block area. Add blocks, small vehicles, and figures of people to encourage community-related block play. Set out scrap paper and felt tip pens to make signs for buildings.

Dramatic Play

Set out a variety of costumes and props to encourage children to explore the role of community helpers. Include costumes and props for mail carriers, firefighters, paramedics, and police officers. Set out poster board and markers for sign making and notepads and pencils for writing tickets.

Set out large hollow blocks or milk cartons, a steering wheel, a bus driver's hat, tickets, and a hole puncher to encourage bus play.

Set out a puppet stage, community helper puppets, and a variety of people puppets to encourage play around community themes.

Literacy

Set out a collection of fiction, nonfiction, and bilingual books on community. Include a tape player and community-related storybooks cassettes, community worker hand puppets and flannel board sets, and materials for making journals and books.

Manipulatives

Add community and career puzzles, matching games, and board games to the manipulative area.

Music

Set out cassettes with songs about neighborhoods, communities, and workers who help us.

Science

Set up a terrarium, aquarium, or vivarium for children to examine. Include hand-held magnifiers for the children to use as they look at the contents. Set up inclined planes or pulleys for children to experiment with force and momentum.

Sensory

Pour an inch or two of sand or dirt on the bottom of the sensory table and add small cars, trucks, and wooden or plastic building materials to encourage city-related play.

Fill a tub with water and add boats to explore another form of transportation that takes place in many communities.

ACTIVITIES: INVESTIGATING THE THEME

Creative Development

Car Painting. Cover a table with butcher paper and tape it down so that it is tight and secure. Set out a few toy cars from the block area and a shallow pan of tempera paint. Tell the children that they can dip the wheels in the paint and "drive" the car around the table to make paint tracks.

Community Buildings. Collect a variety of boxes, making sure you have more than enough for each child to have one. Set out boxes, construction paper, tissue paper, glue, crayons, markers, and scissors. Encourage children to make buildings that they might find in their community.

Community Mural. Set out a large piece of butcher paper and tempera paints. As a class, work together to paint a mural of your community.

Signs. Set out construction paper, felt tip markers, and crayons and invite children to make signs they see in their community. They may want to make stop signs, traffic signals, restaurant signs, bus stop signs, or railroad track signs.

Skyscrapers. Set out a variety of boxes, tubes, collage materials, glue, and masking tape. Encourage children to make their own community buildings or businesses.

Critical Thinking

Community Builders. Give the children problems to solve through constructive play. Set out empty milk cartons, frozen juice cans, cardboard boxes, cardboard tubes, and figures of people in the block area. Challenge the children to make a community for the figures of people to live in. Ask the children to think about what the people need. Do they need a place to live? Places to work? Places to get food and clothes? Places to have fun? Make a list of the children's ideas and post it in the block area. Next, encourage the children to think about how they will arrange their community. Help them build the community and label the buildings. Introduce the concept of transportation. Ask how the people will get around. Children will probably know about cars, but encourage them to think about how people who don't have cars will get around.

What is a Community? Lead a large group discussion on the topic of community. You might want to begin by asking the following questions:

> What is a community?
>
> How small can a community be?
>
> How big can a community be?
>
> What do you need to have a community?
>
> What do you want to know about our community?

What Would You Take? Here is an activity that Gloria Needleman presented at the 1996 NAEYC conference. It fosters empathy for people who are forced to leave their homelands. Read a story about refugees or introduce a persona doll that is a refugee. Bring a suitcase to circle time. Introduce the word *refugee.* A refugee is someone who is forced to leave his or her country and move to a new one. Refugees don't have a choice. They have to move because of things like war or not having enough food to eat. Often, they have to move quickly and leave all their things behind. Ask the children what they would do if their parents decided that tomorrow they were going to live in another place and could only take what fit in one suitcase. Ask the children, "How would you decide which of your favorite things to take? How would you feel about leaving your home?"

Emotional Development

Wait Your Turn. Many children have difficulty waiting. Sometimes we have to wait for a turn, and sometimes we have to wait for someone to pay attention to us. There are lots of people in our community, and sometimes when we are out in the community we have to wait our turn. Sometimes we have to wait at the bus stop for a bus to come. Sometimes we have to wait in line at the bank to cash a check. Sometimes we have to wait in line at the grocery store to buy our food. Sometimes we have to wait at the clinic to see your doctor or dentist. Ask the children to share examples of times when they have had to wait. Ask them, "How does it feel to have to wait for a turn?" Invite the children to role-play waiting. One child could be the parent, another the child, and others could be community workers. Help the children think of ways to wait that are helpful and positive.

Welcome! Help children develop skills in welcoming people. Ask the children, "Have you ever moved to a new neighborhood or town? How does it feel to move to a new neighborhood? How does it feel to be the new kid at school?" Help the children recognize that people might feel scared, shy, or lonely in these situations. Ask the children for ideas about how they could make a person feel welcome. Divide the children into groups of three. Ask them to pretend that one of them is new, and it's their first day here. The other two children can show how they would try to make the person feel comfortable and welcome. Talk about the positive things the children did to make the person feel welcomed.

A Community Called Hope. Cover a table with a large piece of butcher paper. Set out crayons and felt tip markers. Invite children to work together to draw a community that is full of hope. Ask the children the following questions:

What would it be like to live in a city of hope?

How might it feel to live in a city of hope?

Who would live in our city?

Where would we play in a city of hope?

Where would we go in a city of hope?

What would it look like?

 Don't Get Lost! Young children tend to wander off, and some may have experienced being lost. Others may have a fear of being left or lost in a store or other community place. Ask children the following questions:

Do you know what being lost means?

Has anyone ever been lost?

Where did you get lost?

Has anyone ever gotten lost at a store? at a shopping mall? at a park? in the neighborhood? at a fair or carnival?

How does it feel to be lost?

Tell them that children get lost when they get separated from their parents. Invite children to help you role-play getting lost. You could pretend to be the parent and one of the children could wander away from you in a store. Ask the children to suggest what the child should do. Discuss what children should do to keep from getting lost.

 I Know My Community Well. Foster children's self-esteem, pride, and confidence in their ability to participate in their neighborhood and community. At circle time, ask the children to share something they know about the community, a place they like to go in the community, or something they like to do in the community. Children who live in small towns might like to identify the larger communities their families go to shop and receive medical care or other services.

Health, Safety, and Nutrition

Car Safety. Explore transportation safety: wearing seat belts, using car seats, crossing streets at the crosswalk, looking both ways when crossing the street. Set out tricycles and traffic signs. Use chalk to draw an intersection on the sidewalk or play yard. Invite children to role-play being safe drivers and safe pedestrians. One child could be the "traffic light" at the intersection.

 Danger! Help children identify dangerous objects and situations that they might come across in their neighborhood or community. Collect a variety of dangerous objects. For instance, you could include a broken bottle, a book of matches, a cigarette lighter, cigarettes, a beer can, a medicine bottle, a syringe. If you can't find a certain object, cut out magazine pictures and mount them on construction paper. You might want to collect pictures of busy intersections, railroad tracks, abandoned buildings, and barking dogs. Show the objects or pictures to the children. Ask them if they can identify each. Ask them if they know what they should do if they come across any of these objects or situations.

Germs. When we are around other people or in public places, we can give people our germs and pass colds from one person to the next. One of the ways that we spread germs is through coughing and sneezing. Demonstrate how we spread germs by filling two balloons with confetti. Blow up the first balloon. Let go of the neck while still holding onto the balloon. The confetti will fly out, just like our germs when we cough and sneeze. Blow up the second balloon. Release the air and keep your hand over the opening, just like you cover you mouth when you sneeze. Ask the children, "What happens when we don't cover our mouths? What happens when we do cover our mouths?" Invite the children to pretend to sneeze and cover their mouths. Remind the children to wash their hands after they have covered their mouths.

Stoplight. Introduce children to Garrett Morgan, the African American who invented the stoplight after witnessing an accident between a car and buggy. Teach children this popular poem:

> Red on top,
> Green below.
> Red says stop,
> Green says go.
> Yellow says wait,
> even if you're late.

Traffic Signs. Ask the children if they know what the various traffic signs mean. Talk about what each sign "says." Invite the children to make their own traffic signs. Put stop signs or traffic signals on the outside of each classroom interest area and use the signs to tell the children if the interest area is open or closed. Use the traffic signs with the tricycles in the large-motor room or playground.

Language Development

Home Language. *Learn the words for* community, community places, *and* people *in American Sign Language and the home languages of the children in your classroom.*

Community Picture Cards. Glue magazine pictures of city scenes, buildings, streets, and transportation vehicles onto construction paper, or use a commercial set of community teaching pictures. Hold up one picture at a time and ask open-ended questions like the following:

Who can tell me about this picture?

What do you see?

Where is it?

How does it help our community?

How is this picture like our community?

How is this picture different from our community?

What else can you tell me about this picture?

Community Picture Stories. Sit down with a small group of children and some community teaching pictures. Show the children one picture at a time. Ask the children what they see in the pictures. Encourage the children to make up stories about the community places and the people in the pictures. If possible, write down the children's stories.

Crossing Streets. Here's a simple poem to help children remember to stop at the curb and look both ways before they cross the street.

At the curb before I cross
I stop my running feet *(point to feet)*
And look both ways to left and right *(look left and right)*
Before I cross the street.
Lest autos running quietly
Might come as a surprise.
I don't just listen with my ears *(point to ears)*
But look with both my eyes. *(point to eyes)*

(*Creative Resources for the Early Childhood Classroom*, second edition, Judy Herr and Libby Yvonne. Albany, NY: Delmar Publishers, 1995; p. 481. Used with permission.)

Name That Place in Our Community. Bring pictures of a variety of places in your community to circle time. Hide the pictures from the children's view. Give the children clues about a picture one at a time. Describe its location, color, shape, size, who goes there, or who works there. Let children guess the location after each clue. When a child guesses the location, give her the picture to hold while you continue to play the game.

Our Community. Invite the children to write a class book about their community. Decide together what things to include in the book. You could include a page for each of their favorite places in the community. You might also want to consider making an alphabet book about your community.

Math

Community Graph. Graph children's answers to the question, "What is your favorite place to go in the community?"

Community Match. Make four or more sets of community matching cards. Find duplicate photos in magazines, or use a color photocopier to duplicate photographs of places in a community. Place the cards in a basket and encourage children to find the matching sets.

Community Places and Things Matching Game. Make four or more sets of matching cards (see above activity). This time have children match a place in the community with objects that are found there. For instance: grocery store and food, gas station and cars, banks and money, post office and letters, library and books, fast food restaurant and hamburger and fries, bakery and bread, hardware store and tools, police station and police officer, fire station and firefighter or fire truck, health clinic and nurse, drug store and medicine. Choose places and objects that are found in your community.

Community Sort. Collect a variety of pictures of community scenes. Write the name of the location on the back of each card. Place the pictures in a basket. Make sure that the set reflects cultural diversity within your community or, if your community is relatively homogeneous, in the region or country. Set out the basket along with a sorting tray. Invite children to classify the community pictures any way they like.

Park the Cars. Make a simple parking lot by drawing parking spaces that fit your block vehicles on a piece of poster board. If you want, number the parking spaces. Set out the same number of small cars and ask the children to see if they can find a parking space for each car.

People Match. Make eight or more sets of people matching cards. Find duplicate photos of people in magazines, or use a color photocopier to make duplicates. Make sure that the collection of photographs represents the diversity of age, gender, economic class, culture, race, and physical ability present in our world. Glue the photos to index cards, and write the person's identity on the back of each card. Place the cards in a basket and encourage the children to find the matching sets.

Shape a Building. Set out a variety of construction paper shapes, sheets of paper, and glue. Invite the children to arrange the construction paper shapes to make a building. Perhaps they might want to use the shapes to make a building that they know.

Similar to Me. Tape a large piece of paper to the wall. Show children pictures of people from all over the United States and the world, and then see if they can name all of the ways we are similar to one another. Write the children's answers on the paper.

Towers and Skyscrapers. Invite children to build towers and skyscrapers with the unit blocks. Challenge them with the question, "How tall a tower can you make?" Count the number of blocks that each child uses. Then encourage the children to work together to make a tower. See if they can build a taller tower by working together than they could when they were working alone.

Music

We're All One Community. Sing this simple song at morning circle time or at clean-up time to foster a sense of group identity and cooperation.

Tune: *Round the Village*

Let's all stand together
Let's all stand together
Let's all stand together
We're all one community.

Let's all hold hands together
Let's all hold hands together
Let's all hold hands together
We're all one community.

Let's all work together
Let's all work together
Let's all work together
We're all one community.

Let's all have fun together
Let's all have fun together
Let's all have fun together
We're all one community.

(adapted from *Sing a Song All Year Long,* Connie Walters and Dianne Totten. Minneapolis: T. S. Denison & Company, 1991. Used with permission.)

Physical Development

Find a Place for Everyone. Play a cooperative version of musical chairs. Arrange the chairs in a circle, and play music. When the music stops, challenge the children to get up, change seats, and make sure that everyone has a place to sit. Take a chair away each time you stop the music. By the end, the children will all be piled onto one chair.

Firefighters Relay. Divide the class into two teams. Set out two empty buckets about 15 feet away from the starting line. Give each team a bucket of water and a cup. Invite the children to work as teams and take turns scooping up a cup of water, walking or running to the empty buckets, pouring the water into the buckets, returning to the starting line, and passing the cup to the next person on the team.

50

Keep It Up. Have the children sit in a circle. Tell them that in a community everybody has to work together in order to make the community work. Show them a balloon or beach ball and toss it in the air. See if they can work together to keep the ball in the air without it falling to the ground.

Outside Games. Introduce children to street games that are common to your geographic region, and invite children to teach you street games that they play. You might include hopscotch, jump rope, kick the can, four square, or jacks.

Peace Tug. Tie jump ropes together and ask children to work in groups or three or four. Invite the children to work together to make a shape or a letter. Encourage them to come up with shapes, letters, and numbers on their own. Invite them to see if they can sit down and pull themselves up by all holding onto the rope and pulling hard.

Red Light/Green Light. Choose one child to be the caller. The rest of the children stand in a line. The caller turns her back to the others. When she says "green light," the children can move forward. When she says "red light," and turns around, all of the children must stop. If the caller catches a child moving after she has said "red light," the child has to go back to the starting line. The first child to reach the caller and tap her on the shoulder gets to take her place in the next round of the game.

Simon Says. Play a different version of this traditional game. Use the format to invite children to role-play being a community helpers. For instance, "Simon says be a garbage collector. Simon says be a tow truck operator. Simon says be a firefighter. Simon says be a paramedic." Invite children to think of community helpers they could be.

Tricycle Day. Have a day when children can bring their tricycles to school. Block off the parking lot so that children can safely ride in a large area. Use traffic cones and sidewalk chalk to make roads and parking spaces. Children could make traffic signs ahead of time.

Upset the Workers. Make picture cards of different community workers. Make two to four duplicates of each community worker you include. Ask the children to sit in a circle and give each child a card. When you call out a worker, all the children who have that card jump up and exchange places. To make the game more complex, the teacher can take a seat after calling the first worker, which leaves one of the children without a place to sit. That child becomes the next caller.

Science

Air Pollution. Many communities struggle to reduce air pollution. Introduce children to the cause and effect of air pollution. Light a candle. Hold a piece of white ceramic tile over the flame with a pair of tongs so that you don't burn yourself. Turn the tile over and blow out the flame. Show the tile to the children. Ask them, "What do you see on the tile?" Introduce the term *soot*. Pollution leaves soot in the air and on buildings the same way the flame and smoke leave soot on the tile. Take a walk and look for signs and sources of soot and air pollution.

Cars and Air Pollution. Ask a parent or staff person to drive her car up to the door of the building. Take the children outside to watch the adult start the car. Hold a large paper coffee filter next to the exhaust pipe. Show the children the filter. Ask them, "What do you see on the paper?" Introduce the term *exhaust.* Gasoline engines create exhaust, which is like soot. It is in the air and on buildings. Take a walk and look for areas where there might be a lot of exhaust. Congested intersections and freeway ramps tend to have poorer air quality because of idling car engines.

Food Chains. Help children understand how nature takes care of itself by teaching them about predators (creatures that eat meat) and prey (creatures that are eaten by predators). Make sequence cards to illustrate food chains in your backyard, neighborhoods, and region. For example, a food chain in my backyard is the sun, an oak tree, songbirds, mice, and a snowy owl. The sun makes the tree grow. The birds nest in the tree. They eat birdseed in the tree and drop seeds on the snow. The mice eat the seeds that the birds drop. And the owl sits in the tree and eats the mice that live under the snow. Children may think this is cruel and mean. Help them understand that the animals are hungry.

Roll That Car. Invite the children to help you make some ramps for rolling cars. Gather some large pieces of cardboard, a roll of duct tape, and some toy cars. Tape the pieces of cardboard together and tape one end to a chair. Tape another cardboard ramp to the top of a table or shelf unit. Tape a third ramp to a stack of blocks so that you have three ramps, each of which are a different height. Ask the children to roll their cars down the ramp and watch how far they roll. Encourage them to measure how far their cars roll. Ask them what makes the cars roll the farthest and shortest distance. Talk with children about the concepts of gravity, force, and distance. The force of gravity pulls the car down the ramp. And the higher the ramp, the farther the car rolls.

Terrarium. To create a terrarium, use an empty aquarium or a large glass or plastic jar. Cover the bottom with ½ to 2 inches of gravel or small rocks. Then add a thin layer of charcoal (available from garden supply stores). Top with 2 to 4 inches of potting soil. Form the soil into mounds and valleys rather than having a flat surface. Add small houseplants. Ask the salespeople at the garden supply store for suggestions, given the size of your container and the light conditions. Make sure that the root systems are covered with soil. Decorate the terrarium with pebbles, rocks, or a piece of driftwood or moss. Sprinkle the soil with water. Cover the jar or terrarium with a lid or plastic wrap and watch the plants grow.

Vivarium. Make an ecosystem for an animal. Use a 5- or 10-gallon aquarium with a screen cover. Follow the same directions for making a terrarium (see above activity). Add a water dish and small reptiles, amphibians, or insects. Change the water every day and feed the animals regularly.

Social Development

Address Match. Talk with the children about how mail carriers read the address on our mail and match that with the address on our mailbox. Make simple mailbox-shaped cards with each child's address written on them. Encourage the children to see if they can match the addresses on the envelopes with the addresses on the mail-boxes.

Community Helpers. Set out a collection of hats worn by community helpers. Encourage the children to guess which helper is needed in each of the following situations: a doctor's car breaks down on the way to work, a teacher's dog is sick, a taxi driver gets in a car accident, a construction worker gets sick, a nurse has a house that is too cold because the furnace is broken, a firefighter needs food to cook dinner. Invite the children to wear the appropriate hat as they act out these simple situations.

Cooperative Skyscrapers. Invite the children to work cooperatively with a partner to build a tower. Ask each child to find a partner. Give each pair the same number of unit blocks or large hollow building blocks. Tell them to build a tower by taking turns putting one block on the tower at a time. If the tower collapses, they can start over. Repeat a second time, but this time have two pairs join together to make a small group of four. Again, they are to build a skyscraper by taking turns adding one block at a time.

Good Citizenship Award. Make "Good Citizenship Award" badges. Give one to a child in the class each day or each week. Talk with the children about what makes a good citizen. You might want to include things like looking out for others and following the rules.

Greetings. Role-play how you greet and talk to different people. Say to the children, "Let's pretend I'm a grandmother you know, maybe someone who lives on your street or in your neighborhood." Then ask the children, "How would you greet me? How would you talk to me? What are some things you wouldn't want someone to say to a grandmother or an elder in our community?"

Helping Hands in Our Community. Trace hands on construction paper and cut out the shapes. Invite the children to name something they can do with their hands that is helpful to the community. If you want, you can ask children to identify something that people do with their hands that is hurtful to communities.

Let's Vote On It. Introduce voting as a way communities make decisions. Teach the children how to vote. Start with an issue that is selected by the children and is of interest and importance to them. Gloria Needleman, an early childhood teacher at the University of Chicago Laboratory School, introduced voting to her preschool classroom during the recent presidential elections. The first issue they chose to vote on was whether or not children who didn't play with toys had to help clean up.

Community

SOCIAL
DEVELOPMENT

Our Wish for Our Community. Ask the children if they know what *wish* means. Ask each child what they wish for. Then ask the children what they wish for their neighborhood or community. Invite the children to make a poster or mural of all their wishes for their neighborhood or community. Here is a poem that children can recite as they make wishes:

> If my mind was a wishing well,
> I'd find a wish that I could tell—
> A thought from me to you,
> A wish for smiles and fun—
> Something you can do
> To warm you like the sun.

(*The Peaceful Classroom*, Charles Smith. Beltsville, MD: Gryphon House, 1993; p. 163. Used with permission.)

People Paper Dolls. Help children develop social skills with a variety of people. Take a full length picture of each person who visits your class or that you visit on field trips throughout the year. Enlarge the photographs on a color photocopier so that each is 10 inches high. Glue the photos to cardboard and cut them out. Make stands for the dolls out of wood molding and set them out in the block area to foster dramatic play.

Say Hello. Go out to greet the mail carrier, garbage collector, or delivery person who routinely serves your center or school. Make a card and a treat, like a plate of cookies, for the people who serve your program.

We're on the Bus. Simulate a bus by arranging two rows of chairs so they are all facing in the same direction. Set out an additional chair and a steering wheel for the bus driver. Talk with the children about how people act when they ride the city bus. Invite children to role-play positive behavior when riding the bus. At a later time you could invite children to role-play additional public behavior, like eating at a restaurant or greeting adults and elders they meet on the street.

What If? To encourage the children to think about the consequences of their actions, ask them the following questions:

> What would happen if we said, "Ii!" to the people we meet in our neighborhood and community?
>
> What would happen if we called the people in our community names?
>
> What would happen if we fought with the people in our community?
>
> What would happen if we helped the people in our community?

What's My Address? Help children learn to recognize and eventually recall their street addresses. At circle time, tell the children "Our houses are on streets that have a name, and our houses have a number. The house number and name of the street is called our address. We can learn our street address." Print each child's address on an envelope. Show an envelope to the group. Read the address and see if the children can guess whose address it is. Give clues about the child's identity, if necessary. When the children correctly identify the child, give the child the envelope to hold.

Who Is Missing? Help children recall the members of a group. Set out pictures of people from each cultural group in the community. Set them all faceup for the children to see. Mix up the pictures and take one out. Lay the rest back down faceup. Ask children to look at the pictures and guess which one is missing. The child who guesses correctly can shuffle the pictures, pull one out, and lay out the pictures again.

ACTIVITIES: AFFIRMING OURSELVES AND ONE ANOTHER

Human Rights

People have the right to live in safe, healthy communities that they choose.

> **BARRIER:** Sometimes people don't have enough money to live in places that are safe and healthy. Sometimes people of color, poor people, or gay and lesbian people aren't welcome or safe in a certain community because of racism, classism, or homophobia.

Communities have the right to self-determination, which means that the people in them get to decide together things like how they want the community to grow, what they want it to look like, and how they want to educate their children.

> **BARRIER:** Sometimes people in communities disagree about these decisions and have a hard time figuring out what to do. Sometimes there are pressures from outside a community that keep people from being able to make their own decisions.

Everyone has the right to have a voice in decisions that get made in their community.

> **BARRIER:** Sometimes the ways that decisions are made exclude people. For example, people with disabilities are excluded if public information is not available in Braille or on tape or if the public meetings are not physically accessible or are not interpreted into American Sign Language. People who don't have a lot of education are excluded if the information and the meetings use language that they don't understand. People whose first language is not English are excluded if interpreters aren't available or materials are not translated.

All people deserve to be treated with respect.

> **BARRIER:** Some people treat others disrespectfully because they are different. Disrespect includes ignoring, teasing, name-calling, and rejecting people. It makes you feel like you aren't good enough and don't belong.

BIG AS LIFE

All people deserve fair treatment; no one deserves to be treated badly because of who they are.

BARRIER: There is a history of people being treated badly because of who they are in our country, and people are still not treated fairly.

DISCUSSION QUESTIONS: Help children think about fair and unfair treatment of other people. Ask questions that bring up personal issues, such as "How do you decide who would make a good friend? What are fair things to consider? Are there unfair things to consider? What if you and your friend have different ideas about how something should be done? What if someone teases you or calls you names because of who you are? What could you do or say? Who could you ask for help?"

Also ask questions that raise larger societal issues, such as, "What do you think all people need to live and be healthy? Does everyone get what they need? Why do you think some people don't get what they need? What can we do to make our school or our community more fair for everyone?"

Cultural Identity

Cultural Communities. Learn about the different neighborhoods, retail stores, and business centers in your community that represent the cultures of the children and families in your classroom. Take photographs of the neighborhoods and make a book about the cultural neighborhoods in your community.

Diversity

Different Places in a Community. Explore all of the different types of places that make up a community. There are places for people to live, places for people to work, places for people to shop, places for children, and places for elders. Invite children to use the unit blocks to build a community that has all of these different places.

A Foreign Child. Use a doll who looks like a preschool child. Use the doll to tell the children a story about a child who has recently moved here from another country and speaks another language. Ask the children, "How do you think the child feels? What are all of the things this child would need to learn? How can we be a friend to someone who moves from another country?"

How Does It Feel? Invite children to imagine how their community might feel to different people. Older children can take on the role of a different person and look at their community from that person's perspective. Roles could include a homeless person, a toddler, an elderly person, a person who doesn't speak English, a person who is blind, a family that doesn't have a car, or a person of color in a mostly white community. Children can explore what would be good, what would be hard, and how the person would feel. To help them identify real issues for people, ask questions like the following:

If you didn't have a home, where could you sleep at night?

Where could you eat if you didn't have money for food?

If I couldn't see to drive a car, how could I get to the doctor?

If I needed to use a cane to get around, would the streets be easy for me to walk on?

Who Lives in Our Community? Explore all of the different types of people living in your community. Take a walk through the community and notice all the different kinds of people who live there. There are people of all ages: babies, children, teenagers, adults, and senior citizens. There are people from many different cultures. There are boys and girls, men and women. There are people with disabilities and people who are able-bodied. There are people who go to work, people who go to school, and people who don't have jobs. There are people who are homeless, people living in nursing homes, people living in group homes, and people living with families. Discuss how people in your community are similar to one another and how they are different from one another.

Bias and Stereotypes

Back of the Bus. Simulate a bus by arranging two rows of chairs so they are all facing in the same direction. Include enough seats for everyone to participate. Set out an additional chair and a steering wheel. Pretend to be the bus driver and ask children where they would like to go. Once you get to the pretend destination, stop the bus and tell the children that you want to talk to them about something that happened on a bus a long time ago. Ask them to look around and see where they are sitting on the bus. Ask them, "How did you choose where you were going to sit on the bus?" Tell them that there used to be a rule in our communities that African Americans had to sit in the back of the bus. Ask the children if they think that rule is fair. How would they feel if there was a rule that said all boys have to sit in the back of the bus? Or all children with blond hair have to sit in the back of the bus? Help children recognize that is wasn't a good rule because it was unfair.

Community Barriers. Take a walk through the neighborhood or local shopping district to see if there are barriers to people with disabilities. Write a letter to the local newspaper or to the businesses you visited to let the community know about what you found.

Thank You Rosa Parks. Read a book about Rosa Parks. Tell children that she lived in a community and she didn't like the rule that African Americans had to give up their seats on the bus or sit in the back of the bus. She was a member of a group of people who had been challenging unfair laws, including the one about sitting in the back of the bus. She talked about it with her friends, who supported her decision to challenge the law. One day she refused to give up her seat. Because Rosa Parks and many other strong and brave people like her stood up to the unfair laws time and time again, now everybody can sit on the bus wherever they want. Invite children to role-play Rosa Parks refusing to give up her seat on the bus.

Community Service

Community Mural. As a class, design and paint a mural on the outside of your classroom, school, or center. Ask the parents for help. You could also work with a local high school or college and get students to help. You may be able to get the service of a local artist or a grant to fund the project.

World Relief. Gather shoes, eyeglasses, bedding, and clothes for children in a third world country. Perhaps one of the families in your center has family in another country that could use or help distribute these gifts. Otherwise you could contact your local international center, refugee resettlement committee, or legislator to help you identify a country to send the items to.

Trash Patrol. Go on a walk around the neighborhood and pick up trash and litter. Talk with the children about how it feels to clean up the neighborhood. Ask them to think of other things they could do to make their community cleaner and more beautiful.

Social Action Suggestions

Dear Mayor. Invite each child to write a letter to the mayor with suggestions for how to make the neighborhood or community a better place to live.

Drug-Free Zone. Join forces with other neighborhood groups to create a drug-free zone in the neighborhood around your center or school.

Neighborhood Clean-Up. As a class, select an area of the community within walking distance of the school that needs monitoring, care, and maintenance. Perhaps it is a boarded-up building that is currently empty but could become a dangerous play space for children or a site of drug dealing. The class and parents could monitor the building and report problems to the authorities. A vacant lot or alley could be kept clean by the children and parents.

Park Safety. Request that the police increase their patrol to ensure that the local park is a safe place for young children to play.

Safe Streets. Start a petition that requests increased police presence in the sections of your community that are dangerous.

Traffic Safety. As a group, work together to get the city to install traffic signs near your center or school.

Activities: Opening the Door

Classroom Visitors

Ask local community leaders to visit your class and talk to the children about their role in the community.

Invite senior citizens who have lived in the community their entire life to talk with the children about the community.

Field Trips

Take a walk through your neighborhood or the commercial district of your community.

Charter a school bus and take a tour of your community.

Visit a local historical museum.

Take a trip to the local community garden.

Parent Involvement

Ask parents and grandparents to share ways that they are involved in the community, whether through work, recreation, volunteering, or their social connections.

Parent Education

Invite a social worker or parent advocate to talk about community services available to families with young children. Invite a representative from the city government to talk about the state of children in your community and any plans the city may have for increasing services to children and parents. Invite a community organizer who works on local justice issues to talk about local issues of concern to parents and help them identify ways they can get involved.

Ask grandparents and elders in the community to talk about what the neighborhood or community used to be like. They could also write stories for the children about the history of your neighborhood or community. Parents and grandparents might have old photographs of places that are familiar to the children. Use a photocopier to duplicate the photographs. Help the children compare how the sites looked long ago to how they look today.

Classroom Resources

Children's Books

A is For Aloha, Stephanie Feeney (Honolulu: University of Hawaii, 1985).

A is for Africa, Ifeoma Onyefulu (New York: Cobblehill, 1993).

A To Zen: A Book Of Japanese Culture, Ruth Wells (New York: Simon, 1992).

The Adventures Of Taxi Dog, Debra and Sal Barracca (New York: Dial, 1990).

At The Laundromat, Christine Loomis (New York: Scholastic, 1993).

At The Library, Christine Loomis (New York: Scholastic, 1994).

At The Mall, Christine Loomis (New York: Scholastic, 1994).

At This Very Minute, Kathleen Rice Bowers (Boston: Little Brown, 1983).

Beautiful Junk: A Story Of The Watts Towers, Jon Madian (Boston: Little Brown, 1968).

Birthdays! Celebrating Life Around The World, Eve B. Feldman (Mahwah, NJ: Bridge-Water, 1996).

The Car Washing Street, Denise Lewis Patrick (New York: Tambourine, 1993).

City Seen From A To Z, Rachel Isadora (New York: Morrow, 1992).

City Sounds, Craig Brown (New York: Green-willow, 1992).

Count Your Way Through Africa, Jim Haskins (Minneapolis: Lerner, 1989).

The Day Gogo Went To Vote: South Africa, 1994, Elinor Batezat Sisulu (Boston: Little Brown, 1996).

Emergency! Gail Gibbons (New York: Holiday, 1995).

The Garden Of Happiness, Erika Tamar (San Diego: Harcourt, 1996).

Gloria Goes To Gay Pride, Leslea Newman (Boston: Alyson Wonderland, 1991).

A Handful Of Seeds, Monica Hughes (New York: Orchard, 1996).

Hi, Ann Herbert Scott (New York: Philomel, 1994).

Houses And Homes, Ann Morris (New York: Morrow, 1995).

I Got Community, Melrose Cooper (New York: Holt, 1995).

I is for India, Prodeepta Das (Parsippany: Silver Burdett, 1996).

If I Lived In Japan, Rosanne Knorr (Marietta, GA: Longstreet, 1995).

In The Diner, Christine Loomis (New York: Scholastic, 1994).

It Takes A Village, Jane Cowen-Fletcher (New York: Scholastic, 1994).

Jonathan And His Mommy, Irene Smalls-Hector (Boston: Little Brown, 1992).

Ogbo, Ifeoma Onyefulu (San Diego: Harcourt, 1996).

On The Go, Ann Morris (New York: Morrow, 1994).

The Park Bench, Fumiko Takeshita (Brooklyn, NY: Kane/Miller, 1989).

Pearl Moscowitz's Last Stand, Arthur Levine (New York: Tambourine, 1993).

Somewhere In Africa, Ingrid Mennen and Niki Daly (New York: Viking, 1997).

Somewhere In The World Right Now, Stacey Schuett (New York: Knopf, 1997).

My Steps, Sally Derby (New York: Lee, 1996).

Talking A Walk: A Book In Two Languages/Caminando: Un Libro En Dos Lenguas, Rebecca Emberley (Boston: Little Brown, 1994).

Talking Walls, Margy Burns Knight (Gardiner, ME: Tilbury, 1995).

Talking Walls: The Stories Continue, Margy Burns Knight (Gardiner, ME: Tilbury, 1996).

Tar Beach, Faith Ringgold (New York: Crown, 1992).

A Taste Of The Mexican Market/El Gusta Del Mercado Mexicano, Nancy Maria Grande Tabor (Watertown, MA: Charlesbridge, 1996).

The Tortilla Factory, Gary Paulsen (San Diego: Harcourt, 1995).

This Is My House, Arthur Dorros (New York: Scholastic, 1992).

This Is The Way We Eat Our Lunch: A Book About Children Around The World, Edith Baer (New York: Scholastic, 1995).

This Is The Way We Go To School: A Book About Children Around The World, Edith Baer (New York: Scholastic, 1990).

Uncle Jed's Barbershop, Margaree K. Mitchell (Boston: Houghton, 1995).

Uncle Willie And The Soup Kitchen, Dyanne DiSalvo-Ryan (New York: Morrow, 1997).

We Are A Rainbow, Nancy Tabor (Watertown, MA: Charlesbridge, 1997).

We Keep A Store, Anne Shelby (New York: Orchard, 1990).

Weddings, Ann Morris (New York: Lothrop, 1995).

White Socks Only, Evelyn Coleman (Morton Grove, IL: Whitman, 1996).

Who Belongs Here? An American Story, Margy Burns Knight (Gardiner, ME: Tilbury, 1993).

Music

Banton, Mega, Ricky Genral, and Shirley McLean. *Positively Reggae* (Sony, 1994).

"Peace We Want"

Hartmann, Jack. *Make a Friend, Be a Friend* (Educational Activities, 1990).

"What Would It Be Like"

Lefranc, Barbara. *I Can Be Anything I Want To Be* (Doubar, 1990).

"America"

"Name of the Game"

McGruff & Scruff and the Crime Dogs (Beckley-Cardy).

Steve and Gregg. *We All Live Together.*

"We All Live Together"

"The World Is A Rainbow"

Visual Displays

Constructive Playthings
Home and Community Helpers Picture Packet
My Community Picture Packet
Traffic Signs Picture Packet
American Indians Yesterday and Today Teaching Pictures
Black America Yesterday and Today Teaching Pictures
Living Together in America Teaching Pictures
Spanish Americans Yesterday and Today Teaching Pictures

Educational Equity Concepts, Inc.
Mainstreaming for Equity Posters

Lakeshore
Children of the U.S. Poster Pack
Children of the World Poster Pack
Our Community Picture Collection

Videos

Here We Go (Constructive Playthings, 1986).

Computer Software

Community Exploration CD-ROM by Jostens Learning, Educational Record Center

Teaching Kits

Community Awareness Resource Chest, Lakeshore

Children Riding on Sidewalks Safely (CROSS) Curriculum Kit, National Association for the Education of Young Children

Graeme, Jocelyn, and Ruth Fahlman. *Hand In Hand: Multicultural Experiences For Young Children* (Reading, MA: Addison-Wesley, 1990).

Walk in Traffic Safety (WITS) Curriculum Kit, National Association for the Education of Young Children

Additional Resources

National Fire Prevention Association
1 Batterymarch Park
P.O. Box 9101
Quincy, MA 02269-9101
(800) 344-3555
Fire prevention week campaign, fire safety materials, home fire safety, and classroom materials.

Fireproof Children
One Grove Street, Suite 210
Pittsford, NY 14534
(716) 264-1754
Fireproof education kits, handbook, video, and preschool education kit.

FOODS

"I'm hungry. What's for breakfast? Yuck, I hate that!" "Mmmm, yummy in my tummy." "Oooh, you eat that nasty stuff?" Young children have strong feelings about food. Some are attracted to food because they have big appetites and love to eat. Others find food an intense sensory experience. The texture, taste, smell, and color of food determines each child's attitude toward it. Children like to identify and examine foods. They enjoy finding out where foods come from. And they particularly enjoy cooking foods. A unit on foods provides vast opportunities for children to share their cultures with others, be exposed to new experiences, face their fears of trying new and different things, and challenge preconceived ideas they have about foods.

UNIT 3:

Foods

 Look for this symbol to find activities you can use for circle time.

WEB

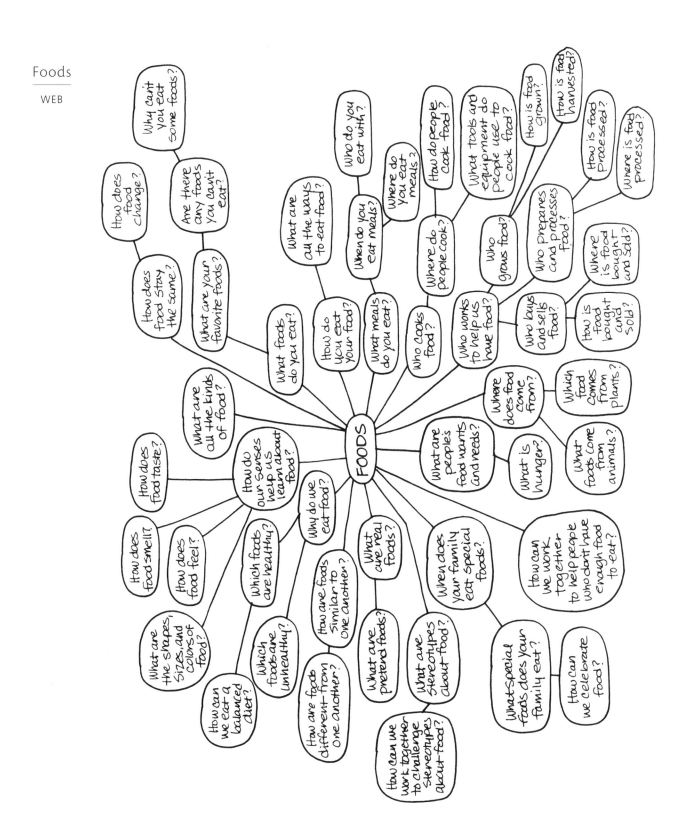

BIG AS LIFE

OUTLINE

I. What foods do you eat?
   A. What are your favorite foods?
   B. Are there any foods you can't eat?
   C. Why can't you eat some foods?
II. How do you eat your food?
III. What are all the ways to eat food?
IV. What meals do you eat?
   A. When do you eat meals?
   B. Where do you eat meals?
   C. Who do you eat with?
V. Who cooks food?
   A. Where do people cook?
   B. How do people cook food?
   C. What tools and equipment do people use to cook food?
VI. Who works to help us have food?
   A. Who grows food?
      1. How is food grown?
      2. How is food harvested?
   B. Who prepares and processes food?
      1. How is food processed?
      2. Where is food processed?
   C. Who buys and sells food?
      1. Where is food bought and sold?
      2. How is food bought and sold?
VII. Where does food come from?
   A. Which food comes from animals?
   B. Which food comes from plants?
VIII. How do our senses help us learn about food?
   A. How does food taste?
   B. How does food smell?
   C. How does food feel?
   D. How does food sound?
   E. What are the shapes, sizes, and colors of food?
IX. Why do we eat food?
   A. Which foods are healthy?
   B. Which foods are unhealthy?
   C. How can we eat a balanced diet?
X. What are all the kinds of food?
   A. How are foods similar to one another?
   B. How are foods different from one another?
   C. What are real foods?
   D. What are pretend foods?
   E. How does food stay the same?
   F. How does food change?
   G. What are stereotypes about foods?
   H. How can we work together to challenge the stereotypes about foods?
XI. What are people's food wants and needs?
   A. What is hunger?
   B. How can we work together to help people who don't have enough food to eat?
XII. When does your family eat special foods?
   A. What special foods does your family eat?
   B. How can we celebrate food?

MATERIALS LIST

ART

skin-colored paints, markers, crayons, and construction paper

butcher paper roll

cooking magazines

food coupons

empty food containers

fruit- and vegetable-shaped sponges for painting

BLOCKS

a variety of multicultural people figures, including figures of people with disabilities

plastic or wooden farm animals (for example, Farm Animal Collection, *Lakeshore, Nasco*)

small farm vehicles and implements, fencing, and a play barn or silo (for example, 1-2-3 Market Stand, *Nasco*; Barn and Fence, *Kaplan*; Big Bruiser Deluxe Farm Set, *Beckley-Cardy*; Giant American Farm Scene Play Mat, *Nasco*; Silo and Stable, *Kaplan*)

dollhouse furniture (for example, Hardwood Dollhouse Furniture, *Constructive Playthings*)

DRAMATIC PLAY

multicultural food and cooking sets (for example, Child-Size Cooking Set, Complete Set of Four Lifelike Meals, Culturally Specific Play Food Sets, Produce, Fruit, and Vegetable Sets, *Constructive Playthings*; Dozen Eggs, *ABC School Supply*; Fruit Assortment, Hispanic Cooking Set, Vegetable Assortment, *Lakeshore*; Wok Set, *Kaplan*; Asian Cooking Set, International Bread Set, *Constructive Playthings, Lakeshore*)

kitchen equipment (for example, Coffee Maker, Food Mixer, *Nasco*; International Cook Set, *Kaplan*; Kitchen Utensils, Pop-Up Toaster, *Constructive Playthings*; Microwave, *Constructive Playthings, Sandy and Son, Nasco*; Picnic Set, *Kaplan*)

grocery store props (for example, Checkout Cash Register, Grocery Crates, *Constructive Playthings*; Grocery Store, *Lakeshore*; Magic Scan Checkout Counter, *J. L. Hammett*; Shopping Cart, *Constructive Playthings*)

restaurant props (for example, Chef Costume, *J. L. Hammett*; Kitchen Apron, Chef's Hat, *Edvantage*)

kitchen: baking sheets, pots, frying pans, spatulas, rotary eggbeaters, wire whisks, potato mashers, spoons, mixing bowls, measuring cups, measuring spoons, pitchers, salt and pepper shakers, aprons, empty food containers, cookbooks, recipe cards, recipe rebus charts

grocery store: cash register, pretend money, paper sacks, empty food containers, pretend food, grocery carts, grocery store sign, grocery store advertisements, food coupons

farmers' market: pretend fruits and vegetables, bushel baskets, strawberry baskets, cash box, play money, aprons, grocery bags, scrap paper and felt tip pens to make signs

restaurant: chef hats, aprons, cooking utensils, pretend food, dishes, napkins, tablecloths, menus or an order board, cash register, receipt pads, pretend money, sign

LARGE MOTOR

wheelbarrow and gardening tools, garden tractor riding toys, grocery carts

LITERACY

children's books: fiction, nonfiction, and bilingual books about food (see resource list at the end of the unit)

cassette player and theme-related storybook cassettes in different languages

magnetic and flannel board sets about food (for example, Farm Life Flannel Board Unit, Vegetables and Fruits Flannel Board Concept Kits, *Lakeshore*; Fruits and Vegetables Flannel Board Sets, Grandpa's Farm Flannel Board Set, *The Story Teller*; Healthful Food Magnetic Set, *Environments*)

card games and flash cards (for example, Bilingual Phot-O-Food Cards, *Kaplan*)

MANIPULATIVES

food and farm life puzzles (for example, Didacta Shopping Puzzle, Market Puzzle, *Sandy and Son*; Eating An Apple Puzzle, Food Groups Puzzle, *Nasco*; Farm Giant Floor Puzzle, Fruit Puzzle, Giant Stand-Up Farm Puzzle, Good Habits Puzzles, Vegetables Puzzle, *Constructive Playthings*; Our Teeth Puzzle, *J. L. Hammett*; Farmer Puzzle, *Lakeshore*; The Farm Giant Floor Puzzle, *Beckley-Cardy*; Make-a-Meal Puzzles, *Constructive Playthings, Edvantage*)

card, board, lotto, and sorting games about food (for example, Harvest Time Board Game, *Childswork/Childsplay*; Fruit Count Matching Game, *J. L. Hammett*; Nutrition Lotto, *Lakeshore*; Orchard Game, *Sandy and Son*; The Very Hungry Caterpillar Game, *Constructive Playthings*)

food-related counting and sorting materials (for example, Half Dozen Eggs Shape Sorters, One Dozen Eggs, *Nasco*; Count 'n Sort Produce, Food

Blocks, Orange Grove Abacus, Fruits and Vegetables Sorting/Counting Materials, *Constructive Playthings*; Fractional Fruit Plate, *Sandy and Son*)

other food-related manipulatives (for example, Food and Nutrition Theme Box, Food Group Pyramid Mats, What Comes From What? Discovery Kit, *Lakeshore*)

MUSIC

fruit- and vegetable-shaped shakers (for example, Egghead Shakers, Fruit and Corn Shakers, *West Music*)

SCIENCE

a collection of grains and the flours that are made from them, in jars

a collection of different kinds of beans in small jars

measurement sets (for example, 12-Piece Measurement Set, *Lakeshore*)

SENSORY

field corn

nuts in the shell

dirt, plastic farm animals, fencing, and farm vehicles

magnetic "fishing" game

plastic eggs and green raffia for "grass"

supplies for making mud pies: muffin tins, wooden utensils

Teaching Through the Interest Areas

Art

Set out cooking magazines, food coupons, empty food containers, and food-shaped sponges for making food-related collages and paintings.

Blocks

Set out plastic or wooden farm animals, figures or people, play farm implements and vehicles, fencing, and a pretend barn and silo to encourage farm-related play.

Dramatic Play

Add a variety of kitchen utensils to the dramatic play area to encourage cooking-related play. Include baking sheets, pots, frying pans, spatulas, rotary eggbeaters, wire whisks, potato mashers, spoons, mixing bowls, measuring cups, measuring spoons, pitchers, salt and pepper shakers, aprons, empty food containers, cookbooks, recipe cards, and recipe rebus charts.

Encourage children to play farmers' market. Set out pretend fruits and vegetables, bushel baskets, strawberry baskets, a cash box, play money, aprons, grocery bags, and scrap paper and felt tip pens to make signs.

Encourage the children to role-play going to the grocery store and purchasing food. Set out a cash register, pretend money, paper sacks, empty food containers, pretend food, grocery carts, a grocery store sign, grocery store advertisements, and food coupons.

Set up the dramatic play area as a restaurant, pizza parlor, bakery, or ice cream shop. Include chef hats, aprons, cooking utensils, pretend food, dishes, napkins, tablecloths, menus or an order board, a cash register, receipt pads, pretend money, and a sign.

Literacy

Set out a collection of nonfiction, fiction, and bilingual books on food. Include a tape player and food-related storybook cassettes, food and farm life flannel board sets, food paper bag puppets, and materials for making journals and books.

Manipulatives

Add food and farm life puzzles, food sorting games, food matching games, food board games, and plastic fruit and vegetables for counting.

Music

Set out a variety of cassettes that contain food-related songs.

Set out materials like plastic containers, cardboard tubes, masking tape, baby bottles, plastic juice bottles, field corn, and dried beans or rice for making simple shakers. Set out oatmeal containers for making drums and hollowed out coconut shells for clappers.

Science

Set out jars filled with a variety of grains and flours. Talk about the fact that people eat bread that they make from the grains that they grow. People living in different places grow different grains and make different kinds of bread.

Set out collections of dried beans. Fill small jars with different types of dried beans.

Sensory

Fill the sensory table with field corn (which is not human food) for a different dry sensory experience.

Make a fishing game by cutting fish shapes out of construction paper and attaching a paper clip to each one. Make simple fishing poles out of dowels and string. Tie a magnet to the end of each string. Set the fish in the sensory table and encourage the children to try to hook the fish.

Fill the sensory table with nuts in the shell, which can be cracked and eaten later.

Put a layer of dirt on the bottom of the sensory table. Add miniature farm animals, fencing, and farm vehicles to encourage farm play.

Place objects in plastic eggs. Hide the eggs in green raffia made to look like grass.

Give children water to add to the dirt in the sensory table. Set out muffin pans and aluminum and wooden utensils for making mud pies. If the children make mud pies outside, set the mud creations in the sun to dry. You could also use sand for this activity.

ACTIVITIES: INVESTIGATING THE THEME

Creative Development

Build a Barn. Collect a variety of boxes, making sure you have more than enough for each child to have one. Set out boxes, construction paper, tissue paper, glue, crayons, markers, and scissors. Encourage the children to make a barn where farm animals might live.

Eggshell Collage. Ask parents and staff to save eggshells. Crush the shells. Invite children to glue the eggshells onto colored construction paper.

Food Collage. Encourage the children to make a collage out of magazine pictures of their favorite food. For a more involved activity, trace each child's body and invite them to paste the pictures of their favorite foods to the outline of their body.

Fruit and Vegetable Prints. Cut a variety of fruits and vegetables in half. Consider using potatoes, carrots, heads of cabbage, ears of corn, apples, grapefruit, and star fruit. Dip the fruits and vegetables in thick tempera paint and stamp designs on butcher paper.

Kitchen Gadget Prints. Gather a variety of kitchen gadgets and cookie cutters that could be used for painting. Set out paper and paint in shallow pans. Encourage the children to dip the objects in the paint and make prints with them.

Spatter Paint Place Settings. Cover a table with newspaper. Set pieces of dark colored construction paper around the table like place mats. Invite the children to set the table the way they would at home. Fill a spray bottle with paint and let the children spray paint over their place settings. Remove the utensils and plates to reveal a negative image of the place settings on the construction paper.

Critical Thinking

The Great Divide. Give children a problem that needs solving. Serve a snack that has not yet been cut up. For instance, you could serve a pan of bar cookies or brownies, a whole pizza, melon, cake, or a pie. Show the children the snack. Ask them, "Does anyone know what the problem is? What can we do so that everyone gets some snack? How can we make sure that everyone gets a piece?"

Emotional Development

Are You Thankful? Lead a discussion on thankfulness. Ask the children, "What foods are you thankful for? What foods would you really miss if you couldn't have them anymore? How could we show that we are thankful for the food we eat?" Invite children to say something they are thankful for before eating the snack.

Try It—You'll Like It! Help children learn to accept new and different food experiences. Introduce children to foods that may be new to them. You might set out foods like an avocado, mango, papaya, star fruit, or persimmon. Ask the children if they can think of ways to get to know these foods. Encourage them to be open to trying new things. Ask them, "What would happen if you said 'Yucky' and walked away?" Encourage children to try the foods by explaining how we miss out when we are afraid or don't like to try new things.

Health, Safety, and Nutrition

Brush Your Teeth. Use a toothbrush and a model of teeth to demonstrate how to brush teeth after eating. Teach children this finger play and song. Sing them while the children brush their teeth after lunch.

BRUSHING TEETH

I jiggle the toothbrush again and again *(pretend to brush teeth)*
I scrub all my teeth for a while.
I swish the water to rinse them and then *(puff out cheeks to swish)*
I look at myself and I smile. *(smile at one another)*

(*Creative Resources for the Early Childhood Classroom*, second edition, Judy Herr and Libby Yvonne. Albany, NY: Delmar Publishers, 1995; p. 351. Used with permission.)

CLEAN TEETH

Tune: *Row, Row, Row Your Boat*

Brush, brush, brush your teeth
Brush them every day.
We put some toothpaste on our brush
To help stop tooth decay.

(*Creative Resources for the Early Childhood Classroom*, second edition, Judy Herr and Libby Yvonne. Albany, NY: Delmar Publishers, 1995; p. 186. Used with permission.)

Chew, Don't Choke. Remind children of the importance of chewing their food thoroughly. Tell them, "Choking is when a big piece of food gets caught in your throat. People cough when they choke, and sometimes they can't breathe. Choking on food is dangerous, and we don't want anyone to choke on their food at school." At snack time, ask each child to show you how they can take a small bite, chew their food, and swallow.

Dental Health. Gather some white ceramic tiles and food that often stains, like coffee, grape juice, mustard, berry jelly, spaghetti sauce, or cranberries. Put one food on each tile and let it dry so that it stains the tile. Set out a cup of water, a toothbrush, and toothpaste for each tile. Talk with the children about how food gets stuck in between and on our teeth. Invite the children to brush the tiles and see if they can clean them. Talk with the children about ways to brush our teeth. After children have had a chance to clean the tiles, demonstrate proper toothbrushing techniques.

Healthy and Unhealthy Foods. Help children learn to identify the foods that make up a healthy diet. Collect a variety of empty food containers. Include juice boxes, pop bottles, cookie boxes, potato chip bags, candy wrappers, and canned goods. Try to have representatives from each area on the food pyramid. Ask children to sort the foods into two categories: healthy and unhealthy. Talk with the children about why some foods are healthy and some foods are unhealthy.

Homemade Toothpaste. Gather plastic zip-lock bags for each child, baking soda, salt, and wintergreen or spearmint extract. Invite each child to put 4 teaspoons baking soda, 1 teaspoon salt, 1 teaspoon water, and 1 drop of flavoring in a bag. Seal the bag and mix the ingredients.

Language Development

> **Home Language.** *Learn the words for* food, hungry, eat, *and perhaps different types of foods in American Sign Language and the home languages of the children in your classroom.*

Bananas. Here's an entertaining finger play that is easily adapted. Repeat this simple verse, inserting the children's favorite fruit.

> Bananas are my favorite fruit, *(make fist as if holding banana)*
> I eat one every day. *(hold up one finger)*
> I always take one with me *(act as if putting one in pocket)*
> When I go out to play. *(wave good-bye)*
> It gives me lots of energy *(make a muscle)*
> To jump around and run. *(move arms as if running)*
> Bananas are my favorite fruit *(rub tummy)*
> To me they're so much fun! *(point to self and smile)*
>
> (*Creative Resources for the Early Childhood Classroom*, second edition, Judy Herr and Libby Yvonne. Albany, NY: Delmar Publishers, 1995; p. 304. Used with permission.)

Food Picture Cards. Glue large magazine pictures of all different types of food onto construction paper, or use a commercial set of food pictures. Hold up one picture at a time and ask open-ended questions like the following:

> Who can tell me about this picture?
>
> What do you see?
>
> What kind of food is it?
>
> Who do you think eats it?
>
> How do you think it tastes?
>
> What makes you think that?
>
> When have you eaten it?

Food Picture Stories. Sit down with a small group of children and some pictures of people growing, processing, preparing, or eating food. Show the children one picture at a time. Ask the children what they see in the pictures. Encourage the children to make up a story about the people and food in the pictures. If possible, write down the children's stories. Older children can write their own stories and read them to one another.

Food Books. Make individual books according to the different types of food on the food pyramid or the culturally based foods that are part of the children's diets. Invite the children to look through magazines and cut out pictures of food that they eat. Then have the children glue the pictures to pieces of construction paper or story manuscript paper. Ask them to tell you about the foods they chose, and write their words below the pictures. Older children can write their own stories about the food they eat.

Name That Food. Bring a variety of pretend foods and empty food containers to circle time. Hide the objects from the children's view. Give the children clues about one of the objects. Describe the color, shape, size, and food type. Let children guess after each clue. When a child guesses correctly, give him the object to hold and continue to play the game. You could also use pictures of food cut from magazines instead of the pretend food and empty food containers.

Math

Animals and Food Products Match. Make a game where children match the pictures of animals that provide us with food with pictures of the food products that we get from these animals. Glue the pictures onto oaktag and cover them with clear contact paper for durability.

Big and Small, Short and Tall. Set out a variety of pretend fruits and vegetables. Ask the children which one is the biggest, the smallest, the longest, the shortest, the lightest, and the heaviest.

Can You Find…? Collect a variety of grocery store advertisements and food coupons. Give each child an ad or some coupons. Ask the children with coupons to lay them out so that they can see all of them at once. Call out a number and see if children can find that numeral on their coupon or ad.

Counting Eggs. Purchase 12 plastic eggs from a discount store and number them 1 through 12. Write the number on the side of each egg so that it is easy to read. Place the eggs in a Styrofoam or cardboard egg carton. Set out a tray of counting objects and invite the children to fill the eggs with the correct number of objects. You could also use small jars, margarine tubs, or coin purses instead of the plastic eggs.

Food Match. Make four or more sets of food matching cards. Find duplicate photos in magazines, use a color photocopier to make duplicates, or trace stencils of food shapes. Include foods from all the major categories and foods that represent the diets of the children in your class or community. Place the cards in a basket and encourage children to find the matching sets.

Food Shapes. Make shapes with the children by pouring pancake batter onto a skillet. Slightly water down the pancake mix, pour it into a squeeze bottle, and cut the nozzle so that it is easy to squeeze out the pancake mix. You could use cookie cutters to cut shapes out of bread, tortillas, or other types of soft flat breads.

Food Sort. Collect pictures of a variety of foods. Glue the pictures onto index cards. Write the name of each food on the back of the card. Place the cards in a basket. Make sure that the set reflects cultural diversity present in your classroom. Set out the basket and invite the children to classify the foods. Provide labels for each of the food groups and lengths of yarn for marking the boundaries of their food groups on the floor. Instead of pictures, pretend food and empty food containers can be used in this activity.

Foods I Know and Don't Know. Collect photographs of a variety of different types of foods. Include foods common to each of the cultures in your class or community. Glue the photographs to index cards. Write the name of the food on the back of the card. Invite the children to look at each picture and sort them into two categories: "Foods I Know" and "Foods I Don't Know." Help the children learn about the foods that are unfamiliar to them. Make a chart identifying who knows and doesn't know about each of the foods. The children who are familiar with a food can help introduce it to the others.

How Much Does It Weigh? Set out a balance or make a simple balance by hanging margarine tubs from each end of a hanger. Set out a variety of pretend foods. Invite children to put the pretend food in the balance and see which weighs more, which weighs less, and how the weights of the different foods compare to one another (for example, how many apples equal a banana).

Pizza Fractions. Cut four 12-inch circles out of heavy cardboard, or ask a pizza restaurant to give you a few pizza circles. Pizza or cake circles can also be purchased at a local paper discount store. Decorate the cardboard circles with red, brown, and yellow construction paper to make the four circles look like pizzas. Use the pizzas to introduce fractions. Keep one of the pizzas whole. Cut the second pizza in half. Cut the third pizza into thirds, and the fourth pizza into fourths. Children can count the number of pieces in each pizza.

Recipe Cards. Create rebus charts of simple recipes (like making a peanut butter sandwich) or the life cycle of a food-producing plant (like an apple tree). Break the process down into simple steps, and use a line drawing to illustrate each step. Arrange the pictures from top to bottom and left to right to foster prereading skills, and write the words to each step beside or underneath the picture. You could set out several copies of a recipe card and thc ingredients to complete the recipe as a free-choice time or small group activity. You could use the life cycle rebus chart to make sequence cards and matching games.

Set the Table. Ask the children to help set the snack table so that they can practice one-to-one correspondence by placing one napkin and cup in front of each chair.

Music

Muffins and More. Sing "Do You Know the Muffin Man," inserting different types of breads and bread products. Make the song more inclusive by occasionally singing "Do You Know the Muffin Woman."

Physical Development

Balance It. Give children an opportunity to practice balancing a wicker basket of pretend fruit. Encourage the children to find different ways of balancing the fruit basket. Invite them to try balancing it on top of their heads.

Beanbag Toss. Invite children to make simple beanbags by filling socks with beans and tying the end in a knot. Challenge children to throw their beanbags into apple baskets or high into the air. They could also use the beanbags to play catch with one another, or they could balance the beanbags on various parts of their bodies.

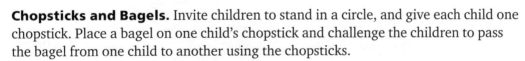

Chopsticks. Set out four sets of chopsticks and objects of different sizes, such as pretend food, large pasta shells, and dried beans. Invite the children to use the chopsticks to pick up the food and move it from one plate to another.

Chopsticks and Bagels. Invite children to stand in a circle, and give each child one chopstick. Place a bagel on one child's chopstick and challenge the children to pass the bagel from one child to another using the chopsticks.

Cooking Tools. Using kitchen gadgets can give children an opportunity to develop their fine-motor skills. Set out rotary eggbeaters or whisks and bowls of soapy water. Use kitchen tongs to pick up cotton balls and transfer them from one bowl to another. A turkey baster can be used to absorb liquid and transfer it from one container to another, and a garlic press can be used to squeeze playdough "spaghetti" or "hair."

Egg Roll. Bring a raw egg and show the children how it rolls on a table. Invite the children to pretend they are eggs by lying on their backs and bending their knees up against their chests, hugging their legs, and clasping their hands together. Encourage children to try to make their bodies roll around on the carpet or a mat.

Food Tasting. Introduce children to the different food groups by setting out platters of food. You could have a fruit tasting, vegetable tasting, bread tasting, or cheese tasting activity. Encourage children to use all of their senses to explore the foods. Invite them to taste, smell, feel, touch, and listen to food.

Hot Potato. Invite children to play the circle game commonly known as "hot potato." The object of the game is to pass the potato from one child to another as quickly as possible without dropping it. Music is played while the potato is being passed, and whoever is holding the potato when the music stops is traditionally "out" of the game, so the circle gets smaller and smaller. You could substitute a potato with another food item.

Pass the Melon. Set out a large watermelon and challenge the children to figure out a way to use their bodies cooperatively to get the melon from one side of the room to another without using their hands.

Playdough Cookies. Set out playdough, rolling pins, cookie presses, cookie cutters, and plastic knives. Invite the children to pretend they are making cookies. Use dried beans for decorating the playdough cookies.

Upset the Fruit and Vegetable Basket. Make picture cards of different fruits and vegetables. Make two to four of the same cards. Ask children to sit in a circle, and give each child a card. When you call out a fruit or vegetable, all the children who have that card jump up and exchange places. To make the game more complex, the teacher takes a seat after calling the first fruit or vegetable, which leaves a child without a place to sit. That child become the next caller.

What Is It? Set out a selection of fresh fruits and vegetables. Blindfold each child. See if they can identify the foods by using their sense of taste, touch, and smell.

Science

Bean Seeds. Line a clear plastic glass with a damp piece of blotter paper. Place some bean seeds between the paper and the glass. Keep the paper damp and watch the seeds germinate.

Food from Seeds. Plant seeds of quick growing vegetables like radishes or lettuce. Cut the tops off milk cartons. Fill them with a lightweight soil mix made especially for starting seeds, leaving 1/2 inch at the top. Place the seeds on top of the soil and sprinkle a light layer of soil over the seeds. Water lightly to moisten the soil, but be careful not to disturb the seeds. Cover with a plastic bag and place them on a sunny windowsill.

Food Pyramid. Make or purchase a poster of the food pyramid. With the children, collect a variety of food containers that match each of the areas of the food pyramid. Keep a count of the number of servings from each category that you and the children eat throughout the day.

Grow Wheat. Fill a plastic tub with 1 pound or so of vermiculite (available at garden centers) so that it is 2 inches below the rim of the tub. Sprinkle 1 pound of wheat seeds on top of the vermiculite. Water the tub until the seeds are moist. Cover loosely with plastic wrap and set it in filtered sunlight. Remove the plastic after two days and don't water the seeds for a week.

Plants from Food. Take an aluminum pan or a terra cotta saucer. Place a layer of small pebbles, gravel, or sand on the bottom. Cover with potting soil. Slice off the top 2 inches from a carrot, beet, onion, or pineapple and set it in the potting soil. Keep the soil moist and watch the plant grow.

Sweet Potato Vine. Insert toothpicks into a sweet potato. Place the potato on the lid of a widemouthed quart glass jar full of water. The toothpicks prop up the potato so that half of it sticks up out of the water. Set it near a sunny window. Soon roots will sprout from the bottom and leaves from the top. If tended, it will grow into a lovely trailing vine.

Social Development

Cooperative Fruit Salad. Set out a variety of fruits in a large bowl. Invite each child to pick out a piece of fruit. Help children wash and cut their piece of fruit. Ask the children to add their fruit slices to a bowl. Mix it up and serve the fruit salad for a snack.

Mind Your Manners. Set out decorative cups, plates, napkins, and a tablecloth at snack time. Invite the children to practice their table manners, such as waiting to eat until everyone is seated, saying please and thank you, asking for more, using a napkin, and clearing the table when everyone is done.

We're Responsible. Teach children how to be socially responsible with food. Introduce them to simple concepts such as sharing food with others, recycling food containers and grocery bags, and composting. You may want to start a recycling program in your classroom.

ACTIVITIES: AFFIRMING OURSELVES AND ONE ANOTHER

Human Rights

Everyone has the right to have enough healthy food to eat and clean water to drink.

BARRIER: Some people don't have enough money to buy good food or land to grow it. Where some children live, there isn't enough food for everyone because of things like war or drought. Some children go to school or live in old buildings where the pipes make the water unhealthy to drink.

Everyone has the right to eat the foods that come from their culture and make them feel at home without being teased or ridiculed.

BARRIER: Sometimes food that comes from a culture that's not our own can look, smell, or taste strange to us. Some foods (staples like masa harina, dal, chickpea flour, and spices, for example) aren't available in every community, school, or child care center.

DISCUSSION QUESTIONS: Help the children think about what people need for food and water and why they don't get it. Ask them questions like, "What do you think all people need to live? Why do you think people don't get the food and water they need? What different choices could we make so everyone has enough to eat and drink?"

Cultural Identity

Family Foods. Explore some of the traditional ethnic foods of the children in your class. Ask the parents to help you select a food that is specific to the cultures in your class and relatively simple to prepare. With the children, cook a dish from each child's culture and serve it for snack.

Foods from Native Americans. Introduce children to many of the foods that we eat today that were introduced to the world by the indigenous peoples of the Americas: avocado, corn, cassava melon, cashews, chilies, gum, grits, hominy, hickory nuts, beef jerky, kidney beans, potatoes, pumpkins, peanuts, popcorn, pineapple, peppers, passion fruit, papaya, pecans, quinoa, squash, sunflower seeds, sweet potatoes, turkey, tapioca pudding, tomatoes, tortillas, wild rice, yams, and zucchini.

Whenever possible, bring in samples for children to explore, or prepare a dish using the food. Display pictures that show the foods being grown, harvested, and eaten.

Multicultural Feast. Send a note home with the children inviting families to a special multicultural feast. Ask each family to bring a food dish from their family's native culture to share with the other families.

Our Garden. Invite children and parents to share what types of foods they grow and what form of gardening they use. Some families may plant their gardens in rows, others may use raised beds. Some may keep the varieties of plants separate, others may combine varieties and use companion planting. One version of a Native American planting technique is to grow corn, beans, and squash together. Form a mound of soil and put a few corn, bean, and squash seeds in a 1-inch-deep hole. When the plants are seedlings, thin the corn and squash to one plant each, because they need a lot of room. It won't hurt for a few pole bean plants to climb up the corn stalk, so don't thin the pole beans.

Place Settings. Ask parents what types of dishes and eating utensils they routinely use at dinner and how they set their table. From parents, find out where you can purchase the eating utensils and dishes. Trace each place setting onto a vinyl place mat. Invite children to try to place the correct dishes and eating utensils on each place mat.

Diversity

All Kinds of Foods. Explore a different kind of food each day. Explore different types of fruits, vegetables, breads, and dairy products. Invite the children to look at, smell, handle, and taste the different foods. Ask the children, "How are these similar to one another? How are these different from one another? What do you like about them?"

Are All the Oranges Alike? Serve oranges for snack. Peel and section the oranges. Ask the children if they know what is on the plate. Then ask, "How are all of these the same? How are they different?" Invite the children to take three to four orange sections. Ask them to see if the sections look, smell, and taste alike. Repeat this activity with a variety of foods.

Diversity at the Grocery Store. Take a walk to a local grocery store. Look at the food on the shelves. Does the grocery store sell the foods that the cultural groups in your neighborhood eat? Can people with disabilities get in and out of the store? Can they move around quickly?

Food from Nature and Food from Stores. Use pictures to introduce children to food we get from hunting, gathering, or gardening. Compare these to pictures of food that we get from the store. Use the pictures to make a sorting game. With older children, explore issues related to foods from nature. Ask the following questions:

> What natural foods are harvested in our area?

> How do people harvest wild foods today?

How does food harvesting affect the lives of people in our community today?

What changes do we see in foods from the past to the present?

How We Eat. Explore different ways of eating food. Set out different types of eating utensils, such as baby silverware, adult silverware, Japanese soup spoons, and different types of chopsticks for the children to try.

Lots of Bread. Help children experience different types of bread. Plan a bread-tasting party for snack time. Include a variety of breads (cornbread, tortillas, Mexican sweet bread, matzo, rusk, lefse, pita bread, steamed buns, chapatis, scones, black bread, fry bread, piki bread.) Talk with the children about how people from different cultures eat different kinds of bread. Introduce the different breads. Ask the children if they have ever eaten any of them before. Give each child a sample of the breads. Talk about the name of the bread and where the bread comes from. Follow up with books about bread, or bake bread for another snack.

No Seconds. Use this activity to introduce the children to the concept of hunger. At snack or lunch, give each child one small serving. As children finish and begin to ask for seconds, talk with them about how it feels to want more. Ask the children, "How would you feel if we didn't have enough for seconds? How would it feel if you were still hungry and there wasn't any more food left?"

Not Everyone Gets Enough. Give each child a paper plate with a line drawn down the middle. Invite children to cut out and glue pictures of food they like on one side of the plate. Give each child a few grains of rice to glue on the other side of the plate. Talk with the children about how some people don't get to eat the foods they like, and some people don't have enough food to eat.

One Food, Many Kinds. Explore different types of the same food. For example, set out different types of apples, grapes, potatoes, or lettuce. Invite the children to compare and contrast the foods. Ask them, "How are all of these apples similar to one another? How are all of these apples different from one another?" Cut up the foods and invite children to smell and taste each of the different types of food. Ask them again to identify the similarities and differences. Also ask the children, "Which ones do you like the best?"

One Food, Many Ways. Explore different ways to prepare the same food. Choose a readily available food that the children are familiar with. You might choose rice, potatoes, or apples. Over the course of days, prepare a variety of dishes using the particular food. For instance, you might make steamed rice, rice pudding, and rice balls. With potatoes you could make baked potatoes, mashed potatoes, french fries, potato pancakes, and potato soup. With apples you could make applesauce, apple pie or apple crisp, caramel apples, dried apples, and apple butter.

Bias and Stereotypes

I Hate It. Help children identify preconceived ideas they may have about some foods. For instance, some children may think they hate broccoli or sweet bell peppers. But when vegetables are served raw with dip, children discover that they like them. Ask the children, "Are there any foods that you don't like?" Make a note of the foods the children name. Encourage them to take another look at those foods by saying, "Let's see if we can learn about those foods and try them in some new ways—some of you might decide you like them after all."

What Do We Eat? Clarify the children's stereotypes about ethnic foods. For example, one African American four year old I knew thought that all Chinese people ate rice (and that's all they ate!). Another kindergartner thought that eating Spanish rice would make him speak Spanish. Prepare some ethnic dishes to help children realize that we eat foods from many different cultures. Use storybooks, persona dolls, and discussions to help children recognize that not all people of an ethnic group eat the same food.

What's On the Inside? Set out a variety of canned goods for the children to taste. Peel off the labels so that the cans look the same. Tell the children that they can't tell what kind of food is inside by looking at the can, and so they don't know if they will like it or not. Place the cans in front of the children and ask, "What do you think is inside these cans? How can you find out what is inside? Which one are you going to choose to eat from?" Then ask the children what they need to do to get to know someone. Can they tell if they will like someone by looking at their outsides? Reinforce that its what's on the inside that counts, and we can't judge people by simply looking at them. Return the focus of the activity to the canned goods. Open the cans and let the children try the different foods to see which ones they like and which ones they don't like.

Women and Men Cook. Help children recognize that both men and women can cook professionally and for their families. Invite a male chef to visit the classroom, or visit a restaurant, bakery, or meat market where men prepare food.

Community Service

Food Drive. Collect canned goods and take them to a local food bank.

Public Awareness Campaign. Help the children make a poster or flyer sharing what they've learned about healthy foods and good nutrition. Duplicate the flyer or poster and distribute it to other classrooms, parents, and the community.

Social Action Suggestions

Fair Advertising. Collect a variety of cereal boxes or other prepared foods that are marketed to young children. As a group, "read" the labels and find out how much sugar, fat, and salt is in each serving. Talk about how some products claim to be healthy or good for children but really are unhealthy. As a class, write to the company that manufactures the food and complain about marketing unhealthy food to children.

Food for Children. As a group work together with parents and staff to advocate for full-funding for the Child Care Food Program or WIC.

Safe Food to Eat. Explore the use of pesticides on foods the children eat. A few years ago there was a concern about the pesticides used on apples and the presence of chemicals in apple juice, which babies and children often drink. Children could write a letter to local grocery stores or the state attorney general advocating for pesticide-free food.

ACTIVITIES: OPENING THE DOOR

Classroom Visitors

Ask a chef, dietitian, or nutritionist to come to the classroom and talk about healthy foods.

Field Trips

Take a field trip to a local grocery store, restaurant, ethnic bakery, or a farm.

Parent Involvement

Ask parents to come into the classroom and talk about or prepare traditional foods eaten in their family.

Make a class cookbook. Ask parents to share their favorite family recipes. Make a book and distribute it to all of the families.

Ask parents to share their family's favorite ethnic recipes or recipes of dishes their children enjoy. Adapt the recipes to meet the requirements of the Child Care Food Program, and incorporate the dishes into the program's food service.

Parent Education

Invite a nutritionist or dietitian to talk to parents about healthy foods and encouraging children to eat a balanced diet. Invite a dentist or dental hygienist to talk about dental health and preventative dental care. Invite your program's cook to share recipes for snacks children love.

CLASSROOM RESOURCES

Children's Books

Benny Bakes A Cake, Eve Rice (New York: Mulberry, 1993).

Biggest Sandwich Ever, Rita Golden Gelman (New York: Scholastic, 1981).

Bread Is For Eating, David and Phyllis Gershator (New York: Holt, 1995).

Bread, Bread, Bread, Ann Morris (New York: Morrow, 1993).

Char Siu Bao Boy, Sandra S. Yamate (Fort Atkinson, WI: Highsmith, 1991).

Corn Belt Harvest, Raymond Bial (Boston: Houghton, 1991).

Cleversticks, Bernard Ashley (New York: Crown, 1992).

Daddy's Store, Mary Glick.

Each Orange Had 8 Slices, Paul Giganti Jr. (New York: Greenwillow, 1992).

Eat Up, Gemma, Sarah Hayes (New York: Morrow, 1994).

Eating Fractions, Bruce McMillan (New York: Scholastic, 1992).

Eating The Alphabet: Fruits And Vegetables From A TO Z, Lois Ehlert (San Diego: Harcourt, 1989).

Everybody Cooks Rice, Norah Dooley (Minneapolis: Carolrhoda, 1991).

Feast For 10, Cathryn Falwell (Boston: Houghton, 1996).

The First Strawberries: A Cherokee Story, Joseph Bruchac (New York: Dial, 1993).

Fruit And Vegetable Man, Roni Schotter (Boston: Little Brown, 1993).

Good Morning, Let's Eat! Karin Luisa Badt (Danbury, CT: Children's Press, 1994).

Growing Vegetable Soup, Lois Ehlert (San Diego: Harcourt, 1987).

Halmoni And The Picnic, Sook Nyul Choi (Boston: Houghton, 1993).

How My Parents Learned To Eat, Ina Friedman (Boston: Houghton, 1984).

Ininatig's Gift Of Sugar: Traditional Native Sugarmaking, Laura Waterman Wittstock (Minneapolis: Lerner, 1993).

Jalapeño Bagels, Natasha Wing (New York: Simon, 1995).

Lunch, Denise Fleming (New York: Holt, 1996).

Mango, Mango, Anne Schreiber (Rockville, MD: Kar-Ben, 1994).

Milk: From Cow To Carton, Aliki (New York: Harper, 1992).

Mr. Sugar Came To Town, adapted by Harriet Rohmer and Cruz Gomez (San Francisco: Children's Book, 1990).

Now I Will Never Leave The Dinner Table, Jane Read Martin (New York: Harper, 1996).

Pancakes, Pancakes, Eric Carle (New York: Simon, 1991).

Peas, Nicholas Heller (New York: Greenwillow, 1993).

Pots And Pans, Anne Rockwell (New York: Macmillan, 1993).

People Of Corn: A Mayan Story, Mary-Joan Gerson (Boston: Little Brown, 1995).

Potluck, Anne Shelby (New York: Orchard, 1991).

The Sacred Harvest: Ojibway Wild Rice Gathering, Gordon Regguinti (Minneapolis: Lerner, 1992).

Saturday Sancocho, Leyla Torres (New York: Farrar, 1995).

Shapes For Lunch! Melinda Lilly (New York: Price, 1997).

Three Stalks Of Corn, Leo Politi (New York: Simon, 1994).

Too Many Tamales, Gary Soto (New York: Putnam, 1993).

The Tortilla Factory, Gary Paulsen (San Diego: Harcourt, 1995).

Tortillas For Emilia, Maria Angeles (Littleton, MA: Sundance, 1996).

Uncle Willie And The Soup Kitchen, Anne Di Salvo-Ryan (New York: Morrow, 1997).

Vegetable Soup, Jeanne Modesitt (New York: Simon, 1991).

A Weed Is A Flower: The Life Of George Washington Carver, Aliki (New York: Simon, 1988).

What Food Is This? Rosmarie Hausherr (New York: Scholastic, 1995).

Music

Bonkrude, Sally. *Celebrating Differences With Sally B* (Musical Imaginings, 1992).

"Bread Poem"

"Billions of People"

"Crunchy Munchy Bread"

Grammer, Red. *Hello World!* (Smilin' Atcha, 1995).

"Buono Appetito"

"We're Rich"

Hinojosa, Tish. *Cada Niño/Every Child* (Rounder, 1996).

"Barnyard Dance/Baile Vegetal"

Jordan, Sarah. *Healthy Habits* (Educational Record Center).

Pirtle, Sarah. *Two Hands Hold The Earth* (Gentle Wind, 1984).

"I Talk To My Food"

Raffi. *Singable Songs for the Very Young* (Troubadour, 1976).

"Aikendrum"

———. *The Corner Grocery Store* (Troubadour, 1979).

"Going On A Picnic."

Rogers, Sally. *Peace By Peace* (Western, 1988).

"I Can't Imagine"

Shih, Patricia. *Big Ideas!* (Glass, 1990).

"Eating Is Fun, Eating Is Serious"

Tune Into Kids. *Color The World* (Endeavor, 1992).

"Candy Monster"

Visual Displays

Constructive Playthings
Food and Nutrition Picture Packets

Sandy and Son
Fruits Poster
Vegetables Poster

Videos

Eat Well! Be Well! (Educational Activities, 1986).

Dental Health Stories (Educational Activities).

Fruit (Educational Record Center).

Teaching Kits

Dental Health Resource Chest, Lakeshore

Foods and Nutrition Resource Chest, Lakeshore

Graeme, Jocelyn, and Ruth Fahlman. *Hand In Hand: Multicultural Experiences For Young Children* (Reading, MA: Addison-Wesley, 1990).

Exploring the Supermarket: The Bank Street Early Childhood Explorer Series (Reading, MA: Addison-Wesley, 1988).

Additional Resources

Chef Combo's Fantastic Adventure
National Dairy Council
O'Hare International Center
10255 West Higgins Road, Suite 900
Rosemont, IL 60018-5616
(800) 426-8271
A nutrition education kit that includes a puppet, teaching pictures, and activity ideas.

The Heart Treasure Chest
American Heart Association
(800) AHA-USA1

Many Hands Media
1133 Broadway, Suite 1123
New York, NY 10010
(212) 924-2944
Multicultural nutrition program for early childhood education.

Public Health Service
Public Affairs
Hubert H. Humphrey Building
200 Independence Avenue SW, Room 701-H
Washington, DC 20201
(202) 690-6867

World Hunger Education Service
P.O. Box 29056
Washington, DC 20017
(202) 298-9503

FRIENDS

"All my friends at school are brats and babies." "Erin, meet my new best friend Derek." "You're not the friend of me." "Sit by me, sit by me. You're my friend, right?" "If you don't play, I'm not gonna invite you to my party." "She can't be my friend because she has icky clothes." "Anybody can be my friend; I like everybody." Learning how to make and be a friend are major social skills children need to develop in the early years. Children risk isolation and rejection by their peers if, by the age of five or six, they don't know how to join other children's play, invite other children to join them, negotiate about roles and rules, incorporate and build on other's ideas, express their feelings and thoughts clearly and in an acceptable way, and manage conflict in a play group. By this time, most children's friendships have become so complex and sophisticated that children who have not learned basic friendship skills will not be able to enter into or maintain their roles in the relationships. Children tend to choose friends who are like them, and thus friendships often fall along gender and cultural lines. A unit on friends helps young children acquire basic friendship skills, increases their appreciation of the importance of relationships in their lives, and expands their circle of friends.

Friends

FRIENDS

 Look for this symbol to find activities you can use for circle time.

WEB

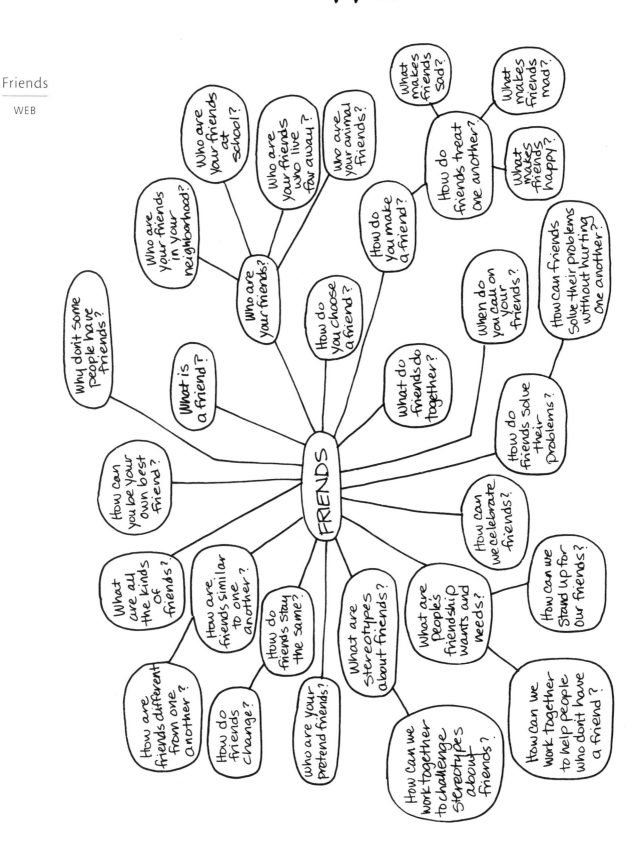

BIG AS LIFE

OUTLINE

I. What is a friend?

II. Who are your friends?
   A. Who are your friends in your neighborhood?
   B. Who are your friends at school?
   C. Who are your friends who live far away?
   D. Who are your animal friends?
   E. Who are your pretend friends?

III. How do you choose a friend?

IV. How do you make a friend?
   A. How do friends treat one another?
      1. What makes friends happy?
      2. What makes friends sad?
      3. What makes friends mad?
   B. What do friends do together?
   C. When do you call on your friend?
   D. Why don't some people have friends?

V. How do friends solve their problems?

VI. How can friends solve their problems without hurting each other?

VII. How can you be your own best friend?

VIII. What are all the kinds of friends?
   A. How are friends similar to one another?
   B. How are friends different from one another?
   C. How do friends stay the same?
   D. How do friends change?
   E. What are stereotypes about friends?
   F. How can we work together to challenge stereotypes about friends?

IX. What are people's friendship wants and needs?
   A. How can we work together to help people who don't have a friend?
   B. How can we stand up for our friends?

X. How can we celebrate friends?

MATERIALS LIST

ART

skin-colored paints, markers, crayons, construction paper, and felt

magazines with photos of people

people stencils

double easels

BLOCKS

a variety of multicultural people figures, including figures of people with disabilities

dollhouse furniture (for example, Hardwood Dollhouse Furniture, *Constructive Playthings*)

green carpet squares

plastic trees

toy playground equipment

DRAMATIC PLAY

puppet theater

people puppets

adaptive equipment for children and dolls with disabilities

preschooler dolls (for example, Friends Dolls, Children and Elders with Mobility and Visual Impairment Dolls, *People of Every Stripe*; Multi-Ethnic School Dolls, *Lakeshore*)

multicultural cooking sets (for example, Asian Cooking Set, Hispanic Cooking Set, *Lakeshore*; Culturally Specific Play Food Set, *Constructive Playthings*)

pretend phones (for example, Talk 'n Listen Phones, *Constructive Playthings*)

LARGE MOTOR

equipment to encourage partner and group play (for example, Classic Hardwood Rocking Boat, Jump Rope Set, Rainbow School Parachute, *Lakeshore*; Rickshaw, *Environments*)

LITERACY

children's books: fiction, nonfiction, and bilingual books about friends (see resource list at the end of the unit)

cassette player and theme-related storybook cassettes

multicultural child puppets (for example, Children of America Doll Puppets, *Lakeshore*)

MANIPULATIVES

multicultural puzzles about children and friends (for example, Children with Special Needs Puzzles, *Kaplan*; Judy Fantasy Inlay Puzzles, *Nasco*; Multi-Ethnic Kids Floor Puzzle Set, Valentine's Day Puzzle, *Lakeshore*; Multicultural Children Puzzle, *Constructive Playthings*; Wheelchair Friends Puzzle, *Environments*)

board games about friendship (for example, Princess Board Game, *Animal Town*; Ring Around the Rosy Game, *Constructive Playthings*; The Kindness Game, The Nurturing Game, You and Me: A Game of Social Skills, *Childswork/Childsplay*)

feelings lotto games

lacing shapes of people

figures of people for counting, matching, and sorting

SCIENCE

magnets and a collection of things that are and aren't attracted to them (for example, Giant Power Magnet, Have A Ball Magnet Set, Magnets Exploration Lab, Mysterious Magnet Tube, *Lakeshore*; Group Magnetic Wand Kit, Magnet Play, Magnets Are Fun, *Beckley-Cardy*)

SENSORY

water and equipment to encourage cooperative play (for example, pipes and connectors, water pumps, and water wheels)

Friends

MATERIALS

Teaching Through the Interest Areas

Art

Set out skin-colored art materials, stencils of people, double easels, and magazines with photos of people.

Blocks

Add green carpet squares, plastic trees, pretend playground equipment, and people figures to encourage children to create park-like settings in their block play. Include figures of people with differing abilities.

Dramatic Play

Add a variety of people puppets and a puppet theater to encourage puppet play around the friendship theme.

Add adaptive equipment to the dramatic play area to encourage friendship play among able-bodied children and children with disabilities.

Literacy

Set out a variety of fiction, nonfiction, and bilingual books on friendship. Include a tape player, friends-related storybooks and cassettes, flannel boards with figures of people, and materials for making journals and books.

Manipulatives

Set out puzzles of people and friends, feelings lotto games, lacing cards shaped like people, and figures of people for counting, matching, and sorting.

Music

Set out a variety of cassettes with songs about friendship and getting along with others.

Science

Set out a variety of magnets and objects that attract and don't attract. Include iron filings, magnetic balls, and magnets (horse shoe, wand, and ring). Add a chart for recording things that attract and things that don't.

Sensory

Set out pipes and connectors, water pumps, and water wheels to encourage children to play together cooperatively.

ACTIVITIES: INVESTIGATING THE THEME

Creative Development

Classroom Friendship Wreath. Trace children's hands onto skin-colored construction paper. Invite the children to cut out the shapes. If this is too difficult for the children, draw a circle around the hand tracing and ask the children to cut out the circle. Draw a circle in the middle of a large piece of butcher paper or poster board. Glue the paper hands around the circle with the fingers facing outward. Let the hands overlap slightly to form a wreath to decorate the classroom door.

Draw Me/Draw You. Ask children to find a partner and sit across from each other at a table. Encourage the children to draw a picture of their partner's face. Help them notice the details of each other's physical features. Encourage children to exchange their drawings when they are done. Ask the children to bring their drawings with them to circle time. Hold up one picture at a time and see if the children can guess which child is the subject of the drawing and which is the artist.

Friendship Bracelets. Set out lengths of yarn and multicolored beads. Invite children to string beads onto yarn to make a friendship bracelet.

Friendship Collage. Make a collage of friends. Invite children to go through magazines and find pictures of people who look like friends. Cut out the magazine pictures and glue them onto a piece of construction paper.

Friendship Mural. Make a classroom mural of all the things friends like to do together. Tape a large piece of butcher paper to a table. Set out crayons and felt tip markers. Invite the children to come to the table and draw pictures of fun things friends do together. Ask the children to write their names by the pictures they draw so that the class can recognize everyone's contribution to the mural.

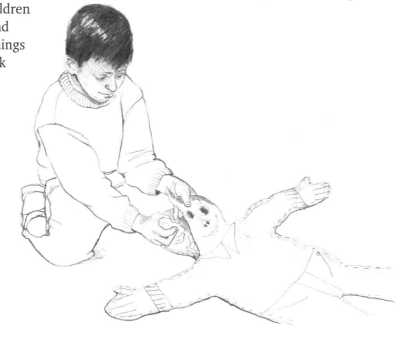

My Own Mobile. Invite the children to make a mobile that will help others get to know them. They can choose a variety of things to hang from a hanger, such as fabric, trim, or trinkets. They could choose to cut pictures from a magazine, or use photographs that you've taken of them during the year. Ask each child to bring their mobiles to circle time and share them with the rest of the class. Hang the mobiles from the ceiling for all to enjoy.

Paper Doll Friends. Invite the children to make paper dolls that could be their friends. Cut two simple body shapes out of butcher paper or paper bags for each child. Set out a variety of art materials to decorate the dolls. Include crayons, markers, feathers, buttons, construction paper scraps, yarn, and glue. Invite the children to decorate the dolls any way they like. Place the second body shape underneath the decorated one and staple the two together around the edge. Leave an opening so the children can stuff the dolls with crumpled newspapers. Once the paper dolls are stuffed, staple the opening closed.

People-Color Fans. Set out containers of skin-colored paint, paintbrushes, a hole punch, and brass fasteners. Invite the children to paint skin colors on plain white index cards or oak tag cut into 3-by-5-inch rectangles. When the cards are dry, punch a hole in corner of each card. Fasten them together. Open up the fan to show all of the colors people come in.

Weaving. Talk with the children about how some people use fabric to tell stories about their lives. Some people make quilts, some dye their fabric in bright colors and patterns, some embroider pictures on fabric, and still others weave rugs and wall hangings. Show children samples of weaving, needlework, and quilting.

Make a simple loom by cutting notches ½ inch apart on the top and bottom of a piece of cardboard. Warp the loom by wrapping a thin piece of yarn around the cardboard from top to bottom so that the yarn is in each of the slits. Secure by tying the ends. You should have vertical lines of yarn ½ inch apart. Begin weaving by threading a plastic needle with another piece of yarn in and out of the vertical lines. Weave 2 inches at the top to form a secure edge.

Set out the loom and demonstrate how to weave the yarn between the threads on the loom. Let the children try to follow the in and out sequence. Leave the materials out for a week or two so that children can add to the weaving. When finished, display the weaving along with other samples of weaving and stitchery.

Critical Thinking

A Friend Like You. Use friendship photos or figures of people to help children think about the various activities they could do with friends of different ages. Show the children pictures of an older person interacting with a child or people figures of an elder and a child. Ask the children, "If you were friends with an older person, what could you do together?" Show them a picture or people figures of a teenager and a young child together. Ask the children, "If you were friends with an adult, what could you do together?" Continue asking these questions about the various age combinations. Expand the activity to include pictures of friendships between children who are able-bodied and children with disabilities, as well as friendships between people of varying genders and cultures.

 Far Away Friends. Hold up two play figures of children and explain that these two children live very far away from each other but they want to be friends, Ask the children, "What could these two children do together even though they live very far away from each other? How can we be friends with people who live far away?"

Emotional Development

Child of the Day. Set aside a day to get to know and celebrate each child. Invite the child to bring photographs or items from home to share with the rest of the class.

 How Would You Feel If...? Help children become aware of feelings associated with prejudice and increase their sensitivity to the feelings of others. Cut an 8-inch circle out of oaktag and divide the circle into six sections. In each section draw a face to represent a different emotion. Make a spinner for the circle. Present a variety of common classroom scenarios in which friends ignore, tease, or reject each other. Pass the circle around and ask children how they would feel if their friend treated them that way. Ask the children to move the spinner so the arrow points to the face that matches how he or she would feel in the given situation.

 I Can Be a Good Friend. Foster children's self-esteem and confidence in their friendship skills. At circle time, ask each child to show the class something they can do to be a good friend to others. Make a chart listing all of the kind things we can do for others.

 I Like You. Help children focus on the good and positive qualities in each of us. At circle time, pick one child to stand in the middle. Ask each child to identify something they like about that child. Encourage them to say, "*(Child's name)*, I like you because…"

 Pass a Hug. At circle time, bend over and give the child next to you a hug. Ask the child to pass it along to the next person until the hug comes all the way back to where it began. You might want to end circle time or each day by passing a hug.

 Show Those Friendly Feelings. Ask children how their friends make them feel and how they feel about their friends. Children may talk about liking their friends and feeling warm and happy. To encourage children to think of ways to use their bodies to say, "I like you," ask them questions like "If you couldn't talk, how would you say, 'I like you?'" Go around the circle and invite the children to turn to the person next to them and say "I like you" with their bodies.

 What Is a Friend? Facilitate a group discussion about friendship. Ask children questions like:

> What is a friend?
>
> When do you call on a friend?
>
> How do friends make you feel?

What makes friends happy?

What makes friends sad?

What makes friends mad?

What Would You Do If...? Help children explore how they might feel and respond to being treated badly. Show children pictures of children in a variety of everyday interactions. Use each picture to create and tell the children about a situation in which one child makes fun of, rejects, or teases another child because of his identity. Ask the children:

How would that make you feel?

What could you do if someone made fun of you?

What could you do if someone calls you names?

What could you do if someone says you can't play?

Health, Safety, and Nutrition

Don't Give Your Friend a Cold. Talk with the children about being very sick and having a cold. How did they feel when they were sick? Did they cough? Sneeze? Explain that coughing and sneezing are ways that germs spread, and germs cause colds. Take a mister and spray it in the light. Fine drops of water will be suspended in the air. Explain that when we have a cold, we sneeze and cough and spread germs in much the same way, especially when we do not put our hands over our mouths.

There's a Cold Going Around! To play this game, tape a piece of construction paper high over the cheek of each child. Explain that you will spray one of them, giving that person the cold. To give the person a cold, the spray must show on the construction paper. A child with a cold becomes sick and moves to a "sick bay." When one child is sent to the sick bay, then one of the children already in the sick bay gets well and moves out to rejoin the group. The game is over when everyone has had a cold and made a trip to the sick bay.

At the end of the game, review how colds are spread. Remind the children that the mist from the bottle is a cough or sneeze. Ask them how they could prevent spreading germs.

Language Development

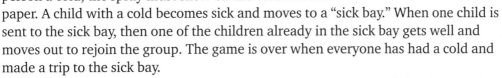

Home Language. *Learn the words for* friend, hello, good-bye, *and other greetings in American Sign Language and the home languages of the children in your classroom.*

All Our Children. Make a book about all the children in the class. You may want to involve families in putting the book together. Read about a different child each day at circle time. For each child, include the following:

What can you do?

What can't you do?

Who do you love?

Who loves you?

What do you look like?

Who do you look like?

What are your favorites?

Who is your favorite person?

What's your favorite toy?

What's your favorite color?

What's your favorite song?

What's your favorite thing to do?

What's your favorite food?

What makes you happy?

What makes you laugh?

Friends Picture Cards. Use a commercial set of teaching pictures or make your own by cutting out large magazine pictures of pairs and groups of children and gluing them onto construction paper. Hold up one picture at a time. Ask open-ended questions like the following:

Who can tell me about this picture?

What do you see?

Who is in this picture?

Where are they ?

What are they doing?

How are they feeling?

How are these friends like you and your friends?

How are these friends different from you and your friends?

 Friends at Play. Here's a counting finger play about friends. Ask the children what they like to do with one friend? with two friends? with three friends? and so forth. Incorporate their suggestions into the rhyme.

One little child with nothing to do *(hold up one finger)*
Found a friend to play with
And then there were two *(hold up two fingers)*
Two little children, playing happily

Along came another and then there were three
  (*hold up three fingers*)
Three little children
  playing grocery
  store
Along came a
  customer and
  then there were
  four (*hold up
  four fingers*)
Four little children
  with cars and
  trikes to drive
Along came a
  friend in a
  wagon, and
  then there were
  five. (*hold up five
  fingers*)

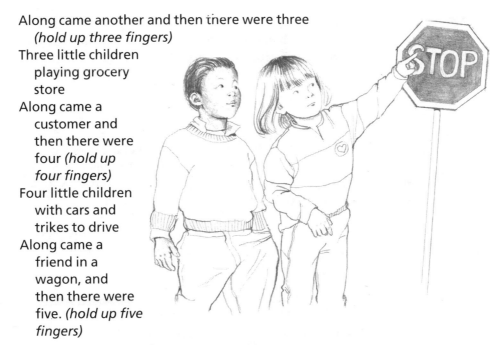

(*Busy Fingers Growing Minds: Finger Plays, Verses and Activities for Whole Language Learning*, Rhoda Redleaf. St. Paul: Redleaf Press, 1993; p. 55. Used with permission.)

Friends Picture Stories. Sit down with a small group of children and some pictures of friends. Show the children one picture at a time. Ask the children what they see in the pictures. Encourage the children to make up stories about the friends in the pictures. If possible, write down the children's stories.

Introductions. Help children gain experience introducing one friend to another. At circle time, ask children to reach out and hold hands with the person next to them. Have the children take turns introducing the person on their left. Ask them to hold their friend's hand up in the air and say, "Hey everybody, this is my friend, (*child's name*)." All the children respond, "Hello, (*child's name*)." Do this activity in English as well as the other languages spoken in your class. Ask children for other ideas of how to introduce one friend to another.

"My Friends" Book. Invite each child to make a book about his friends. Include pages for topics such as friends at home, friends at school, adult friends, and what I do with my friends, as well as other topics that make sense to you. Invite the children to draw or cut out a picture for each page. You could ask them, "What would you like to say about your friends at home? What would you like to say about your friends at school?" Write down what the children say. Repeat for each aspect of friendship included in the books.

Name Game. Explore how children got their names. Ask parents if there is any significance to their child's name. For instance, was the child named after someone? Does the name have a special meaning? Did someone else name the child? Or did the child get the name in a ceremony? Share the stories with the children at group time. You might also to get a book of baby names and look up the meaning of the children's names. Help each child make a name poster that includes the meaning of the child's name.

"We're Friends" Book. Make a class book about friendship. You could focus on ways that friends treat each other. For instance, include pages on what friends do together, how friends help each other, when friends play together, fun things friends do together, when friends fight, and how friends solve their problems.

Math

Calling My Friend. Set out two telephones and a homemade book of the children's telephone numbers. If a child doesn't have a phone number, invite him to make one up. Encourage the children to pick a friend to call, find the friend's number in the book, and then dial the number on the telephone.

Copy Me. Ask children to find a friend to work with. Set out stringing beads and laces or pattern blocks. One child goes first and makes a pattern with the beads or blocks, then the other child tries to copy it. Take turns by alternating who goes first and who copies the pattern.

 Friends Count. Set out a basket of people figures and ask children to group them in pairs of friends. Set the figures on the floor in sets of two. Then help the children count the friends by twos. At circle time, pair up the children and count them by twos.

Friends Match. Make four or more sets of friends matching cards. Find duplicate photos of people who look like they are friends in magazines, or use a color copier to make duplicates of animal photos. Include photographs of friendships between able-bodied children and children with disabilities, and friendships across cultures, genders, and generations. Place the cards in a basket and encourage children to find the matching sets.

 Friend Shapes. Challenge the children to work with a partner and make shapes with their bodies. Ask them, "How can you make a circle with your bodies? Is there another way to make a circle? Can you make a square? Can you make a triangle?"

How Many? Ask each child to name all his friends. Write down all of the names on a piece of paper. Ask the child to count how many friends were named. On the bottom of the paper, write "(_Child's name_) has (_number_) friends."

 Patty-Cake Count. Pair up children and teach them a simple patty-cake sequence (clap your hands, touch your right palm to your partner's left palm, clap your hands, touch your left palm to your partner's right palm). Have the children count out loud at they touch palms. Teach them chants that involve counting.

People-in-My-World Sort. Collect a variety of pictures of people representing diversity in race, culture, gender, age, economic class, and physical ability. Glue the pictures to index cards. Place the pictures in a basket. Set out the basket along with a sorting tray. Invite the children to classify the people pictures any way they like.

Music

Friendship Songs. Songs are wonderful ways of reinforcing theme-related concepts. Here are five songs about friendship to sing with the children.

THE MORE WE ARE TOGETHER

Tune: *Have You Ever Seen a Lassie?*

The more we are together, together, together,
The more we are together, the happier we'll be.
For your friends are my friends, and my friends are your friends.
The more we are together the happier we'll be.

We're all in school together, together, together,
We're all in school together, and happy we'll be.
There's (*child's name*), and (*child's name*), and (*child's name*), and
   (*child's name*),
We're all in school together and happy we'll be.

(*Creative Resources for the Early Childhood Classroom*, second edition, Judy Herr and Libby Yvonne. Albany, NY: Delmar Publishers, 1995; p. 293. Used with permission.)

THE MORE WE WORK TOGETHER

Tune: *Have You Ever Seen a Lassie?*

The more we work together, together, together
The more we work together, the happier we'll be
For your friends are my friends, and my friends are your friends.
The more we work together the happier we'll be.

I LIKE YOU

Tune: *Skip To My Lou*

I like you; there's no doubt about it.
I like you; there's no doubt about it.
I like you; there's no doubt about it.
You are my good friend.

You like me; there's no doubt about it.
You like me; there's no doubt about it.
You like me; there's no doubt about it.
I am your good friend.

I like me; there's no doubt about it.
I like me; there's no doubt about it.
I like me; there's no doubt about it.
I am my good friend.

(*The Friendly Classroom for a Small Planet*, Priscilla Prutzman, Lee Stern, M. Leonard Burger, and Gretchen Bodenhamer. Gabriola Island, Canada: New Society, 1988; p. 105. Used with permission.)

One Little Friend

Tune: *One Elephant Went Out To Play*

One little friend went out to play
Out to the park on a summer day
he had such enormous fun
He called for another little friend to come.

(*Busy Fingers Growing Minds: Finger Plays, Verses and Activities for Whole Language Learning*, Rhoda Redleaf. St. Paul: Redleaf Press, 1993; p. 55. Used with permission.)

Physical Development

 Bouncing Balls. Ask children to pick a friend. Give each pair a ball and ask them to bounce the ball back and forth. Then ask them to be creative and think of other ways that they could bounce the ball to a friend.

 Find a Place for Everyone. Play a cooperative version of musical chairs. Arrange the chairs in a circle, and play music. When it stops, challenge the children to get up, change seats, and make sure that everyone has a place to sit. Take a chair away each time you stop the music. By the end, the children will all be piled onto one chair.

Friends Puzzles. Take a close-up photo of the children in your class playing together. Take photos of pairs, triads, small groups, and large groups. Use a color photocopier to enlarge the photos. Glue the photocopies to pieces of oaktag or poster board and cut into puzzle pieces. Older children can make their own puzzles.

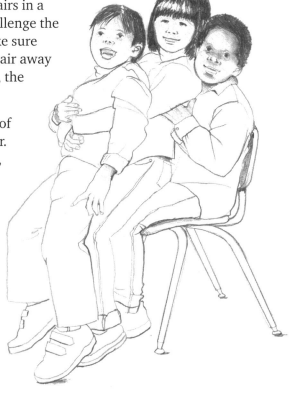

 Mirror Friends. Ask the children what happens when they stand in front of a mirror and move their bodies. What do they see in the mirror? What does the reflection do? Ask the children to find a partner and stand facing each other. Tell them to pretend that one child is looking into a mirror and the other child is the reflection. One child must copy the other child's move, just as if he was the reflection in a mirror. Give the children a chance to change roles often.

 Musical Hugs. Children move around the room while music plays. When the music stops, everyone hugs another person. Each child must find a different person to hug every time the music stops. The children could also greet one another by shaking hands, saying hello, or greeting the other person in another language.

Red Rover. Here's a cooperative twist on a traditional children's game. Ask children to form two lines that are facing one another, and at least 10 to 15 feet apart. The children in one line select a child in the line across from them to come and join them by saying, "Red Rover, Red Rover, let (*child's name*) come over." In this version, change the word *come* to a movement, like jump, run, hop, crawl, dance, gallop, or crab walk, so the emphasis is on how the child gets from one side to the other. When the child reaches the other side, the children in that line clap and welcome the newcomer. Repeat the activity with the other line calling a child over. Continue until all of the children have had a turn.

Touching Game. Play a group game about finding and touching body parts. Invite children to stand up. First ask them to find and touch different body parts on their own body. Then ask them to use their hand to touch a friend. Then ask children to touch various body parts on their friend. You can then ask children to touch physical features related to race (hair, eyes, nose, mouth, skin).

Science

Animal Friends. Involve the children in learning about and selecting an animal for the classroom. Some popular classroom pets are hamsters, gerbils, guinea pigs, mice, rats, and rabbits. My favorites are guinea pigs, rats, and dwarf rabbits. Consider the personality, sleeping habits, space requirements, and heartiness of the animal you choose. Once the class has decided on the type of pet, begin gathering supplies. You will need a cage and food and water dishes. Help the children learn about how they can be friends with the pet. Find out about the care their animal will need—the type and amount of food it eats, the type of exercise it needs, how to keep its cage clean, and how to hold it.

Me and My Shadow. Sometimes we think of our shadows as friends who follow us everywhere. Encourage children to think about what makes a shadow. Provide the children with a variety of light sources (flashlight, desk lamp, slide projector) and invite them to find partners and explore light and shadow. To cast a shadow on a wall, one child points a light source at the wall, and the other stands between the light source and the wall. To expand this activity, you may want to trace the child's silhouette on paper. If it is a sunny day, go outside and look for your shadows. Trace shadows on the sidewalk with colored chalk.

Ladybugs. Ladybugs are friends to gardeners because they eat aphids that destroy flowers and garden plants. To create an environment for observing ladybugs, pour a thin layer of soil in a large jar or aquarium. Wet the soil down so that it is moist like a damp sponge. Add some twigs and small stones so that the ladybugs will have a place to hide. Gather some ladybugs or order some from a garden supply company. You can also purchase ladybugs at some garden centers. Place them in the container and feed them aphids from infected plants. They eat a lot but won't need any water—that need is met by eating the aphids. Encourage children to let the ladybugs crawl on their fingers and hands. After a week of observing the ladybugs, help the children be friends of nature by letting the ladybugs go free in a garden.

Social Development

Cooperative Drawings. Here's a chance for each child to make a contribution to a cooperative effort. Divide the class into small groups of five to six children. Ask the children to sit in a circle, and give each child crayons and paper. Ask the children to draw a picture on their piece of paper. After two minutes, ask the children to pass the picture to the person on their left. Ask the children to add to the picture.

Friendliest Kids. Make a bulletin board entitled, "We're The Friendliest Kids Around." Every time a child does something friendly, write it up and post it on the bulletin board.

Friends Work It Out. Help children learn how to resolve their conflicts with one another. Teach them the following five-step problem-solving method:
1. Find out what happened.
2. Name the problem, our feelings, our wants, and our needs.
3. Think of solutions.
4. Make a choice.
5. Do it!

Some teachers encourage children to ask one another if they want a hug after they have resolved their conflict.

I Want It. Children need help learning to take turns and share. Bring a popular classroom toy to circle time. Set it on the floor in front of the children. Ask them to pretend that two children both want to play with it. Ask the children, "What can they do? How can they work out this problem?"

The Kindness Pledge. Invite children to take the kindness pledge each morning at circle time.

> I pledge to myself, on this day.
> To try to be kind, in every way.
> To every person, big and small,
> I will help them if they fall.
> When I love myself and others, too,
> That is the best that I can do!

(*The Kindness Curriculum: Introducing Young Children to Loving Values*, Judith Anne Rice. St. Paul: Redleaf Press, 1995; p. 9. Used with permission.)

Make a Friend. Help children learn how to make a friend. Begin by asking the children, "How do you make a friend?" Then use a puppet or persona doll to role-play the steps of greeting a friend and asking him to play. Have the puppet think to herself, "Gee, I sure would like to play with someone. I'll look around the room and see who's here. Oh, there's a boy at the sand table. I'd like to play in the sand. I'll just walk over there." Pretend to walk the puppet over to the sand table and introduce herself by saying, "Hi, my name is Marissa. What's your name? Can I play with you?" Incorporate the children's ideas into the role-play. Follow up by inviting the children to practice walking up to one another, introducing themselves, and asking another child if he would like to play.

Our Wish for Our Friends. Ask children if they know what a wish is. Ask each child what their wish is. Then ask the children what their wish is for their friends. Go around the circle and invite each child to wish something for another child in the class. Here is a poem that children can recite as they make wishes:

> If my mind was a wishing well,
> I'd find a wish that I could tell—
> A thought from me to you,
> A wish for smiles and fun—
> Something you can do
> To warm you like the sun.

(*The Peaceful Classroom*, Charles Smith. Beltsville, MD: Gryphon House, 1993; p. 163. Used with permission.)

Stand Up to Hitting and Kicking. Help children develop assertiveness in the face of hitting, kicking, or other forms of physical aggression. Use a doll or puppet to role-play the experience of being hit. Ask the children, "How do you think the puppet feels? What can the puppet do when others hit him?" Discuss the children's answers. Tell the children that you know how to stand up for yourself, which is a way to respond that is strong and doesn't hurt anyone. You have to stand tall and proud, look at the other person, speak in a strong voice and speak your truth (what you know, what you feel, and what you need). Use the puppet to model standing up for yourself. Reenact the hitting incident and have the puppet stand tall, look at the puppet who hit him, and say in a strong voice, "No hitting! I don't like it when you hit me. Use your words instead!"

Who Is Missing? Help children recall the friends in their class. Take pictures of each child in the classroom. Set them all faceup for the children to see. Pick up the pictures, shuffle them, and take one out. Lay the rest down faceup. Ask the children to look at the pictures and guess which one is missing. The child who guesses correctly can shuffle the pictures, pull one out, and lay them out again.

ACTIVITIES: AFFIRMING OURSELVES AND ONE ANOTHER

Human Rights

Everyone has the right to choose the friends they want.

BARRIER: Sometimes we don't think of someone as a possible friend because we believe the stereotypes about him or her. Sometimes other people don't think it's okay for us to be friends with people who are different from us.

Everyone has the right to be treated with respect.

BARRIER: Name-calling, teasing, leaving people out, and refusing to hold someone's hand are some of the ways children are mean or disrespectful to one another.

Everyone has the right to keep their bodies and their feelings safe.

BARRIER: Sometimes we hurt other people by accident. Sometimes when people are mad they forget that it isn't okay to hurt other people's feelings or bodies. Sometimes we are afraid to say no to others. Sometimes we make fun of other people's feelings when they are mad, sad, or scared.

DISCUSSION QUESTIONS: Help children think about what people want and need from their friends. Ask them questions like, "Who do you think needs to have a friend? How do you make friends with someone you don't know yet? What makes someone a good friend to you? How do you want your friends to treat you? What do your friends do that makes you feel angry? What do you do when you get mad at your friend? What do you think gets in the way of making friends with someone? Why do you think some people don't have friends? How can we help people who don't have friends?"

Cultural Identity

Family Friends. Explore family friends. Ask the children, "Who are your family's friends? What do you do with family friends?" Give the children an opportunity to share what their families do when they get together with their friends.

Games from My Home Culture. Introduce children to games from the cultures represented in your classroom that childhood friends might play.

BIG AS LIFE

Special Friends. In some cultures, there are special names and roles for family friends. Sometimes there are ceremonies in which a special friend is named and recognized. These special friends have an important role to play in a child's life. Invite parents to visit the classroom and talk with the children about the role of special friends in their family and culture. For example, Latino American cultures use the role of the compadre, comadre, and padrenos (godparents) as special adults in children's lives.

Diversity

Ask First. Young children may assume that a person with a disability is helpless and fall into the pattern of automatically helping and caring for the person with a disability in a paternalistic way. Give able-bodied children a chance to role-play offering help to a person with a disability. Teach the children how to ask permission before helping a person with a disability ("Do you want me to help you?"), wait for the person with the disability to respond, and accept the children's answers. Present them with a variety of situations:

> "Suppose a child named Mikkel was in our class and he was blind. What do you think we would have to do to make it easy for him to know where things are and recognize the children in our classroom?"

> "What if a child named Angela was in our class and she used a wheelchair to move around. What do you think we could do so that she would be able to go all the places that other children go in our classroom?"

> "What if a child named Derius was in our class and he was Deaf and used American Sign Language. How could we learn to talk to Derius and play with him?"

> "What if a child named Hua was in our class and she had prosthetic arms. How would we make sure she could use the toys that are in our classroom?"

Biracial and Interracial Friends. Learn about people who are interracial. Show children photographs of interracial families and people who are biracial. Talk about how people of one culture can marry people of another culture. People with one skin color can marry people with another skin color. They can have children together and we say that children whose parents come from different cultures are biracial. Invite children to draw a picture of an interracial family or a person who is biracial.

Color Doesn't Change Anything. Set out color paddles or make your own by placing color cellophane inside embroidery hoops. Ask children to hold hands with a friend. Ask them to look at their friend and say what they like about each other. Give each pair of friends a color paddle. Invite them to look at one another through the paddle. Ask them what is different about their friends? Ask them if their friend's skin color changes or if their friend's color is different. Does this change their friendship? Help them recognize that it doesn't matter what color of skin a person has, because it is what's on the inside that counts.

Friends are Alike and Different. Explore the ways in which friends can be similar to and different from one another. Invite the children to think about all the ways they are like their friends and different from their friends. For instance, do friends like the same toys? Do friends wear the same clothes? Do friends live in the same house? Do friends have the same hair? Do friends have the same skin? Do friends have the same parents? Do friends like the same foods? Are friends the same age? Do friends have the same kinds of bodies?

Friends

BIAS AND
STEREOTYPES

Just Like You. Help children explore the concept of alike and different. Display a variety of pictures of people that represent different cultures and abilities. Ask the children to find a friend and pick out all of the pictures of people who look like their friend. If a child seems unsure about selecting a particular picture, encourage him to look closely at his friend. Talk about the common features between the people in the pictures and the children.

We're All Human. Help children explore ways that friends are similar to and different from one another. Display pictures of diverse people who appear to be friends. Show children the pictures and discuss them. Ask the children, "How are the friends in these pictures similar to one another? How are you similar to your friends? How are you like the friends in these pictures?"

Fun Differences. Here's a simple song that promotes positive attitudes toward differences. Follow up by charting all the ways friends can be alike and different.

> Tune: *Skip to My Lou*
>
> What if all your friends looked just like you?
> What if all your friends talked the same way too?
> What if all your friends toys were blue?
> What a boring world this would be.
>
> I'm glad we're different each and every one.
> I'm glad that we all have our own song.
> I'm glad that we're special each and every one
> It's fun to be different you see.

Bias and Stereotypes

Are You One or the Other? Some children make the mistake of believing that a biracial child is from one culture or another. Children may say to their biracial playmate, "That's not your mom. She's white and you're brown." Give children an opportunity to stand up to rejection by role-playing situations where children say, "You can't be...," to other children. This technique is valuable for combating many of the stereotypic comments children make to one another. Consider role-playing other examples as well. For example, children may make any of the following prescriptive comments: "You can't have two moms," "You can't get married when you grow up 'cause only boys can marry girls," "You can't wear a dress 'cause only girls wear dresses," and "You can't be a firefighter 'cause only boys can be firefighters."

Find the Stereotypes. Talk with the children about how we often send our friends greeting cards. Ask the children, "When do you get cards? When does your mom get cards?" Take a walk to a local drug store or card shop. Look at the cards on display. Are there any cards with African Americans, Native Americans, Asian Americans, or Latinos on them? Are there any cards with people with disabilities? Are there any cards that are stereotypic? Ask the children how they think those cards will make people feel. Ask the children if they can imagine how it might feel to be left out or see a stereotypic picture of yourself, especially on a day like a birthday or a holiday. Ask the children if they think they could do anything to change the kinds of cards that the store carries or the kinds of cards the card companies make. Depending on what they come up with, you may want to suggest talking to or writing the store manager or the card company.

Pick a Friend. Help children explore their preferences in picking friends. Show children pictures of boys and girls of different ages, cultures, economic classes, and abilities. Show children the pictures. Ask them, "Who would you like to be your friend?" After the child chooses a picture of someone who could be his friend, ask "What makes this child look like a friend to you? Do you see any other children who could be your friend?" Help children recognize any biases they might have, such as not picking a child who has a disability, or who wears dirty clothes, or has a different skin color.

Community Service

A Friend is Someone to Lean On. Help children recognize when people need their friends to help them. Encourage children to think about times when they need their friends by asking, "When do you need help from a friend? Are there any times when your mom or dad needs help from a friend? Are there people in our community who might need a friend to help them?"

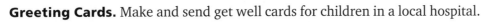

Gift Baskets. Make gift baskets to give to senior citizens. Collect personal care items, food, books, bedding, and greeting cards. Take a field trip to deliver the baskets personally.

Greeting Cards. Make and send get well cards for children in a local hospital.

Senior Friends. Form an ongoing relationship with residents of a local nursing home. Visit every week or two, and alternate the location. One week the children could go to the nursing home, and the next week the senior citizens could come to the children's school or center. Sing, play games, watch videos, cook and eat snacks, and take field trips together.

Social Action Suggestions

Television Violence. Work together to protest the amount of violence on television. Request that television stations help children learn how to be friends.

ACTIVITIES: OPENING THE DOOR

Classroom Visitors

Invite senior citizens, police officers, or firefighters to visit the classroom to show and talk about how they are friends to children.

Field Trips

Take a field trip to a local park where children can play together. Or take a field trip to a nursing home or senior citizen center.

Parent Involvement

Encourage parents to set up play dates for their children and other class members so that the children can get together outside of school.

Parent Education

Invite a local expert or advocate on child abduction to give a presentation on how to teach children about strangers and prevent child abductions. You could also offer to make identification cards that include each child's photograph and fingerprints.

Invite a child development specialist or multicultural education coordinator to talk with parents about preventing prejudice and promoting children's positive interaction with people who are different from themselves.

CLASSROOM RESOURCES

Children's Books

Adventures of Connie and Diego, Marcia Garcia (San Francisco: Children's Book, 1994).

Aekyung's Dream, Min Paek (San Francisco: Children's Book, 1988).

All About You, Catherine Anholt and Laurence Anholt (New York: Viking, 1991).

Almond Cookies And Dragon Well Tea, Cynthia Chin-Lee (Chicago: Polychrome, 1993).

Amigo Means Friend, Louise Everett (Mahwah, NJ: Troll, 1997).

Andrew Jessup, Nette Hilton (New York: Ticknor, 1993).

Anna's Secret Friend, Yoriko Tsutsui (New York: Puffin, 1989).

Be Good To Eddie Lee, Virginia Fleming (New York: Philomel, 1993).

Bein' With You This Way, W. Nikola-Lisa (New York: Lee, 1994).

Best Friends Sleep Over, Jacqueline Rogers (New York: Scholastic, 1993).

Best Friends Together Again, Aliki (New York: Greenwillow, 1995).

Big Friend, Little Friend, Eloise Greenfield (New York: Writers and Readers, 1991).

Billy The Great, Rosa Guy (New York: Delacorte, 1991).

Black Like Kyra, White Like Me, Judith Vigna (Morton Grove, IL: Whitman, 1996).

Bo and Peter, Betsy Franco.

The Bracelet, Yoshiko Uchida (New York: Philomel, 1993).

Brusca, María Cristina (New York: Holt, 1994).

Caravan, Lawrence McKay Jr. (New York: Lee, 1995).

A Caribbean Counting Book, Charles Faustin (Boston: Houghton, 1996).

Chicken Sunday, Patricia Polacco (New York: Philomel, 1992).

Come Sit By Me, Margaret Merrifield (North York, Canada: Stoddart, 1998).

Count On Your Fingers African Style, Claudia Zaslavsky (New York: Harper, 1980).

Count Your Way Through Africa, Jim Haskins (Minneapolis: Lerner, 1989).

A Country Far Away, Nigel Gray (New York: Orchard, 1991).

Dancing With The Indians, Angela Shelf Medearis (New York: Holiday, 1991).

Down Home At Miss Dessa's, Bettye Stroud (New York: Lee, 1996).

Eagle Song, Joseph Bruchac (New York: Dial, 1977).

Friends From The Other Side, Gloria Anzaldua (San Francisco: Children's Book, 1995).

Friends In The Park, Rochelle Bunnett (New York: Checkerboard, 1992).

Fruit And Vegetable Man, Roni Schotter (Boston: Little Brown, 1993).

The Generous Jefferson Bartleby Jones, Forman Brown (Los Angeles: Alyson, 1991).

Giving Thanks: A Native American Good Morning Message, Chief Jake Swamp (New York: Lee, 1995).

Got Me A Story To Tell, Sylvia Yee (St. John's Educational Threshold Center, 1977).

Gracias Rosa, Michelle Markel (Morton Grove, IL: Whitman, 1995).

Hawaii Is A Rainbow, Stephanie Feeney (Honolulu: University of Hawaii, 1985).

Hello Amigos, Tricia Brown (New York: Holt, 1992).

Here We Are Together, Aileen Fisher.

I Know Everything About John And He Knows Everything About Me, Louise Fitzhugh (New York: Doubleday, 1993).

Jacks Around the World, Mary Lankford (New York: Morrow, 1996).

Jamaica Tag-Along, Jaunita Havill (Boston: Houghton, 1993).

Jamaica's Find, Juanita Havill (Boston: Houghton, 1987).

Jamaica and Brianna, Jaunita Havill (Boston: Houghton, 1996).

The Land Of Many Colors, Klamath County YMCA Preschool (New York: Scholastic, 1993).

Little Blue And Little Yellow, Leo Lionni (New York: Morrow, 1995).

Loving, Ann Morris (New York: Lothrop, 1990).

Luka's Quilt, Georgia Guback (New York: Greenwillow, 1994).

Manners, Aliki (New York: Morrow, 1997).

Margaret And Margarita/Margarita Y Margaret, Lynn Reiser (New York: Greenwillow, 1993).

Matthew And Tilly, Rebecca C. Jones (New York: Dutton, 1991).

Me And Neesie, Eloise Greenfield (New York: Harper, 1984).

Mine! Hiawyn Oram and Mary Rees (Hauppauge, NY: Barron's, 1992).

Miss Tizzy, Libba Moore Gray (New York: Simon, 1993).

Making Friends, Fred Rogers (New York: Putnam, 1996).

Mrs. Katz And Tush, Patricia Polacco (New York: Bantam, 1992).

My Friends, Taro Gomi (San Francisco: Chronicle, 1995).

My Friend Leslie: The Story Of A Handicapped Child, Maxine B. Rosenberg (New York: Lothrop, 1983).

My Grapes, Megan McGrath (Duluth, MN: Pfeifer-Hamilton, 1993).

My Navajo Sister, Eleanor Schick (New York: Simon, 1996).

Peace Begins With You, Katherine Scholes (Boston: Little Brown, 1990).

Pink And Say, Patricia Polacco (New York: Philomel, 1994).

Rainbow Fish, Marcus Pfister (Carson, CA: Book Nippan, 1997).

Rainbow Fish To The Rescue! Marcus Pfister (Union City: Pan Asian, 1996).

A Ride On Mother's Back, Emery Bernhard (San Diego: Harcourt, 1996).

The River That Gave Gifts, Margo Humphrey (San Francisco: Children's Book, 1987).

Roses For Gita, Rachna Gilmore (London: Mantra, 1996).

Say It, Sign It, Elaine Epstein (New York: Scholastic, 1994).

Secret Valentine, Catherine Stock (New York: Simon, 1991).

Shoes, Shoes, Shoes, Ann Morris (New York: Lothrop, 1995).

Smoky Night, Eve Bunting (San Diego: Harcourt, 1994).

Someone Special Just Like You, Tricia Brown (New York: Holt, 1991).

Street Rhymes Around The World, Jane Yolen (Honesdale, PA: Boyds Mills, 1992).

Three Wishes, Lucille Clifton (New York: Dell, 1994).

Together, George Ella Lyon (New York: Orchard, 1989).

We Are Best Friends, Aliki (New York: Morrow, 1987).

The Woman Who Outshone The Sun, Alejandro Cruz Martinez and Fernando Olivera (San Francisco: Children's Book, 1991).

Why Can't I Be The Leader? Pam Griscom (Portola Valley: Share, 1992).

Wilfred Gordon McDonald Partridge, Mem Fox (Brooklyn, NY: Kane/Miller, 1985).

Yo! Yes? Chris Raschka (New York: Orchard, 1993).

Music

The Children of Selma. *Who Will Speak For The Children?* (Rounder, 1987).

"Hello Friends"

"Unite Children"

Grammer, Red. *Teaching Peace* (Smilin' Atcha, 1986).

"Shake Your Brains"

Hartmann, Jack. *Let's Read Together* (Educational Activities, 1990).

"Everyone Needs To Feel Needed"

"Sharing and Caring"

———. *Make a Friend, Be a Friend* (Educational Activities, 1990).

"Be a Friend—Don't Be a Bully"

"Friends Rap"

"Make a Friend, Be a Friend"

"My Name Is Daniel"

"We Know Your Name"

"You've Got Personality"

———. *One Voice For Children* (Educational Activities, 1993).

"Circle of Friends"

"Everyone's Different"

"Friends"

Lefranc, Barbara. *I Can Be Anything I Want To Be* (Doubar, 1990).

"Name of the Game"

"Will You Be My Friend?"

Pirtle, Sarah. *Two Hands Hold The Earth* (Gentle Wind, 1984).

"I Am A Person"

"There Is Always Something You Can Do"

Raffi. *Singable Songs For The Very Young* (Troubadour, 1976).

"The More We Get Together"

"The Sharing Song"

Rogers, Sally. *Peace By Peace* (Western, 1988).

"Don't You Push Me Down"

"I Wanna Be Somebody"

"I'm So Lucky To Be In The World"

"Mir Peace"

———. *What Can One Little Person Do?* (Round River, 1992).

"No One"

Shih, Patricia. *Big Ideas!* (Glass, 1990).

"Bully"

"Cooperate"

"The Sandbox"

"Three Wishes"

Songs for Peacemakers (Beckley-Cardy, 1994).

Thomas, Marlo, and Friends. *Free To Be…A Family* (A&M, 1988).

"Thank Someone"

Vitamin L. *Walk A Mile* (Lovable Creature, 1989).

"I Want To Get To Know You"

"I Want To Walk A Mile In Your Shoes"

"So Much To Share"

Visual Displays

ABC School Supply
Good Manners Posters

Constructive Playthings
Good Manners Picture Packets
Living Together In America Teaching Picture Packets

Lakeshore
Children of the U.S. Poster Pack

National Black Child Development Institute
Horizons Poster

New Moon
Listen to Girls Poster

Syracuse Cultural Workers
Babies Poster

Videos

Children's Songs Around The World (Educational Record Center, 1989).

Songs For Peacemakers (Educational Activities, 1994).

Computer Software

Dr. T's Sing-A-Long Around the World CD-ROM, Scholastic

All-In-One Language Fun CD-ROM by Syracuse Language Lab, Educational Record Center

Spanish/Español CD-ROM by Twin Sisters Productions, Educational Record Center

Teaching Kits

Different and the Same: Helping Children Identify and Prevent Prejudice (created by Family Communications, Inc., producers of Mr. Rogers' Neighborhood). Available from:

University of Nebraska-Lincoln
P.O. Box 80669
Lincoln, Nebraska 68501-0669
(800)228-4630
fax: (800)306-2330

Additional Resources

Kids Meeting Kids
380 Riverside Drive
New York, NY 10025

YOUTHPEACE
War Resisters League
339 Lafayette Street
New York, NY 10012
(800) WRL-YOUTH
(212) 228-0450
Order an organizing packet that includes resolving conflicts (K -12), parenting non-violently, countering violent toys, uprooting conditions that underlie violence against and by youth, ending militarism.

HEROES AND SHEROES

"I'm a superhero!" "Me too." "Don't you know, girls can't be superheroes." Young children are attracted to people who they perceive as having power. They watch their every move and imitate their words and intonation, body movements, and behavior—that's why children are so attracted to media action heroes. Often early childhood educators simply ban action figures and superhero play from the classroom. A unit on heroes and sheroes gives children the opportunity to clarify real and pretend, identify and get in touch with their own personal power, learn about real heroes and sheroes who work to make the world a better place, and discover ways of being a hero or shero in their everyday lives. I suggest using the word *shero* rather than *heroine* for female heroes because young children tend to think that only boys can be heroes, not girls. Young children use the gender pronouns he and she, and they easily make a connection between he and hero and she and shero. Using the terms hero and shero helps teach children that anybody can be powerful and can work to make the world a better place—boy or girl, man or woman.

UNIT 5:

HEROES AND SHEROES

 Look for this symbol
to find activities you
can use for circle time.

WEB

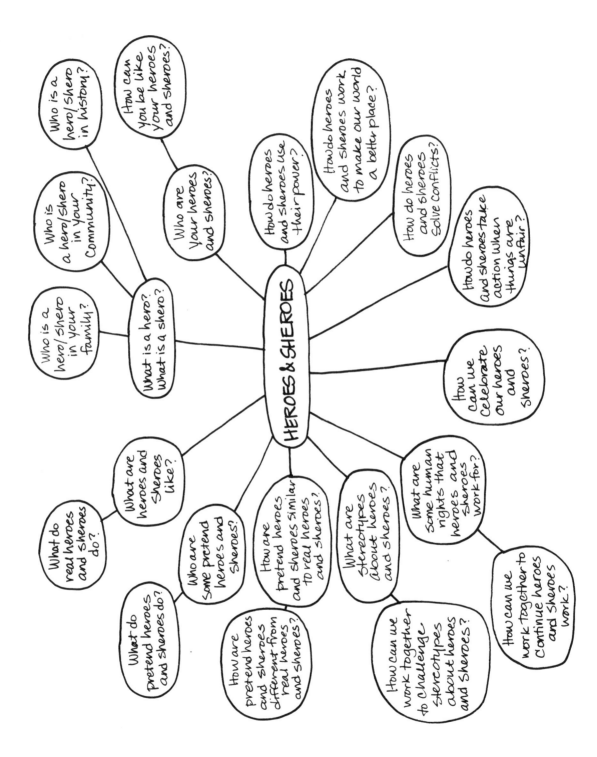

OUTLINE

I. Who are your heroes and sheroes?

II. What is a hero? What is a shero?

    A. Who is a hero/shero in your family?

    B. Who is a hero/shero in your community?

    C. Who is a hero/shero in history?

III. What are heroes and sheroes like?

    A. What do real heroes and sheroes do?

    B. How do heroes and sheroes use their power?

    C. How do heroes and sheroes work to make our world a better place?

    D. How do heroes and sheroes solve conflicts?

    E. How do heroes and sheroes take action when things are unfair?

    F. How can you be like your heroes and sheroes?

IV. Who are some pretend heroes and sheroes?

    A. What do pretend heroes and sheroes do?

    B. How are pretend heroes and sheroes similar to real heroes and sheroes?

    C. How are pretend heroes and sheroes different from real heroes and sheroes?

V. What are stereotypes about heroes and sheroes?

VI. How can we work together to challenge the stereotypes about heroes and sheroes?

VII. What are some human rights that heroes and sheroes work for?

VIII. How can we work together to continue heroes' and sheroes' work?

IX. How can we celebrate and honor our heroes and sheroes?

Materials List

ART

skin-colored paints, markers, crayons, construction paper

gold and silver paint (for example, Jumbo Glitter Painters, Silver and Gold Liquid Paint, *Lakeshore*; Washable Glitter Paint, *Constructive Playthings*)

metallic poster board, foil, and Mylar scraps (for example, Metallic Foil Board and Paper, *ABC School Supply*; Sparkle Colors Cello Toss and Shredded Metallic Mylar, *Environments*)

butcher paper roll

paper cut outs of people (for example, Paper People, *Environments*)

paper shopping bags

paper plates

wooden clothespins

fabric scraps

fine-tipped markers

current events, photojournalism, and news magazines with many pictures of diverse people

BLOCKS

a variety of multicultural people figures, including figures of people with disabilities

action hero figures

play castle and fantasy figures

city mats or carpets

skyscrapers

rescue vehicles

rescue worker figures

DRAMATIC PLAY

superhero props like capes, tunics, hats, eye masks, and wands (for example, Dress-Ups Adventure Set, *Nasco*; RoleOvers Dramatic Play Clothes, RoleOvers Hat Set, *Environments*)

LARGE MOTOR

a variety of sports-related equipment (for example, a baseball tee, plastic baseballs, plastic bats, small basketballs, basketball hoops, soccer nets and soccer balls, plastic bowling balls and bowling pins, plastic golf clubs and golf balls)

LITERACY

children's books: fiction, nonfiction, and bilingual books about heroes and sheroes (see resource list at the end of the unit)

cassette player and theme-related storybook cassettes

community worker flannel board sets

a variety of puppets of people, animals, and fantasy figures (for example, Fairy Tale Hand Puppets, *ABC School Supply*; King Simon and Queen Ruby Puppets, *Beckley-Cardy*)

MANIPULATIVES

puzzles about community helpers, children recycling, and heroes/sheroes (for example, Martin Luther King Jr. Puzzle, *Lakeshore*)

SCIENCE

samples of different kinds of tree bark, leaves, pinecones, and acorns

teaching pictures about trees

SENSORY

sand or cornmeal

action figures

Teaching Through the Interest Areas

Art

Set out paper shopping bags, paper plates, scissors, and a variety of art materials to encourage children to make hero and shero costumes and masks.

Add silver and gold paint to the collection of paints at the easel.

Set out wooden clothespins, fabric scraps, glue, and fine felt tip markers to encourage children to make their own action figures.

Set out current event, photo journalism, and news magazines that include numerous photographs of real people for children to use for collage materials.

Blocks

Add action figures to the block area to encourage superhero and supershero play.

Set out city mats or carpets, skyscrapers, rescue vehicles, and figures of rescue workers.

Add a castle and fantasy figures to the block area to encourage fairy tale and folk hero and folk shero play.

Dramatic Play

Add props like capes, tunics, hats, eye masks, and wands to encourage superhero and supershero play.

Literacy

Set out a collection of fiction, nonfiction, and bilingual books on heroes and sheroes. Include hero- and shero-related storybooks, cassettes, community worker flannel board sets, and materials for making journals and books.

Add a variety of puppets to encourage fantasy hero and shero play. Include lion, wolf, crocodile, dragon, spider, owl, bear, king, queen, wizard, and witch puppets.

Manipulatives

Set out puzzles of community helpers, heroes and sheroes, and children recycling.

Music

Set out cassettes with songs about helping, making the world a better place, courage, the power of children, and working together.

Science

Set out samples of tree bark, tree leaves, pinecones and acorns, and pictures of trees.

Set out recycling- and pollution-related materials.

Sensory

Fill the sensory table with a dry material like sand or cornmeal and add action hero and shero figures.

ACTIVITIES:
INVESTIGATING THE THEME

Creative Development

My Dream. Introduce children to Dr. Martin Luther King Jr. and his dream. Encourage children to finish the sentence, "I have a dream that..." Write down what children say, and encourage them to paint or draw a picture under their words. You could also ask children to paint their wish for the world.

My Hero/My Shero. Set out easels and easel paints. Encourage the children to draw or paint a picture of a hero or shero.

Paint It. Remind children of some of the qualities of a hero or a shero. Invite the children to pick one quality: power, courage, caring, or helpfulness. Ask them to think about that quality, and encourage them to paint a picture of it.

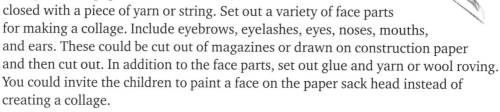

Paper Sack Heroes and Sheroes. Invite children to make a paper sack head modeled after their favorite hero or shero. Have them stuff a lunch sack or medium-sized grocery bag with crumpled newspaper and tie the end closed with a piece of yarn or string. Set out a variety of face parts for making a collage. Include eyebrows, eyelashes, eyes, noses, mouths, and ears. These could be cut out of magazines or drawn on construction paper and then cut out. In addition to the face parts, set out glue and yarn or wool roving. You could invite the children to paint a face on the paper sack head instead of creating a collage.

Planet Earth. Set out paper strips and a bowl of glue that has been thinned with glue. Invite the children to dip the paper strips into the glue, wipe them on the rim of the bowl, and place them on an inflated balloon. Cover the balloon with two to three layers of papier-mâché. Hang from a string to dry. Set out blue, brown, green, and white tempera paints and invite the children to paint the papier-mâché ball to look like the earth. Let the paint dry. Ask children to draw people on skin-colored construction paper. Cut out the children's drawings and glue them around the middle of the earth. Hang the papier-mâché ball from the ceiling for all to enjoy.

Critical Thinking

I'm Growing. Give the children a chance to celebrate their achievements. Invite them to make a poster of all the things that they can do. Write down their answers to the following questions and include them as part of the poster:

What are all the things that you can do?

What could you do when you were a baby?

What do you want to learn how to do?

What will you be able to do when you are seven?

What Does It Take? Hero and sheroes take action based on value choices. Help children think critically about what it takes to be a hero or shero. Read or tell children a story about a child who takes social action. You might read *Sadako, The Story of Ruby Bridges,* or *Rose Blanche.* Afterwards, encourage the children to think about what doing for others involves. Ask the children questions about the book such as the following:

What's the problem in this story?

What did she want to change?

What did she do that makes her a shero?

How do you think she learned to be a shero?

What if you were in her place, what would you do?

Emotional Development

Courage. Introduce children to the word *courage.* We think of heroes and sheroes as having courage. You might describe courage as a special quality that each of us can have. Tell the children that courage is doing something even when you are afraid. Courage is standing up for yourself and others. Children demonstrate courage when they face a chronic or terminal illness or other difficult situation. Read a story about someone who is courageous. Make it a point to listen to the news and read the paper for examples of children who demonstrate courage. Bring these examples and share them with the children.

Heroes and Sheroes Stand Strong. Ask the children, "What are things that some people like but really can hurt you?" As a group, make a list of all the things we need to say no to. For example, the list might include name-calling, teasing, leaving people out, guns, violence, drugs, and bad touch. As a group, talk about how you can say no to these things in our lives. Go through the list the children come up with, and for each one ask them, "How can we say no to *(name-calling, for example)*?" You might want to have the children role-play saying no as well. For example, you could set up a situation involving one child or a group of children teasing another, or you could have a child role-play standing up for herself or a friend. You could set up similar situations involving guns or violence.

I Am a Gift to the World. Set out a collection of small boxes, wrapping paper, ribbons, and cellophane tape. Invite the children to pick a box and wrap it up like a gift. Tell them that like a hero or a shero, they are a gift to the world. Ask each child to think of some things about themselves that make them a gift to the world. Write the qualities that they identify around the outside of the box. Add a gift tag that reads, "(*Child's name*) is a gift to the world."

Personal Shield or Armor. Introduce children to the concept of shields and how some heroes and sheroes use shields to protect themselves and feel safe. Set out felt tip markers and poster board cut in the shape of large shields. Ask the children to think about things that make them feel safe and protected. Invite them to decorate their personal shield using these images.

Positively Speaking. Foster children's self-esteem and confidence in their positive outlooks on life. At circle time, ask each child to tell about or show the class something positive they can do for themselves and others.

Power. Help children explore ways that heroes and sheroes use their power. Ask the children, "What is power? Who do you know who has power?" Help the children recognize that their minds are powerful, their voices are powerful, their bodies are powerful, and their friendship skills make them powerful. Have the children list all the things they know, or have them show how they can talk in a strong voice or how they have strong muscles. Power is trusting yourself, knowing what you can do, thinking for yourself, and acting for yourself and others. Reinforce the children by saying, "See, you are powerful."

Health, Safety, and Nutrition

We Can Jump, but We Don't Fly. In my experience as a teacher, I have known two different preschool children who broke bones by trying to fly like their favorite TV superhero. Talk with children about who can fly and who cannot fly. Ask them leading questions like, "Who's a pretend hero who can fly? Do you think real people can fly like that? What do you think might happen if people try to fly?" Reinforce the reality that people are not birds. People cannot fly. If people try to fly, they will fall down. Ask the children to share their experiences of falling down. Ask them to identify things in the classroom that they shouldn't climb on because they could fall. People can jump, however. Invite the children to identify a place at school where they can climb and jump. Encourage them to practice jumping off the climber or other safe platform and show you how they can land safely on two feet.

Language Development

Home Language. *Learn the words for* hero, shero, power, courage, brave, helper, dream, *and* hope *in American Sign Language and the home languages of the children in your class.*

I Think for Myself. Here is a simple finger play story that I learned from Gloria Needleman at a recent NAEYC conference. It's a great way to reinforce thinking and acting for yourself.

> Once there was a mother who had five children. *(hold up five fingers)*
> One day she had to leave her children at home and go care for a sick friend. She told her children, "I want you to stay home until I return." Then she went to care for her friend. *(hold up four fingers)*
> The first child said, "It's a hot, sunny day. I'm going down to the creek to swim and play." *(fold down the first finger, leaving three remaining)*
> The second child said, "I'm hungry and I want a treat. I'm walking to the store to get something to eat." *(fold down another finger, leaving two remaining)*
> The third child said, "I don't care what you say. I'm going to my friend's house to play." *(fold down another finger, leaving one remaining)*
> The fourth child said, "There goes my friend Mike. I'm going outside and ride my bike." *(fold down the last finger)*
> But the fifth child said, "I don't agree. I will not roam. Because I think for myself and act for myself, I will stand alone." *(turn hand and hold thumb up)*

Remember Martin. Dr. Martin Luther King Jr. may be one of the first heroes children learn about. This poem is one way to introduce children to Dr. King.

> We remember you, Martin
> for all the good things you've done
> You tried to unite all people
> and bring us together as one.
>
> We remember your actions and words
> for what you believed in was good:
> love and peace among people
> the goals of true brotherhood.
>
> (source unknown)

Begin with a Dream. People who want to make changes begin with a dream. Martin Luther King gave a famous speech in which he talked about his dreams for our world. Ask the children to finish the sentence, "I have a dream that…" Write down their dreams and encourage them to draw or paint a picture to accompany their dream. Our visions become real when we take action, when we do something to make them real. To follow up, invite the children to "read" their dreams to the class. As a group, brainstorm things we could do to make the dreams become real.

Dear Hero/Shero. Set out story paper and invite the children to write a letter to a hero or shero. If they could write a letter to any hero or shero, who would they write to? What would they like to say to this hero or shero? Take dictation, and when they are finished, invite them to draw a picture to go with their letter.

Hero and Shero Picture Cards. Use a commercial set of teaching pictures of heroes, sheroes, or famous people. You could make your own by cutting out large magazine pictures of famous individuals and gluing them onto construction paper. Hold up one picture at a time. Tell the children a little bit about the person and what the person has done that was helpful. Ask the children open-ended questions such as

What do you see when you look at this person?

What kind of a person is he or she?

What do you like about this person?

How could you be like this person?

Hero and Shero Picture Stories. Sit down with a small group of children and some pictures of people helping others in courageous ways. Show the children one picture at a time. Ask the children what they see in the pictures. Encourage the children to make up stories about the people in the pictures. If possible, write down the children's stories.

Math

Hero and Shero Lotto. Make a lotto game by dividing an 8-by-11-inch piece of construction paper into nine sections. Glue the photos of a hero or shero to each section. Make four game boards, each a little different. Make a set of game cards that match the pictures on the game boards. Set out poker chips, milk caps, or other type of game markers. Play the game by turning over one card at a time and asking the children to place a marker on the picture of the hero or shero.

Hero and Shero Match. Make four or more sets of hero and shero matching cards. Find duplicate photos of current heroes and sheroes in magazines, use a color photocopier to make duplicates, or reduce and copy teaching pictures of heroes and sheroes. Place the cards in a basket and encourage the children to find the matching sets.

Real and Pretend. Make a sorting game to help children begin to tell the difference between real images of people and pretend images that are unfair (stereotypic). Label one side of a manila file folder "Real" and the other side "Pretend." Gather a variety of photographs of real-life heroes and sheroes from different cultures and pictures of cartoon superheroes and supersheroes. Invite the children to sort the pictures.

Who's That? Make a peek hole cover for pictures by taking a manila file folder and cutting a small hole in the middle of the front cover. Place a picture of a hero or shero inside the folder, facing the front. Ask the children to keep the file folder closed, look through the hole, and guess which hero or shero it is. You could also make folders with increasingly larger peek holes. If the children are unable to guess who it is, take the picture out of the first file folder and place it in one with a larger hole.

Music

Songs of Hope. Here are two songs that promote love, courage, peace, equality, and freedom. Introduce them at circle time, and sing them after reading a story about heroes and sheroes.

I Am Full of Joy and Sunshine

Tune: *I've Been Working on the Railroad*

I am full of joy and sunshine, happy all day long
I am healthy and courageous, I feel so well and strong
Joy and love and wisdom are in my life all day
Health and peace and many blessings go with me on my way.

(*The Joyful Child: A Sourcebook of Activities and Ideas For Releasing Children's Natural Joy*, Peggy Jenkins. Tucson, AZ: Harbinger House, 1989; p. 98. Used with permission.)

Martin Luther King

Tune: *He's Got the Whole World in His Hands*

He had a dream of equality
He had a dream of equality
He had a dream of equality
His name was Martin Luther King.

He believed that we could all be friends
He believed that we could all be friends
He believed that we could all be friends
His name was Martin Luther King.

He led a march for civil rights
He led a march for civil rights
He led a march for civil rights
His name was Martin Luther King.

He won the Peace Prize for all his work
He won the Peace Prize for all his work
He won the Peace Prize for all his work
His name was Martin Luther King.

We can work for freedom
We can work for equality
We can work for civil rights
And keep Martin's dream alive.

(adapted from *Sing a Song All Year Long,* Connie Walters and Dianne Totten. Minneapolis: T. S. Denison & Company, 1991. Used with permission.)

Physical Development

Harriet Tubman. Set up a maze for the children to go through. Turn off the lights. Take the children through the maze from danger to safety. Leave the maze out so that children can take turns being Harriet Tubman helping her people escape from slavery to freedom.

Gutera Uriziga. This is a game from Rwanda that was designed to teach boys hunting skills. Give each child a beanbag and ask them to stand side-by-side in a line. Pick one child to roll a hoop in front of the line. As the hoop rolls by, the children try to throw their beanbags through it. Collect all of the beanbags and repeat, this time with a different child rolling the hoop.

Jumping and Flying. Set out capes or large scarves that children can tie around their necks and use as capes. Invite children to hold their arms out and run around the room as though they were flying. Set out the bouncer or jogging trampoline and encourage children to jump off the tramp.

Like a Hero or a Shero. Invite children to participate in a creative movement activity and move their bodies like heroes or sheroes. Invite them to move their bodies like heroes or sheroes they have learned about. How would a hero walk? How would a shero stand tall and proud?

Squeeze. Set out a variety of squeeze bottles in a sensory table filled with water. For example, use empty mustard, ketchup, chocolate syrup, and liquid soap bottles, as well as eye droppers and turkey basters. Invite the children to squeeze dry, empty bottles toward their faces to feel the air come out. What would happen if you filled the bottle with water and squeezed? The scientific principle here is cause and effect—one motion creates another motion. Squeeze the bottle and water or air comes out the top. Heroes and sheroes also take action that creates action.

Swimmy. Read *Swimmy* by Leo Lionni. Talk with the children about how when we all join together we can be big and strong and make a difference. Invite the children to walk around the room like little fish. Then ask them to find a friend and lock arms and walk around the room. Next ask each pair to join arms with another until there are groups of four walking around the room. Continue in this way until the whole class is joined arm in arm and moving together. Ask them if they feel big and strong when they are walking together.

Tug of Peace. Put children into small groups. Give each group a piece of rope that has been knotted to make a large loop. Ask the children to stand inside the loop and hold the rope at their waists. Encourage them to try to work together to make shapes. Then have all the children sit down on the floor, with the rope still around them. Remind them that heroes and sheroes help each other up. Challenge them to pull the rope so hard that everyone who's sitting gets pulled up to a standing position.

Science

Flying Superheroes and Supersheroes. Children are often interested in superhero and supershero stunts. Make a launch to send action figures and other small unbreakable objects flying. Secure a cylinder-shaped block to the table with duct tape. Place a long block on top of the cylinder so that it makes a teeter-totter, except have one end extend longer than the other. Secure the block to the cylinder with duct tape. Place the action figure on the long end of the block and push the short end down quickly with your hand. The action figure is sent flying through the air. Talk with the children about force and movement.

I'm a Conservationist. Help children learn about conservationists. With children, make a list all the things that a conservationist does to show that they care about planet earth and are making a difference.

Nature Heroes and Sheroes. Introduce children to two pretend characters who help children and adults learn to take care of the earth. Woodsy Owl helps us learn about pollution. His saying is, "Give a hoot, don't pollute." Get free Woodsy Owl materials by contacting the Woodsy Owl Fan Club, P.O. Box 1963, Washington, DC 20250.

Smokey Bear helps children and adults learn about forest fires. He tells us, "Only you can prevent forest fires." Smokey Bear was a real bear that lived a long time ago. When he was a bear cub, there was a big forest fire that killed many animals and burned many trees. But Smokey survived. The United States Forest Service used Smokey's life to create a cartoon bear to help us learn to prevent forest fires because most of the time forest fires are started by people. To get Smokey Bear materials write to the U.S. Forest Service, U.S. Department of Agriculture, Auditor's Building, 201 14th Street SW, Washington, DC 20250.

Plant a Tree. Trees are the largest plants on earth and they produce oxygen for people to breathe. In addition, trees give us shade, protection from wind, fruits and nuts, spices, wood, paper, and maple syrup. They also provide birds and small animals with places to live. Contact your local forestry department or department of natural resources. They often can provide you with inexpensive tree seedlings. Plant a tree on the playground or in the community in honor of a hero or shero for all to enjoy.

Pollution Solution. Use this demonstration activity to motivate children to clean up their trash and throw it away properly. Tell the children to pretend you are going on a picnic by the river. If the weather is nice, take the children outside and tell the story sitting on the grass. Set out a blanket for the children to sit on while they listen to you tell the story. Bring along a picnic basket full of props and a large clear bucket of water to represent the river. Begin the story by having the children get on the bus, arrive at the park, play for a while, and then get hungry for the picnic lunch. Take out some chicken bones from the basket and talk about how good the fried chicken was. Then take out some orange peels and talk about how you ate some fruits and vegetables. Then take out some soda pop and a cup of strong coffee. Talk about how the children got to drink soda and the adults got to drink coffee. Talk about how nice it is to have a good picnic lunch near the pretty river. Look at your watch and tell the children that it is time to go home. Ask them, "What should we do with our trash?" Tell them that some people don't put their trash in trash cans. Some people throw their trash in the river. Pretend to be a careless person and toss the bones, peels, soda, and coffee into the bucket of water. Take a small rubber duck out of the basket and float it on the water. Ask the children the following questions:

How does our river look?

Is it clean and beautiful?

What happens when people pollute?

What can we do about pollution?

The Power of a Seed. Here's a simple experiment that shows how powerful a sprouting seed can be. If a small seed is this powerful, just think how powerful children can be. Fill two clear plastic cups half full with potting soil. Plant three lima bean seeds in each cup. Water the seeds in one cup. Mix some plaster so that it is runny. Pour a thin layer of plaster over the beans in the second cup. Water the seeds in both cups each day. Watch the cups for two weeks.

 Trees in Our Neighborhood. Gather a large piece of paper, a pencil, and a tree identification book. Take the children on a walk through the playground or neighborhood and make a map of where the trees are located. Use the book to try to identify the trees. If there are leaves on the ground, collect them and preserve them by ironing them between sheets of waxed paper. Display the map on the wall and pin the leaves around the outside of the map. Staple pieces of yarn on the map to connect the location of each to the leaf from it.

 We Can Take Care of the Environment. Show children photographs of trashy and polluted areas. Ask them what makes these areas ugly and unhealthy. Then show the children pictures of beautiful parks and outdoor scenes. Ask the children what makes these places pretty. Ask them further questions, such as the following:

What do you think the difference is?

How do you think these polluted areas got that way?

What do you think they looked like before?

Which areas do you prefer?

How can we work together to make our world clean and beautiful?

Social Development

Dove and Eagle Club. Make a bulletin board and decorate it with a dove and an eagle. Add the heading, "Peace and Freedom Begin with Us." Tell the children that the dove is often a symbol of peace and the eagle is often a symbol of freedom. Every time a child helps another or stands up for another, write up the incident and post it on the bulletin board. Read through them periodically throughout the month.

Hero or Shero for a Day. Invite children to come to school for a day dressed up like their favorite hero or shero.

Heroes and Sheroes Walk Away from Trouble. Role-play resisting hurtful or unfair situations. Use examples from the classroom or the children's lives. Also try to use examples that give children an opportunity to role model using their words, saying no with their strong inner voices, saying, "Stop it. I don't like it when you…," saying, "That's not fair!", walking away from trouble, and telling an adult friend who can help them.

Peaceful or Not. Set out toy catalogs, scissors, glue, and a large sheet of butcher paper. Tape the paper to a wall at a height that is within children's reach. Divide the paper in half and label one side "Peaceful Toys" and the other side "Violent Toys." Invite the children to go through the catalogs and cut out pictures of toys that encourage peace, love, and cooperation. Ask the children to glue these pictures to the right side of the wall chart. Then ask them to find pictures of toys that encourage violence and glue these pictures to the other side of the chart.

People in Power. Help children identify people who are in power in your neighborhood or community. Invite public leaders to visit your classroom to see what the children are doing and to talk with the children about the aspects of community life in which they have influence. Take a picture of each person and help children create a chart of the people in power and their areas of focus. You might want to invite such people as the mayor, the chief of police, the fire chief, a city council member, a tribal council leader, and the head of the tenants' union.

Rescue Me. Help children think about situations in which someone might need to be rescued and ways they could work together to rescue someone. For example, ask them, "If we were ice skating on a pond and you fell through the ice, what could we do to save you?" Have the children role-play the accident and helping the victim.

Stand By Me. How can you be a friend to someone who isn't being treated fairly? Help children recognize that they can resist joining in the unfair treatment. They could stand by their friends and tell the others, "Hey, that's not fair," or they could work with their friends to make things fair.

Stand Up to Name-Calling. Help children develop assertiveness in the face of name-calling, teasing, or other forms of rejection. Use dolls or puppets to role-play the experience of being called a name. Ask the children, "How do you think the puppet feels?" and "What can the puppet do when others call him names?" Discuss the children's answers. Tell the children that you know a way to respond that is strong and doesn't hurt anyone. It's called standing up for yourself and others. You have to stand tall and proud, look at the other person, speak in your strong voice, and speak your truth (what you know, what you feel, and what you need). Model standing up for yourself and others with the puppets.

Walk Away. Help children learn that they can ignore name-calling or teasing by turning around and walking away. Ask the children,

> Why do some kids stick their tongues out at people?
>
> Why do some kids make faces and say things like, "na-na na boo-boo"?
>
> Do you think they are trying to make us mad?
>
> Do you think they are trying to get our attention?

Ask the children what they do when someone makes a face at them. Tell them that there is a way to respond that is strong and proud. It's a special skill that Martin Luther King Jr. and other heroes have used. All you have to do is stand tall and proud, turn your head, and walk away. Ask the children to form a circle, and pick two children to stand in the circle facing each other. One child is the teaser and the other child is the hero. The teaser makes faces at and taunts the hero. The child who is the hero stands tall, turns around, and walks away, leaving the teaser alone in the circle. Everyone cheers for the hero who walked away. The hero picks another child to go into the circle and the teaser becomes the hero in this round. Continue until all the children have had a turn being the hero and the teaser.

ACTIVITIES: AFFIRMING OURSELVES AND ONE ANOTHER

Human Rights

Everyone has the right to think about what would make the world a better place and work to make change.

BARRIER: Sometimes people feel overwhelmed by all the work that needs to be done. Sometimes people think that someone else should think about the problems and how to solve them. Sometimes people think that only grown-ups should be thinking about how to make the world better.

Everyone has the right to talk about what things they think are unfair and work to change them so that all people have what they need to live and be healthy.

BARRIER: In some places it's not safe to talk about what's unfair or to work for change.

DISCUSSION QUESTIONS: Help children think about how heroes and sheroes work to change the world, work for peace and freedom, and work to make things more fair for all people. Ask them questions about specific heroes and sheroes such as, "What did this person do to be a hero/shero? How did they make the world better or make things more fair? Do you think it was easy for them to do what they did? What happened to them when they tried to make change? Why do you think they kept going?" Also ask more general questions like, "What do you think makes a person a hero/shero? What kinds of things do you think heroes and sheroes are working for? How do you think they decide what's important? How do you decide what's important to you, what unfair things you might like to change? What kinds of choices can we make to change the world and make sure all people have what they need to live and be healthy?"

Cultural Identity

Folk Heroes and Sheroes. Read or tell folktales from the home cultures of the children in your class. Some folktales have the hero or shero make a mistake to teach us a lesson. Use folktales to start a discussion about heroes and sheroes. Talk with the children about these stories. Ask them, "Do heroes or sheroes make mistakes? How are they like us? How are they different from us?"

Heroes and Sheroes of My People. Introduce the children to both historical and current local heroes and sheroes of the cultures represented in your classroom.

Diversity

Alike and Different. Explore ways that heroes and sheroes are similar to and different from one another. Display pictures of the heroes and sheroes your class has been learning about. Ask the children, "How are all of these people like one another? How are they different from one another?" Help the children recognize that heroes and sheroes can be boys or girls, women or men, young or old, rich or poor, able-bodied or disabled. They can speak any language, have any skin color, and live anywhere in the world.

Many Kinds of Heroes and Sheroes. Introduce children to courageous people from many different cultures. Make sure that you include both women and men. Here are some individuals to consider: Mary McLeod Bethune, Paul Robeson, Jackie Robinson, Fannie Lou Hamer, Langston Hughes, César Chavez, Alicia Alonso, Rosa Parks, Harriet Tubman, Chief Joseph, the Grimke sisters, Daniel Inouye, Sojourner Truth, Dr. Martin Luther King Jr., Dorothy Day, John Brown, Winona LaDuke, Rigoberta Menchu, Nelson Mandela, Mahatma Gandhi. Introduce children to heroes and sheroes who had disabilities. You could include Helen Keller, Franklin Roosevelt, Thomas Edison, or Shirley Chisholm.

Real and Pretend. Explore the differences between pretend and real heroes and sheroes. Set out pictures of cartoon or comic book heroes, male and female super-hero action figures, and any other objects that you can find that have cartoon heroes and sheroes on them. Also set out photographs of real-life heroes and sheroes. Show the children the pictures and paraphernalia of the cartoon superheroes and ask the children questions like these:

> Are these real or pretend?
>
> How do you know?
>
> What makes them pretend?
>
> What kind of things do pretend heroes and sheroes do?

Help the children recognize that these are pretend cartoon characters. They are not real people. Show the children the photographs of real-life heroes and sheroes. Ask the children, "Are these real or pretend? How do you know? What makes them real?" Reinforce the fact that these are real people just like them and they used their lives to help make the world a better place.

You Can Be a Hero or a Shero. Invite the children to brainstorm all the different ways that they can be heroes or sheroes. Make a class book or mural of all the ways to be a hero or a shero.

Bias and Stereotypes

Martin Luther King Jr. Introduce the children to Dr. Martin Luther King Jr. You might want to begin by showing the children a picture of him and reading a book about his life. Talk with the children about how Martin Luther King Jr. worked to change laws that weren't fair. Give the children concrete examples of unfair rules that they can relate to. For example, describe a situation where only children with green shoes could get a drink at the drinking fountain, or only children with red hair can be line leaders, or children with freckles can't watch videos. What can we do where there are unfair rules? Ask the children, "What did Martin Luther King Jr. do?" Invite the children to make a banner of all the things they can do.

Superheroes Aren't Super. Because of cartoons, action movies, and action figures, young children often falsely believe that heroes fight, terrorize, shoot, and kill people in order to "get the bad guy," right the wrong, and make the world a better place. Bring a few superhero comic books to class. Ask the children to select one for you to read to them. Tell the children that you want them to think about the message in the story. Also ask the children the following questions:

> Who are the people in this cartoon?
>
> What do the people in this cartoon do?
>
> How do they solve their problems?
>
> What is the story trying to teach us?
>
> Would your family like it if you did these things?
>
> Why do you think someone drew this cartoon?
>
> Would you like to change it?
>
> How would you change it?

Who Can Be a Hero or Shero? Because young children associate heroism with cartoon characters, they may have adopted the belief that only boys can be heroes. Young children may also think that only European Americans can be heroes or sheroes. Help children recognize that a hero can be a boy or a girl. A hero is a boy or a man. A shero is a girl or a woman. Introduce the children to heroes and sheroes from a variety of cultures. Use pictures or books to introduce children to a variety of real-life heroes and sheroes.

Community Service

Service Award. As a group, the children, parents, and staff could create a service award to honor someone in your community who is a hero or shero to children and families.

Social Action Suggestions

Children's Television. Facilitate a group discussion on children's television. Ask children questions like the following:

> What kind of television shows would help children learn to solve problems peacefully?
>
> What kinds of shows would help us respect all different kinds of people?
>
> What kinds of shows would help children learn how to make the world a better place?
>
> Can you think of television shows that do these things?

Brainstorm ways to support these shows and to thank the people responsible for making them. Also brainstorm shows that encourage children to fight, be selfish, or be sneaky, and think of ways to challenge those shows. You could also work with parents and teachers to protest violent and stereotypic children's cartoons.

Don't Tear It Down. Is there an area or building in your community that is at risk for demolition or a program at risk of being closed? Children can learn about the situation and start a petition to save the site, building, or program. You might want to read *Pearl Moscowitz's Last Stand* by Arthur Levine.

Get Out the Vote. Learn about voting. Get voter registration materials from your local election office or local League of Women Voters. Make signs encouraging parents to vote. Encourage the children to write letters to their parents encouraging them to vote on their behalf.

Martin Luther King Day. Work together to plan a Martin Luther King Day celebration. Work together to protest the ways that cartoon superheroes solve their problems. Or request that your local public television station do more to tell the stories of real-life local heroes and sheroes.

Thanks and No Thanks. As a group, go through the classroom materials and identify which ones are respectful and which are stereotypic. Write thank you letters to educational suppliers that manufacture or distribute quality multicultural, gender-fair, and disability-aware materials. Write a letter to the company and send back any stereotypic items that you may have purchased for your classroom.

ACTIVITIES: OPENING THE DOOR

Classroom Visitors

Invite community activists to come to your class to talk about what children can do to be a hero or shero in your community.

Ask a storyteller to come and tell stories about heroes and sheroes.

Field Trips

Take a trip to a local museum to see a civil rights display.

Take a trip to an organization that is working to improve the community.

Take a field trip to see a play or performance by youth who are working against violence or drugs.

Parent Involvement

Ask parents to come into the classroom and talk about some of their heroes and sheroes.

Parent Education

Invite a local parent educator, psychologist, or social worker to present a workshop on how to foster values and morals in children.

Invite an early childhood educator or parent educator to talk about the role of superhero play in children's development and the need for children to have heroes and sheroes in their lives.

Classroom Resources

Children's Books

Aani And The Tree Huggers, Jeannine Atkins (New York: Lee, 1995).

Allen Jay And The Underground Railroad, Marlene Targ Brill (Minneapolis: Carolrhoda, 1994).

Alvin Ailey, Andrea Davis Pinkney (New York: Hyperion, 1993).

Aunt Harriet's Underground Railroad In The Sky, Faith Ringgold (New York: Crown, 1992).

A Boy Called Slow, Joseph Bruchac (New York: Putnam, 1998).

César Chavez, Ruth Franchere (New York: Harper, 1986).

The Christmas Menorahs: How A Town Fought Hate, Janice Cohn (Morton Grove, IL: Whitman, 1995).

The Day Gogo Went To Vote, Elinor Batezat Sisulu (Boston: Little Brown, 1996).

Diego, Jeanette and Jonah Winter (New York: Knopf, 1994).

Dinner At Aunt Connie's House, Faith Ringgold (New York: Hyperion, 1993)

The Drinking Gourd: A Story Of The Underground Railroad, F. N. Monjo (New York: Harper, 1993).

El Chino, Allen Say (Boston: Houghton, 1990).

Elizabeth Cady Stanton, Carol Hilgartner Schlank and Barbara Metzger (Beltsville, MD: Gryphon, 1991).

Follow The Drinking Gourd, Jeanette Winter (New York: Knopf, 1988).

Frederick Douglass: Portrait Of A Freedom Fighter, Sheila Keenan (New York: Scholastic, 1995).

Frederick Douglass: The Last Day Of Slavery, William Miller (New York: Lee, 1996).

Hanna's Cold Winter, Trish Marx (Minneapolis: Carolrhoda, 1993).

Happy Birthday, Martin Luther King Jr., Jean Marzollo (New York: Scholastic, 1993).

Harriet Tubman: They Called Me Moses, Linda Meyer (Seattle: Parenting, 1988).

Hats, Hats, Hats, Ann Morris (New York: Morrow, 1995).

Hats Off To Hats, Sara Corbett (Danbury, CT: Children's Press, 1995).

Helping, James Levin (New York: Scholastic, 1993).

Heroes, Ken Mochizuki (New York: Lee, 1997).

Ibis: A True Whale Story, John Himmelman (New York: Scholastic, 1990).

John Henry: An American Legend, Ezra Jack Keats (New York: Knopf, 1987).

John Henry, Julius Lester and Jerry Pinkney (New York: Dial, 1994).

Johnny Appleseed, Steven Kellogg (New York: Morrow, 1996).

Let Freedom Ring: A Ballad Of Martin Luther King Jr., Myra Cohn Livingston (New York: Holiday, 1992).

Let's Celebrate Martin Luther King Jr. And His Birthday, Jacqueline Woodson (Englewood Cliffs, NJ: Silver, 1990).

Mandela: From The Life Of The South African Statesman, Floyd Cooper (New York: Philomel, 1996).

Martin Luther King, Rosemary L. Bray (New York: Morrow, 1997).

Martin Luther King Jr.: A Biography For Young Children, Carol Hilgartner Schlank and Barbara Metzger (Henrietta, NY: Rochester AEYC, 1989).

My Dream Of Martin Luther King, Faith Ringgold (New York: Crown, 1996).

My First Martin Luther King Jr. Book, Dee Lillegard (Danbury, CT: Children's Press, 1987).

My Wish For Tomorrow: Words And Pictures From Children Around The World, Jim Henson Productions (New York: Morrow, 1995).

Now Let Me Fly: The Story Of A Slave Family, Dolores Johnson (New York: Simon, 1993).

Passage To Freedom: The Sugihara Story, Ken Mochizuki (New York: Lee).

Paul Bunyan, Steven Kellogg (New York: Morrow, 1988).

Peace Begins With You, Katherine Scholes (Boston: Little Brown, 1994).

Peace Crane, Sheila Hamanaka (New York: Morrow, 1995).

Pearl Moscowitz's Last Stand, Arthur Levine (New York: Tambourine, 1993).

Pecos Bill, Steven Kellogg (New York: Morrow, 1986).

The People Who Hugged The Trees, Deborah Lee Rose (Boulder, CO: Roberts Rinehart, 1990).

A Picture Book Of Anne Frank, David A. Adler (New York: Holiday, 1994).

A Picture Book Of Amelia Earhart, David A. Adler (New York: Holiday, 1998).

A Picture Book Of Eleanor Roosevelt, David A. Adler (New York: Holiday, 1995).

A Picture Book Of Florence Nightingale, David A. Adler (New York: Holiday, 1997).

A Picture Book Of Frederick Douglass, David A. Adler (New York: Holiday, 1995).

A Picture Book Of Harriet Tubman, David A. Adler (New York: Holiday, 1993).

A Picture Book Of Helen Keller, David A. Adler (New York: Holiday, 1992).

A Picture Book Of Jackie Robinson, David A. Adler (New York: Holiday, 1997).

A Picture Book Of Louis Braille, David A. Adler (New York: Holiday, 1997).

A Picture Book Of Paul Revere, David A. Adler (New York: Holiday, 1997).

A Picture Book Of Rosa Parks, David A. Adler (New York: Holiday, 1995).

A Picture Book Of Sitting Bull, David A. Adler (New York: Holiday, 1993).

A Picture Book Of Sojourner Truth, David A. Adler (New York: Holiday, 1996).

A Picture Book Of Thurgood Marshall, David A. Adler (New York: Holiday, 1997).

Rachel Carson, William Accorsi (New York: Holiday, 1993).

The Real McCoy: The Life Of An African-American Inventor, Wendy Towle (New York: Scholastic, 1995).

Rebel, Allan Baillie (New York: Ticknor, 1994).

Richard Wright And The Library Card, William Miller (New York: Lee, 1997).

Roberto Clemente: Baseball Superstar, Carol Greene (Danbury, CT: Children's Press, 1991).

Rose Blanch, Roberto Innocenti (New York: Stewart, 1985).

Ruth Law Thrills A Nation, Don Brown (New York: Ticknor, 1993).

Sadako, Eleanor Coerr (New York: Putnam, 1993).

Save My Rain Forest, Monica Zak (Santa Cruz, CA: Volcano, 1992).

Sequoya, Kathleen Thompson (Austin, TX: Raintree/Steck-Vaughn, 1988).

Sweet Clara And The Freedom Quilt, Deborah Hopkinson (New York: Knopf, 1993).

Swimmy, Leo Lionni (New York: Knopf, 1973).

The Story Of Ruby Bridges, Robert Coles (New York: Scholastic, 1995).

The Story Of "Stagecoach" Mary Fields, Robert H. Miller (Parsippany: Silver Burdett, 1994).

Theodore's Superheroes, Alain Léonard (North Dighton: World, 1993).

Thomas Edison: Great American Inventor, Shelly Bedik (New York: Scholastic, 1995).

What Is Martin Luther King Jr. Day? Margot Parker (Danbury, CT: Children's Press, 1990).

The Wishing Chair, Rick Dupré (Minneapolis: Carolrhoda, 1994).

Young Amelia Earhart: A Dream to Fly, Susan Alcott (Mahwah, NJ: Troll, 1992).

Young Harriet Tubman: Freedom Fighter, Anne Benjamin (Mahwah, NJ: Troll, 1997).

Young Helen Keller: Woman of Courage, Anne Benjamin (Mahwah, NJ: Troll, 1992).

Zora Hurston And The Chinaberry Tree, William Miller (New York: Lee, 1996).

Music

Allen, Lillian. *Nothing But A Hero* (Redwood, 1991).

"Harriet Tubman"

"I And Africa"

Fink, Cathy, and Marcy Marxer. *Nobody Else Like Me* (A&M, 1994).

"A Kid Like Me"

"A Little Like You And A Little Like Me"

"Hello, Hello, Hello"

"Nobody Else Like Me"

"Everything Possible"

Harley, Bill. *I'm Gonna Let It Shine: A Gathering Of Voices For Freedom* (Round River, 1990).

Hartmann, Jack. *Make a Friend, Be a Friend* (Educational Activities, 1990).

"Make A Friend Be A Friend"

———. *One Voice For Children* (Educational Activities, 1993).

"Hold A Dream In Your Heart"

Hinojosa, Tish. *Cada Niño/Every Child* (Rounder, 1996).

"Las Fronterizas/The Frontier Women"

Lefranc, Barbara. *I Can Be Anything I Want To Be* (Doubar, 1990).

"Happy Birthday Martin"

Music For Little People. *Peace Is The World Smiling* (Music for Little People, 1989).

"If I Had A Hammer"

"Kid's Peace Song"

"Turn The World Around"

Pirtle, Sarah. *Two Hands Hold The Earth* (Gentle Wind, 1984).

"Here's A Hand"

Rogers, Sally. *Peace By Peace* (Western, 1988).

"Study War No More"

"The Lambeth Children"

———. *What Can One Little Person Do?* (Round River, 1992).

"What Can One Little Person Do?"

Sprout, Jonathon. American Heroes (Educational Record Center).

Sweet Honey In The Rock. *All For Freedom* (Music for Little People, 1989).

———. *I Got Shoes* (Music for Little People, 1994).

Tune Into Kids. *Color The World* (Endeavor, 1992).

"Do Your Own Thing"

Vitamin L. *Walk A Mile* (Lovable Creature, 1989).

"Endurance"

"Here's To The Hero"

"Family Feeling"

"People Are A Rainbow"

Visual Displays

ABC School Supply
Character Building Chart

African American Images
20th Century Black Personalities
20th Century Hispanic Americans
Black American Achievement
Black Americans Poster
Contemporary Asian Americans
Great Black Americans

Beckley-Cardy
20th Century American Women
20th Century Black Personalities
20th Century Hispanic Americans
Black Americans Poster
Contemporary Asian Americans
North American Indian Personalities

Constructive Playthings
Black Personalities Photo-Posters

Knowledge Unlimited
Heroes of the Twentieth Century
Nobel Peace Prize Winners

Northern Sun Merchandising
Indigenous Heroes Poster

Organization for Equal Education of the Sexes, Inc.
Women At Work Posters
Women of Achievement Posters

Syracuse Cultural Workers
Rosa Parks: The Beginning Poster
Malcolm X Poster
Martin Luther King Jr. Poster

Videos

Brittany Meets Harriet Tubman (Educational Record Center).

Martin Luther King, Jr.: A Peaceful Warrior (Educational Record Center).

Rabbit Ears Heroes and Legends Video Series (Educational Record Center).

Money

"I've got money. Look. See! I got lotsa money." "My mom says I'm getting a new coat the next time she gets some money." When a child can't get something he or she wants we may hear, "Well, just get some money. Go to the cash machine." During the early years, children begin to construct their understanding of money. They enjoy having their own money and using pretend money. Most connect money with getting or not getting the things they want. Certainly, most young children are confused by the numeric value of different forms of currency. They are also confused about how much everyday items cost.

I came up with the idea for a curriculum unit on money a few years ago when teachers from an African American early childhood program said that Monopoly was a favorite board game among the three to five year olds. I was shocked because many of the children I worked with struggled to get through a round of the simple board game Candyland.

A unit on money can introduce children to various forms of money, how money is used, and the relationship between work and money. It will help children develop awareness and attitudes that form the foundation of consumer education. It also provides children with an opportunity for cooperation and sharing.

UNIT 6:

Money

 Look for this symbol
to find activities you
can use for circle time.

WEB

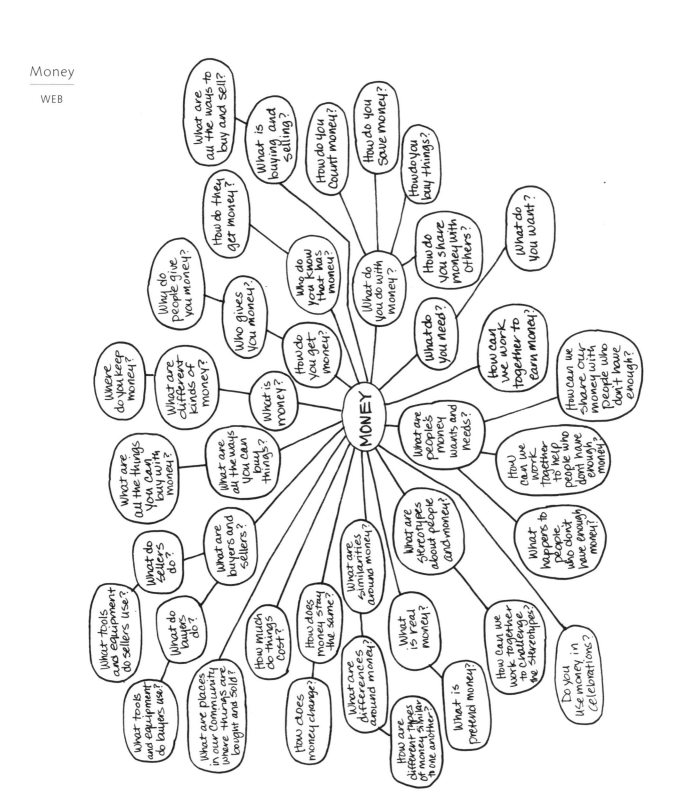

BIG AS LIFE

OUTLINE

I. How do you get money?
   A. Who gives you money?
   B. Why do people give you money?
   C. Who do you know that has money?
   D. How do they get money?
II. What do you do with money?
   A. How do you count money?
   B. How do you save money?
   C. How do you buy things?
   D. How do you share money with others?
III. What do you need?
IV. What do you want?
V. What is buying and selling?
   A. What are all the ways to buy and sell?
   B. Who are buyers and sellers?
      1. What do buyers do?
      2. What tools and equipment do buyers use?
      3. What do sellers do?
      4. What tools and equipment do sellers use?
   C. How much do things cost?
   D. What are places in our community where things are bought and sold?
VI. What is money?
   A. What are different kinds of money?
   B. Where do you keep money?
   C. What are all the ways you can buy things?
   D. What are all the things you can buy with money?
   E. What are similarities around money?
   F. How are different types of money similar to one another?
   G. What are differences around money?
   H. How are different types of money different from each other?
   I. How does money stay the same?
   J. How does money change?
   K. What is real money?
   L. What is pretend money?
   M. What are stereotypes about people and money?
   N. How can we work together to challenge the stereotypes?
VII. How can we work together to earn money?
VIII. What are people's money wants and needs?
   A. What happens to people who don't have enough money?
   B. How can we work together to help people who don't have enough money?
   C. How can we share our money with others who don't have enough?
IX. Do you use money in celebrations?

MATERIALS LIST

ART

skin-colored paints, markers, crayons, and construction paper

butcher paper roll

advertisements and coupons for collage

silver and gold paint for making money (for example, Silver and Gold Liquid Paint, *Lakeshore*)

rubber stamps of coins (for example, Coin Rubber Stamps, *Lakeshore*)

BLOCKS

a variety of multicultural people figures, including figures of people with disabilities

dollhouse furniture

scrap paper and markers or crayons for making signs

DRAMATIC PLAY

pretend money and accessories (for example, Classroom Money Kit, *Beckley-Cardy, Constructive Play-things, Lakeshore*; Realistic Currency, *Beckley-Cardy*; Toy Coins, Jumbo Assortment, *Edvantage*; Pretend and Play Cash 'n Carry Wallet, Pretend and Play Checkbook and Checks, Pretend and Play Shopping Set, *Sandy and Son*)

cash registers and calculators (for example, Calculator, Cash Register, *Beckley-Cardy, Constructive Play-things, Edvantage*; Pretend and Play Bank Set, *ABC School Supply, Sandy and Son*)

puppet stage or play store (for example, Play Store and Puppet Stage, Paraphernalia for Pretending, *Nasco*)

preschooler dolls (for example, Multi-Ethnic School Dolls, *Lakeshore*)

shoe store: cash register and pretend money, purses and wallets, a variety of shoes, shoe boxes, chairs, a full-length mirror, foot-measuring devices

grocery store: cash register, pretend money, purses and wallets, pretend food, empty food containers, a magazine rack with magazines and newspapers, grocery bags, paper and pencils for shopping lists, store sign

clothing store: cash register, pretend money, a variety of men and women's clothes, hats, purses, wallets, jewelry, paper sacks, store sign

LARGE MOTOR

plastic coins for playing relay games and group games like "find the coin," "doggie doggie find the bone," or "button button who's got the button"

hopscotch mats and large plastic coins for markers

money games (for example, Money Toss Game, *Lakeshore*)

flying disks to use as goals for coin tossing games (write a coin amount—5¢, 10¢, 25¢—on each disk)

LITERACY

children's books: fiction, nonfiction, and bilingual books about money (see resource list at the end of the unit)

cassette player and theme-related storybook cassettes

money magnetic sets and flannel board sets (for example, Magnetic Money, *Sandy and Son*)

BIG AS LIFE

MANIPULATIVES

pretend coins and bills and a sorting tray (for example, Cash Box, Coin Bank with Plastic Coins, *Beckley-Cardy*; Sparkling Gem Counters, *Lakeshore*; Coin Bank with Plastic Coins, *Edvantage*)

a bucket of pennies for counting

puzzles about stores and money (for example, Cashier Puzzle, *Constructive Playthings*; Didacta Shopping Puzzle, Market Puzzle, Shop Puzzle, *Sandy and Son*; Sales Clerk Puzzle, *Lakeshore*)

board, card, and lotto games about money (for example, Consumer Sequential Cards, *SRA*; Cool Cash Bingo, Monopoly Junior Game, The Allowance Game, *Lakeshore*; Count Your Change Game, Let's Go Shopping Board Game, Primary Money Chase, *Beckley-Cardy*; Money Dominoes, Primary Money Chase Game, *ABC School Supply*; Sesame Street Shopping Game, Super Market Game, *Nasco*)

SCIENCE

balance scale (for example, Simple Scales, *Beckley-Cardy*)

magnifying glasses

objects made from a variety of materials (wood, paper, plastic, stone, metal, glass)

SENSORY

plastic coins, beads, or jewels

sand

treasure boxes or chests

Money
___
MATERIALS

TEACHING THROUGH THE INTEREST AREAS

Art

Set out a collection of advertisements and coupons to use for making a collage. Add gold and silver paint and markers for making pretend money.

Blocks

Add figures of people, dollhouse furniture, scrap paper, and crayons for making signs. Encourage children to build stores like those that are in their community.

Dramatic Play

Add a cash register and pretend money, purses and wallets, a variety of shoes, shoe boxes, chairs, a full-length mirror, foot-measuring devices.

Set out a cash register, pretend money, purses and wallets, pretend food, empty food containers, a magazine rack with magazines and newspapers, grocery bags, paper and pencils for shopping lists, and a store sign.

Encourage dramatic play involving a clothing store by setting out a cash register, pretend money, a variety of men and women's clothes, hats, purses, wallets, jewelry, paper sacks, and a store sign.

Set up the dramatic play area like a store or restaurant that is a favorite in your community. It might be a flower shop, bakery, video store, meat market, pizza parlor, or ice cream shop.

Literacy

Set out a collection of fiction, nonfiction, and bilingual books on money. Include a tape player and recordings of children's books about money, store and money flannel board sets, and materials for making journals and books.

Manipulatives

Set out the pretend money (coins and paper bills) and a sorting tray, a bucket of pennies for counting, store and money puzzles, shopping sequence cards, and board games that deal with shopping and money.

Music

Set out cassette tapes that include songs about money and shopping.

Science

Set out a balance scale, magnifying glasses, and objects made out of a variety of raw materials (wood, paper, plastic, metal, glass).

Sensory

Bury plastic coins, jewels, or beads in sand. Or place coins in small boxes or treasure chests and bury them in sand in the sensory table. Add scoops or small shovels and encourage the children to hunt for buried treasure.

ACTIVITIES: INVESTIGATING THE THEME

Creative Development

 Being Poor Is Like.... Ask the children what they think it's like to be poor. Set out art materials and invite the children to draw or paint a picture of what they think it is like to be poor.

 Being Rich Is Like.... Ask the children what they think it's like to be rich. Set out art materials and invite the children to draw or paint a picture of what they think it is like to be rich.

Clay Coins. Set out modeling clay, rolling pins, and at least three different sizes of circle-shaped cookie cutters. Invite the children to roll out the clay and cut out coins from the clay. Let the coins dry overnight or until hardened and paint or decorate them.

Coin Crayon Rubbings. Set out a variety of coins, peeled crayons, and butcher paper. Invite the children to place a piece of paper over some of the coins, hold the crayons sideways, and rub the long side across the top.

Coin Prints. Set out ink pads and a variety of coins. Invite the children to press coins onto the pad and then onto a piece of butcher paper.

Let's Draw a Store. Unroll a large piece of butcher paper. Set out a large variety of felt tip markers. Invite the children to cooperate with one another and draw a picture of a store. Before they begin, help the group decide what type of store they want to draw and the parts of the store they want to include in their drawing.

Make a Piggy Bank. Encourage children to save their money by giving them a chance to make their own piggy banks. Collect enough margarine tubs and lids for each child. Cut a slit in each lid large enough so that coins will go through. Set out a variety of art materials and invite the children to decorate their banks.

What I Need Every Day. Ask the children, "What do you need each day to live and stay healthy?" Invite children to paint a picture of the things they need to live.

Critical Thinking

People for Sale. Ask children, "Can people be sold? How would you feel if someone sold you to another family?" Talk with the children about how people should not be bought and sold. When people are bought and sold they don't get to say, "I want to stay with my family. I don't want to go with you. I want to stay here." Tell the children that people who sell other people are called slave masters and people who are bought and sold are called slaves. Ask children what they would do if they were a slave. Read children a story about the underground railroad and how Harriet Tubman helped African Americans escape from slavery.

Money

EMOTIONAL
DEVELOPMENT

What Is Money? Identify what children know about money by leading a group discussion. Ask questions like, "What is money? Where does money come from? How do people get money? How do you know if you have the right amount of money to buy something?"

Who Owns This? To generate discussion among the children about the complex issue of ownership, use a flannel board to tell this simple story. Make or gather simple felt figures for each character (mother, father, boy, baby brother, teacher, two school friends) and the various items mentioned in the story (toys, bed, car, moon, stars).

> "One morning a boy named Chris woke up and ate breakfast with his mother, father, and baby brother. Then he and his brother played with their toys for a little while. His father told Chris it was time for school, so Chris drove with his father to his school. Chris got out of the car and went inside. He saw his teacher and played with his friends and with the toys at school. After school, his father came again and drove him home. That night while Chris was sleeping in his bed, the moon and stars came out and shone in the sky over his house."
>
> (*Social and Moral Development in Young Children*, Carolyn Pope Edwards. New York: Teachers College Press, 1986; pp. 136–137. Used with permission.)

Facilitate a discussion by asking questions such as, "Who owns Chris? Who owns his mother? Who owns his father? Who owns his baby brother? Who owns the toys at home? Who owns the toys at school? Who owns the stars? Who owns the moon?"

Emotional Development

Do We Have Enough or Do We Need More? Children often experience scarcity and shortages in their early childhood classrooms. Ask the children to help you identify things you have plenty of and things that are scarce. Say to the children, "What are some toys and supplies that we have lots of in our classroom? When we have plenty of something, we don't run out and we don't have to share or wait for a turn. Just the opposite, we run out of things when we don't have enough. When we don't have enough of something, there isn't enough for everyone, and people have to wait for a turn. What are some things that we have plenty of? What are some things that are scarce?" Once the children have identified the things the classroom is short on, they can take the list and divide it into wants and needs.

I Can Wait for What I Want. Foster children's self-esteem and confidence in their growing self-control. At circle time, ask each child to tell or show the class one way that he can wait for something he wants.

Jar of Pennies. Sometimes parents and teachers keep a nickel, dime, or quarter jar with the requirement being that you have to deposit a coin every time you use a swear word. Along these same lines, keep a jar and a basket of pennies in the classroom. Each time a child says a self-defeating statement like "I can't," "I'm stupid," or "I'll never be able to do this," fine the child one penny and have him drop a penny into the jar.

Needs and Wants. Introduce the concept of needs. A need is something that you have to have in order to live. If you don't have your basic needs met, you could get sick or die. Basic human needs are food, water, shelter, clothes, and love. Wants are all of the things we would like to have because we think they are nice, or fun, or would make our lives easier, but we don't really need them to live. Toys, candy and gum, videos, and fancy clothes are wants. As the children about their wants and needs.

Not Getting What You Want. Give children an opportunity to explore coping with not getting what they want. Ask children, "How do you feel and how do you act when you don't get what you want?" Recruit children to role-play what happens when their mom or dad says, "No, we don't have enough money" or "No, we can't afford it." Challenge the children to think of all the positive ways they can act when they don't get what they want. Invite the children to role-play positive responses to being told that they can't have what they want.

Sometimes We're Disappointed. Introduce the word *disappointed* by explaining that sometimes things don't turn out the way we want them to, and sometimes we don't get what we want. Often we feel disappointed when this happens. Ask the children how they would feel if they opened a gift and it turned out to have been broken by accident. How would they feel if they got permission to go to the store to get ice cream, only to find the store closed? How would they feel if they couldn't get a candy bar because their parents didn't have enough money? Invite the children to talk about times when they have been disappointed.

Health, Safety, and Nutrition

Dirty Money. Help children recognize that money passes through many hands and can be covered with germs and dirt. Press a coin on an ink pad and place it in one child's hand. Ask the child to pass the coin to the child next to him. Ask the children to look at the mark the coin left on their hands. Remind the children of the importance of washing their hands after touching money. Take the children to the bathroom so that they can wash their hands.

Healthy Choices. Often children's first experience spending money is buying a treat at a store. Set out a food pyramid and pictures of food. Review the pyramid with the children. Put a price tag on each of the pictures of food and give each child some pretend money. Invite the children to "make a healthy choice" and purchase one of the foods.

Language Development

> **Home Language.** *Learn the words for* money, store, bank, buy, *and* sell *in American Sign Language and the home languages of the children in your class.*

If I Could, I Would. Give children an opportunity to think about what they would buy for their parents if they had money. Read the book *A Chair For My Mother* by Vera B. Williams, in which a family loses their possessions in a fire. The mother and daughter save their coins in a jar until they have enough money to buy a chair for the mother to sit in so she can rest her feet after a long day of work. Ask each child to take a turn saying what he would buy for his parents. Write down children's answers for all to see.

Money Picture Cards. Glue large magazine pictures of people handling money onto construction paper. Hold up one picture at a time. Ask open-ended questions like, "Who can tell me about this picture? What do you see? What is this person doing? Why is there money in the picture? What are they doing with the money? What would you do if you were in this situation?"

Money Picture Stories. Sit down with a small group of children and some teaching pictures of people using money or pictures of people who appear to be wealthy, middle-income, or poor. For each picture, ask the children what they see. Encourage the children to make up a story about the people in the picture. If possible, write down the children's stories. Older children could choose a picture, write their own story, and read it to the class.

Our Book About Money. Invite the children to make a class book about money. You might want to include children's answers to these questions: Where does money come from? Who has money? What can you do with money?

Superstore. Create a board game by drawing a simple floor plan of a superstore. Include different departments within the store, such as food, clothes, shoes, toys, housewares, and hardware. For each item that is for sale in the superstore, make two cards—a card with a picture of the item on it, and a card with the name of the item on it. Children play the game by picking up a word card and trying to figure out what the word says. Help them sound out the word and then match the word card to the picture card. The child can then place the picture card in the correct department of the super-store. You could also make a "shopping list" by posting or laying out the word cards.

Math

Can You Buy It? Set up a pretend store. Choose a variety of toys and objects from around the classroom. Make a price tag for each item. Price the toys from 1 cent to 20 cents, so that children will recognize and be able to count the numbers. Give each child a small coin purse with a different number of pennies in each purse. Pretend to be the storekeeper and invite the children to your store to buy some toys. Ask them what they would like to buy. Help them read the price tag and figure out if they have enough money to buy a toy. You might say, "This doll costs 4 cents. How much money do you need to give me? Do you have enough money to buy the doll?"

Estimation. Fill a small jar with pennies. Encourage the children to guess how may pennies are in the jar. Write down their guesses over the course of a week. Allow the children to guess different numbers on different days. Poor the pennies out and count them at the end of the week.

How Many? At circle time, give each child a penny. Ask the class, "How many pennies do we have all together? How do you know?" Give each child two pennies. Again ask. "How many pennies do we have all together?" Children can take turns passing out pennies to one another.

Money Chart. With the children, make a simple money chart. Show that a penny equals 1 cent (a penny by itself), a nickel equals 5 pennies, a dime equals 10 pennies, a quarter equals 25 pennies. With older children, include that a dollar equals 100 pennies. Children could use the chart to count out coins or to make change for each other.

Money Match. Make four or more sets of money matching cards. Use a color photo-copier duplicate pretend money, trace coins, or use coin stamps to print the cards. Children can match pennies, nickels, dimes, quarters, half dollars, and silver dollars. They could also match amounts (three pennies with three pennies, two quarters with two quarters). Place the cards in a basket and encourage children to find the matching sets.

Money Sort. Gather a few sets of pretend money or make money picture cards. Place the money or cards in a basket. Set out the basket along with a sorting tray. Invite children to classify the money or cards any way they like.

More or Less. Write the word *less* on one side of a sorting tray and the word *more* on the other side. Set out small baskets with different amounts of pennies or pretend coins in them. Invite the children to pick out two baskets, count the coins in each, and place the one with a greater number of coins in it on the side labeled more and the basket with fewer coins on the side marked less. Repeat the activity with another set of baskets.

Piggy Bank Count. Purchase 10 small piggy banks from a discount store and number them 1 through 10. Write the number on the side of each piggy bank so that it is easy to read. Set out a bowl of pennies and invite the children to put the correct number of pennies in each piggy bank. You could also use small jars, margarine tubs, or coin purses instead of the piggy banks.

Music

Miss Mary Mack. Teach children this traditional song and encourage them to find a partner and play a clapping game to the rhythm of the song. You could try the following simple patty-cake sequence: Clap your hands, clap right hands with your partner. Clap your hands, clap left hands with you partner. Clap your hands, clap both hands with your partner. As the children get used to the pattern, they can speed up their clapping and chanting.

> Miss Mary Mack, Mack, Mack
> All dressed in black, black, black
> With silver buttons, buttons, buttons
> All down her back, back, back
> She asked her mother, mother, mother
> For fifteen cents, cents, cents
> To see the elephant, elephant, elephant
> Jump the fence, fence, fence
> He jumped so high, high, high
> He touched the sky, sky, sky
> He never came back, back, back
> Until the Fourth of July, July, July

Physical Development

Can You Find the Medallion? Make a large gold medallion. Hide it somewhere in the classroom or the playground. Invite the children to find the medallion. You can say, "You're getting warmer," as the children get closer to the medallion, and "You're getting colder" as children get farther from it.

Hear the Money. Make a simple bank by cutting a slit in the plastic lid of a metal can. Invite the children to hide their eyes and count the sounds they hear as you drop pennies into the can one at a time.

Penny Bucket. Fill a plastic bucket with 8 inches of water and place a quarter on the bottom. Give the children a few pennies each and invite them to drop their pennies into the water one at a time and try to cover up the quarter with their pennies.

Treasure Walks. Take the children on a walk in a park or nature area and invite the children to look for a "treasure."

Treasure Chest. Set out a hatbox or medium-sized decorated box filled with some large-motor props like a yarn ball, tennis ball, small traffic cone, flying disc, scarf, wand, rubber ring, and a length of rope. Tell the children that you have a treasure chest full of things used for inside movement activities. Give each child a turn to reach into the box and pull out an object. Then invite the children to show the class one way they could play with the object.

What Kind of Store? Ask children to think of a store that they go to with their families. Invite them to pantomime the activities that occur in the store and see if the other children can guess what type of store it is.

Science

Shiny Pennies. You will need four bowls and four pennies for this activity. Pour 30 milliliters vinegar into the first bowl, pour 5 milliliters salt into the second bowl, pour 5 milliliters salt and 30 milliliters of water into the third bowl, and pour 5 milliliters salt and 30 milliliters vinegar into the fourth bowl. Label each bowl. Invite the children to put a penny in each bowl. Ask them to check the bowls every 5 minutes for 15 minutes. Which chemicals work to clean the pennies? Which chemicals do not clean the pennies? Let the children clean the pennies with the mixture that works.

Treasure Boxes. Invite each child to select and decorate a box for collecting "treasures" from nature. Children could select an egg carton, shoe box, jewelry box, or other divided container. Take children on a variety of nature walks so that they can collect treasure like seedpods, acorns, shells, leaves, pinecones, dead insects, empty birds' nests, bark, bones, driftwood, and rocks.

Social Development

Buyers and Sellers. Set up a store in the dramatic play area. Invite the children to pretend to operate the store and go shopping at the store. Introduce children to the roles of the sellers and the roles of the buyers. Ask them the following questions:

What do sellers do?

When you go to the store, what does the sales clerk do? What does the sales clerk say?

When you go shopping at a store, what do you do?

What do you say to the clerk when you go shopping?

Money

SOCIAL
DEVELOPMENT

Free Gifts. Help children think about gifts they could give others that don't cost anything. Ask the children if they can think of something they could give their families or community that doesn't cost any money. Write the children's answers on a large piece of paper for all to see.

Give Kindness Coupons. Ask children if they know what a gift is. What are some gifts they like to get? Help them realize that doing kind and thoughtful things for others is a gift. Ask children to think of kind things that they could do for one another. Set out index cards and felt tip markers. Invite the children to make "kindness coupons." For example, they might make a coupon for a hug or help with a puzzle, help putting on snow boots, or help cleaning up the dramatic play area. Place the completed kindness coupons in a basket and label it the "kindness store." At circle time, one or two children can pick a coupon from the store and cash in on their coupons.

Give Away. Ask the children if they know what the word *generous* means? Do they know what the word *giving* means? Show them a bag of cookies or trinkets. Tell them you have a bag that you want to give away. Ask the children what they would do if someone gave them a bag of treats. Help them consider the options of keeping it all, giving it all away, and giving away some and keeping some. Then give the bag to a child in the group. Ask the child what he wants to do with the items. Talk with the children about how they feel about the situation. You may want to have an extra bag of goodies so that children who didn't get any can receive something at the end of the activity. This is an important tradition in many Native American communities. Perhaps children could get involved in a family or community give away.

Let's Make Money. Give children an opportunity to learn that people can use their minds and bodies to produce "goods" that can earn them money. Tell the children that if they work together they could make something to sell. Ask the children, "What could we make together here at school that we could sell?" Brainstorm a list of possibilities. For each product listed, identify what you would need to be able to make it. As a group, look over the list of what you would need. Ask the children, "Which ones could we make and which ones couldn't we make?" Vote on what to make. For example, it could be voting on whether to make cookies or paper airplanes. If parents participate, the class could produce a cookbook or activity book. Involve the children in all the aspects of purchasing supplies, making the product to sell, setting the price, and selling their finished product.

Let's Share Our Books. Help foster children's awareness of ownership and ability to share things with others. Invite all of the children to bring a children's book to school on a special day. Put the child's name on the outside of his book and put all of the books into a basket. At circle time, take out the basket. Invite the children to introduce their books to the rest of the class. Remind the children that these books are not school books. They are owned by each of the children and the owner has the right to decide if he will share the book with others or keep it for himself. Let the children decide if they want to keep their books in the sharing basket for others to look at during free-choice time. If the child does not want to share, he can put the book in his cubby or on a shelf out of reach of the children.

Not Enough. Offer the children a new toy to play with. Choose a car, a doll, a puzzle, or something else that can't be divided easily among the children. Tell them that before they can play with it they need to solve a problem. Ask them, "What do you think the problem is? How can we solve this problem?" Brainstorm as many options as possible and work toward consensus about how to solve the problem, or vote as a group for the best option.

Time, Love, and Money. Help children recognize how their families give time, love, and money to care for their children. Set out a large piece of butcher paper and felt tip markers. Ask the children to brainstorm all of the ways that their families take care of them. The list will likely include giving love, food, clothes, and toys. When the children are finished naming all the ways they are cared for, read the list out loud. Ask the children which things take money. Go through each item on the list and ask, "Does it take money to buy you this?" If the answer is yes, tape a coin next to it. Talk with the children about how caring for another person takes time, love, and money.

We Can Produce a Service. Help children learn that people can also produce a service as a way of earning money. A service is something we do for people and they pay us money for our service. For example, if you need a haircut, you go to the barber and he cuts your hair. Your mom or dad pays him for his service. When we ride on the city bus, we pay the bus driver and she gives us a ride. Ask the children, "What service could we provide that would be helpful to others?" Make a list of all the possible services your class could provide. As a group, vote on a service they would like to offer the school community, families, and neighborhood. Help the children make a plan for how they will develop their skills, offer their service, set a price for their service, and find customers to buy their service. For instance, the children may offer the service of singing, picking up trash, planting flowers, recycling, or planning a party.

We Can Trade. Introduce the concept and practice of trading through an art activity. You might say something like, "If you have something that I want and I have some-thing that you want, we can trade. I'll give you what I have and you give me what you have. And then we'll both be happy. Trading is like swapping. We both get some-thing." Give each child a piece of art paper and glue. Then give each child a small bowl of different collage material. For instance one child might have pieces of yarn, another glitter, another buttons, another construction paper scraps, another gummed stickers. Help the children notice that each of them has an art material and could make their own picture by only using their material. If they want, they could trade bowls with another child as a way of adding other things to their picture.

ACTIVITIES:
AFFIRMING OURSELVES
AND ONE ANOTHER

Human Rights

Everyone has the right to have enough resources to live and be healthy.

BARRIER: In the United States and all over the world, some people have more resources than they need, and some people don't have enough.

Everyone has the right to healthy food and water, clothing, housing, education, and good work to do.

BARRIER: Many people don't have enough money to have all of these things.

DISCUSSION QUESTIONS: Help the children think about what resources people need to live and be healthy. Ask them questions like, "What things do you think people need to live and be healthy? Why do you think some people don't have enough money to get all the things they need? How can we work to make sure all people have enough resources to get the things they need?"

Cultural Identity

Cultural Money Traditions. Explore the cultural traditions related to money of the children in your class. For example, Native American communities often give money to dancers and drummers at a powwow. Chinese Americans may practice a tradition of giving "lucky money" on New Year's. Children in your class could make envelopes out of red construction paper, decorate them with gold glitter, and place pretend money inside.

Let's Swap. Introduce children to the culturally based practices of bartering, swapping, or trading goods and services rather than using money. Set out activities that involve associative play. For example, set out tracing stencils and markers, playdough and cookie cutters, and other activities in which children often swap materials. Follow up with an activity in which each child gets something different and children have the opportunity to swap. For instance, pass out four different types of crackers at snack, and invite the children to trade with one another.

Money from My Homeland. Ask parents to share with the class coins, currency, wallets, purses, and piggy banks from their native cultures.

What Do You Treasure? Invite children to describe who and what they treasure. Remind them that things that are fun or special to us can be free. They don't have to cost any money. Write down their answers on a piece of art paper and invite the children to draw or paint a picture to accompany their words.

Diversity

Alike and Different. Facilitate a discussion with the children about money that will help them recognize that we all spend money, but that people have different amounts of money and spend money on different things. Count up all the different things that we do with money. Ask the children the following questions:

> Who has money?
>
> How much money do people have?
>
> Who has more money? Who has less money?
>
> Why do people have different amounts of money?
>
> What are some things we do with money?
>
> What are all the things people spend their money on?

Does Money Make Us Different? Help children begin to explore the differences money creates. Show the children pictures of people representing different economic classes. Invite the children to look at the pictures. Ask them, "Look at these pictures of people. Which of these people have a lot of money? Which of these people don't have a lot of money?" Depending on the children's answers, place the photographs into two groups. Next, ask them to look at the pictures and ask the children, "How are people with a lot of money and not a lot of money similar to each other? How are people with a lot of money and not a lot of money different from one another?"

Real and Pretend Money. Set out a bowl that contains both real and pretend money. Invite each child to reach in and take out a coin or paper bill. Ask the child, "Is it real or pretend? How do you know?" Next, ask the child to put the money in the real pile or the pretend pile. Conclude the activity by reviewing all the differences between the real and pretend money.

Susan B. Anthony. Introduce children to the Susan B. Anthony dollar. Ask the children how it is similar to and different from a dollar bill. Some of their answers might include that there is a picture of a woman on it, that it is made of metal rather than paper, and that it is round rather than rectangular. Help the children learn about Susan B. Anthony and why she was chosen to be remembered and honored.

Bias and Stereotypes

Clothes Don't Make a Person. Sometimes children judge others by their clothes. Show children a variety of photographs of people, some dressed in expensive clothes and some dressed in inexpensive or old clothes. Ask the children, "Who can be your friend?" If a child responds, "She can't be my friend because she has icky clothes," talk about it. Help the children look at the pictures in detail. You might point out things like the child in the picture is smiling, their same age, or doing something fun that they might enjoy doing too. Introduce the saying, "You can't judge a book by its cover" or "clothes don't make a person." It's not fair to think that someone who has old or dirty clothes isn't nice and someone who has new or clean clothes is a nice person.

Share Something. Children may think that sharing time means bringing something to school that costs money. Invite children to make sharing time a time of the day in which they share something that doesn't cost any money. They could share something they have made, a song, a story, a hope, a wish, or a dream.

Community Service

Community Fundraiser. Make something like cookies or a class quilt. Sell them and donate the profits to a community group.

Coupon Collection. Ask parents to bring in the coupon sections of their Sunday paper. Children can cut out the coupons and deliver them to a food bank.

Social Action Suggestions

Television Boycott. Talk about how the commercials on Saturday mornings try to get us to buy junk food and toys. Show children how they could mute the television when the commercials come on. As a group, boycott Saturday morning commercials.

ACTIVITIES: OPENING THE DOOR

Classroom Visitors

Ask someone who works at a bank, a local entrepreneur, or someone who runs a family business to come to the class to talk about buying and selling.

Field Trips

Take a field trip to a bank or a store.

Parent Involvement

Ask parents to share examples of times when money is given as a gift or shared among family members.

Parent Education

Invite a financial advisor to conduct a workshop on money management or a social worker to talk about accessing or changes in social services like welfare reform.

Invite a parent educator to talk about how to teach children to be responsible about money.

CLASSROOM RESOURCES

Children's Books

26 Letters And 99 Cents, Tana Hoban (New York: Morrow, 1995).

Alexander Who Used To Be Rich Last Sunday, Judith Viorst (New York: Simon, 1987).

Aunt Martha And The Golden Coin, Anita Rodriquez (New York: Crown, 1993).

Believing Sophie, Hazel Hutchins (Morton Grove, IL: Whitman, 1995).

Benny's Pennies, Pat Brisson (New York: Doubleday, 1993).

The Big Green Pocketbook, Candice Ransom (New York: Harper, 1993).

A Chair For My Mother, Vera B. Williams (New York: Greenwillow, 1982).

Emeka's Gift, Ifeoma Onyefulu (New York: Dutton, 1995).

The Farmer And The Poor God, Ruth Wells (New York: Simon, 1996).

Feathers, Ruth Gordon (New York: Simon, 1993).

General Store, Rachel Field (New York: Greenwillow, 1988).

The Gift, Alianna Brodmann (New York: Simon, 1993).

The Gifts of Wali Dad: A Tale Of India, Aaron Shepard (New York: Macmillan, 1995).

The Gold Coin, Alma Flor Ada (New York: Simon, 1994).

The Hundred Penny Box, Sharon Bell Mathis (Boston: Houghton, 1995).

Irene And The Big, Fine Nickel, Irene Smalls-Hector (Boston: Little Brown, 1996).

Let's Find Out About Money, Kathy Barabas (New York: Scholastic, 1997).

Music, Music For Everyone! Vera B. Williams (New York: Morrow, 1988).

My First Look At Shopping, Stephen Oliver (New York: Random, 1991).

Nathan's Hanukkah Bargain, J. D. Green (Rockville, MD: Kar-Ben, 1986).

On Market Street, Arnold Lobel (New York: Scholastic, 1993).

Sam And The Lucky Money, Karen Chinn (New York: Lee and Low, 1997).

Saturday Sanocho, Leyla Torres (New York: Farrar, 1995).

Something Special For Me, Vera B. Williams (New York: Morrow, 1986).

Sukey And The Mermaid, Robert D. San Souci (New York: Simon, 1996).

Three Wishes, Lucille Clifton (New York: Dell, 1994).

Tight Times, Barbara Shook Hazen (New York: Penguin, 1983).

The Tiny Kite Of Eddie Wing, Maxine Trottier (Brooklyn, NY: Kane/Miller, 1996).

The Toothpaste Millionaire, Jean Merrill (Boston: Houghton, 1993).

Music

Music For Little People. *Fiesta Musical,* with Emilio Delgado (Music for Little People, 1994).

"Los Enanos"

———. *Peace Is The World Smiling* (Music for Little People, 1989).

"Everybody Is Somebody"

Rogers, Sally. *Peace By Peace* (Western, 1988).

"Dear Mr. President"

"Magic Penny"

Thomas, Marlo, and Friends. *Free To Be…A Family* (A&M, 1988).

"Doris Knows Everything"

Tune Into Kids. *Color The World* (Endeavor, 1992).

"Take Me As I Am"

Visual Displays

ABC School Supply
Big Money Bulletin Board Set
Five Senses Chart

Videos

Saving With Tom And Martha (Educational Record Center).

Teaching Kits

Exploring the World of Shoppers, Addison-Wesley

Alexander Who Used To Be Rich Last Sunday Literature Based Math Packet, Lakeshore

Read All About It! Money Activity Kit, Lakeshore

SENSES

"Look at that!" "Oooh, what's that smell?" "Mmmm, that tastes good." "Aaah, it's cold." "That noise hurts my ears." Children first learn about the world through their senses, and they need hands-on experiences to foster their perceptual development. A unit on senses gives young children a chance to learn about their sensory body parts and how their senses help them. This unit lends itself well to diversity because you use different senses to explore a wide range of experiences. Within the context of this unit, children can also learn about people whose sensory body parts don't work the way theirs do and how to be respectful of people who are Deaf or blind.

UNIT 7:

SENSES

Look for this symbol
to find activities you
can use for circle time.

WEB

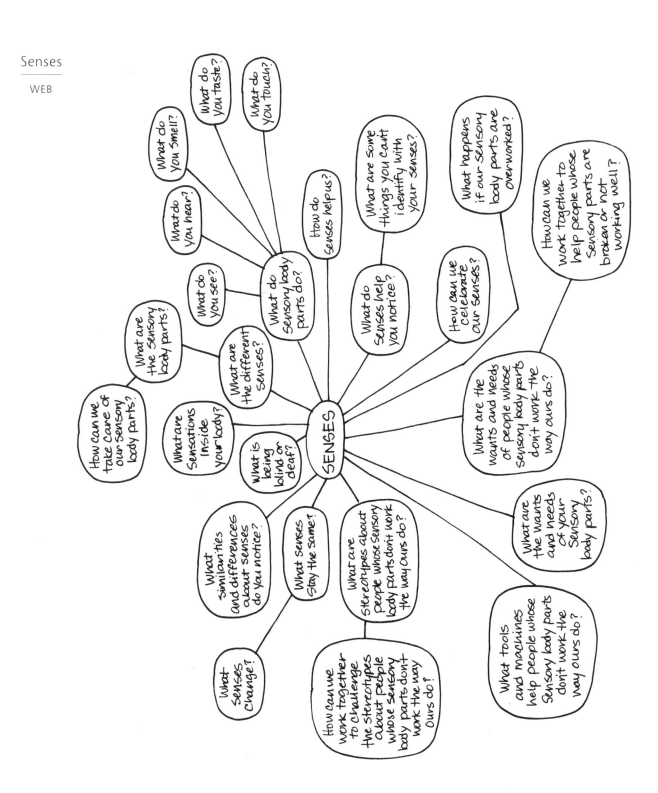

What do you taste?

What do you touch?

What do you smell?

What do you hear?

How do senses help us?

What are some things you can't identify with your senses?

What happens if our sensory body parts are overworked?

How can we work together to help people whose sensory parts are broken or not working well?

What do you see?

What do sensory body parts do?

What do senses help you notice?

How can we celebrate our senses?

What are the sensory body parts?

What are the different senses?

How can we take care of our sensory body parts?

What are sensations inside your body?

What is being blind or deaf?

SENSES

What are the wants and needs of people whose sensory body parts don't work the way ours do?

What are the wants and needs of your sensory body parts?

What similarities and differences about senses do you notice?

What senses stay the same?

What are stereotypes about people whose sensory body parts don't work the way ours do?

What senses change?

How can we work together to challenge the stereotypes about people whose sensory body parts don't work the way ours do?

What tools and machines help people whose sensory body parts don't work the way ours do?

OUTLINE

I. What are the different senses?

    A. What are the sensory body parts?

    B. How can we take care of our sensory body parts?

    C. What are sensations inside my body?

II. What do sensory body parts do?

    A. What do you see?

    B. What do you hear?

    C. What do you smell?

    D. What do you taste?

    E. What do you touch?

III. How do senses help us?

    A. What do senses help you notice?

    B. What are some things you can't identify by using your senses?

IV. What similarities and differences do senses help you notice?

V. What senses stay the same? What senses change?

VI. What happens if our sensory body parts are overworked?

VII. What are the wants and needs of your sensory body parts?

VIII. What is being blind or Deaf?

    A. What are stereotypes about people whose sensory body parts don't work the way yours do?

    B. How can we work together to challenge the stereotypes about people whose sensory body parts don't work the way ours do?

    C. What are the wants and needs of people whose sensory body parts don't work the way yours do?

    D. What tools and machines help people whose sensory body parts don't work the way yours do?

    E. How can we work together to help people whose sensory body parts don't work the way ours do?

VIII. How can we celebrate our senses?

MATERIALS LIST

ART

skin-colored paints, markers, crayons, and craft paper

butcher paper roll

rolls of different colors of cellophane (for example, Cellophane Rolls, *ABC School Supply*)

foam paints (for example, Rainbow Foam Paint Set, *Lakeshore*)

paint tools (for example, Paint Rollers and Scrapers, *Constructive Playthings*)

double easel or Plexiglas easel (for example, See-Through Adjustable Double Easel, The Giant Magic Drawing Board, *Lakeshore*)

scented markers (for example, Lifesavers Scented markers, Mr. Sketch "Scented" markers, *Nasco*; Smelly Markers, *Lakeshore*)

a variety of molding doughs and clays (for example, Lakeshore Scented Dough, *Lakeshore*)

clay tools (for example, Clay Extruders, Clay Hammers, *Constructive Playthings*)

colored sand

BLOCKS

a variety of multicultural people figures, including figures of people with disabilities

colorful blocks

foam blocks (for example, Foam Building Blocks, *Environments*; Sof-Blox, *ABC School Supply*)

hollow blocks

tracks for rolling cars and balls (for example, Build and Roll Raceway, *Lakeshore*)

DRAMATIC PLAY

preschooler dolls, including dolls with disabilities (for example, Multi-Ethnic School Dolls, Adaptive Equipment for Dolls with Disabilities, *Lakeshore*; Friends, Elders, and Dolls with Visual or Hearing Impairment, *People of Every Stripe*)

eyeglass store: eyeglasses, sunglasses, mirrors, eye chart, order forms, cash registers, play money, store sign

beach: plastic tarp, plastic wading pool, beach towels, straw hats, sandals, thongs, sunglasses, empty sunscreen bottles, sand toys

LARGE MOTOR

a variety of different-textured balls (for example, Colors Beanbag Set, *Lakeshore*; Flying Fleece Ball, Koosh Ball, Yarn Balls, *J. L. Hammett*)

LITERACY

children's books: fiction, nonfiction, and bilingual books about senses (see resource list at the end of the unit)

cassette player and theme-related storybook cassettes

flannel board sets about the senses

bookmaking and journaling materials

MANIPULATIVES

multicultural puzzles about senses (for example, Children with Special Needs Puzzles, *Kaplan*; Senses Puzzle, *Nasco*; Special Needs Kids Puzzles, *Sandy and Son*)

a variety of design and construction sets (for example, Bristle Blocks, Flexiblocks, Transparent Design Tiles, Prism Brick Sets, *Constructive Playthings*; Parquetry Design Blocks, Magnashapes, *Lakeshore*) card sets (for example, Beginning Signing Primer Cards, Finger Alphabet Cards, Finger Alphabet Lotto, Sign Number Cards, *Sandy and Son*; Giant Beaded Number Cards, *J. L. Hammett*; Touch Giant Number Cards, *Environments*)

matching and listening games (for example, Feel and Match Textures, *Nasco*; Scent Match, *Constructive Playthings*, *ABC School Supply*; Scenterville Orchard Game, *Sandy and Son*; Sound Tracks Listening Lotto Game, Perfection Game, Tactile Dominoes, Texture Match Game, *Constructive Playthings*; What Do You Hear? Matching Game, *AGS*; Look Hear, *ABC School Supply*; Sound Hearing Cassette Tape and Book, *Sandy and Son*)

zip, tie, snap, button, and buckle boards (for example, Buckle, Lace, and Tie Dressing Frames, Zip, Snap and Button Dressing Frames, Beads and Laces, *Lakeshore*)

tactile materials (for example, Bag of Feelies, *Sandy and Son*; Multi-Shape Touch Boards, *Constructive Playthings*; Mystery Box, Pathfinder Motor Skills Board, *Lakeshore*)

light table (for example, Light Table Activity Center, *Constructive Playthings*)

MUSIC

a variety of hand instruments (for example, Percussion Instruments, Resonator Bells, Bars, and Xylophones, *West Music*; Shake, Rattle, and Roll, *Nasco*; True Tone Handbells, *Lakeshore*; Xylopipes, *Constructive Playthings*)

SCIENCE

visual materials (for example, Fisher Price Binoculars, Fisher Price Micro Explorer Set, Fisher Price Telescope Set, *Nasco*; Giant Hands-On Color Mixing Center, Color Discovery Tubes, Magnifiers, *Lakeshore*; Giant Periscope, Magnifiers, *Constructive Playthings*; Unbreakable Prism, *Constructive Playthings*, *Lakeshore*)

SENSORY

food coloring or flavoring, plant essences

ice cubes, snow, or crushed ice

sand or dirt, muffin tins, sand molds, wooden or aluminum utensils

bubbles (for example, Big Bubble Kit, Incredible Bubble Science Kit, *Lakeshore*)

Teaching Through the Interest Areas

Art

Set out scented felt tip markers, foam paint, a variety of molding doughs and clays, a variety of collage materials, and colored sand.

Blocks

Add colorful rainbow blocks, hollow blocks, and foam blocks to the area to provide a variety of sensory experiences in block building.

Dramatic Play

Add eyeglasses, sunglasses, mirrors, eye chart, order forms, cash registers, play money, and a store sign to encourage playing optometrist or eyeglasses store.

Lay a plastic tarp or shower curtain on the floor. Set a plastic wading pool on top of the tarp and fill it with beach sand. Add beach towels, straw hats, sandals, thongs, sunglasses, empty sunscreen bottles, and a few sand toys.

Literacy

Set out a collection of fiction, nonfiction, and bilingual books on senses. Add a tape player and storybook cassettes, senses flannel board sets, and materials for keeping journals and making books.

Manipulatives

Add a feeling box, senses puzzles, beaded number and alphabet cards, texture matching games, and listening lotto games.

Music

Set out cassettes with a variety of different types of music.

Science

Set out visual materials like color paddles, color tubes, prisms, magnifiers, telescopes, periscopes, and binoculars. Add a collection of smelling jars and a collection of material with different textures.

Sensory

Use food coloring, flavoring, or plant essences to color or scent the water in the sensory table.

Add ice cubes, snow, or crushed ice to the water table.

Give children water to add to the sand or dirt in the sensory table. Set out muffin pans, sand molds, and aluminum and wooden utensils. If children make mud pies outside, set them in the sun to dry.

ACTIVITIES: INVESTIGATING THE THEME

Creative Development

Draw Me/Draw You. Ask children to find a partner and sit across from each other at a table. Encourage the children to draw a picture of their partner's face. Help them use their sense of sight and touch to notice the details of each other's physical features. Encourage children to exchange their drawings when they are done. Ask the children to bring their drawings with them to circle time. Hold up one picture at a time and see if the children can guess which child is the subject of the drawing and which is the artist.

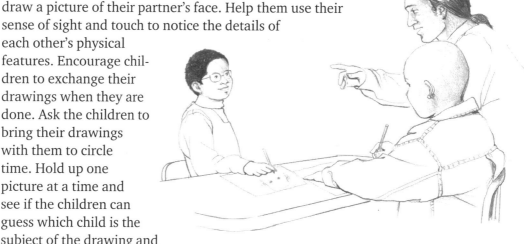

Drawing in the Dark. Set out crayons and paper and invite the children to take a seat at the table. Turn off the lights so that the room is very dark, and ask the children to draw a picture in the dark.

Light Mobile. Spread newspaper on a table. Lay down a sheet of waxed paper. Sprinkle skin-colored crayon chips, bits of skin-colored string, and small squares of tissue paper on top of the waxed paper. Lay another piece of waxed paper on top. Cover with newspaper and press with a warm iron until the crayon chips melt. Children can take their waxed paper design and cut them into shapes. Punch holes in the top and bottom of the pieces and tie them together with yarn. Hang from the ceiling near a window so that children can see the impact of the sun on their designs.

Marbled Patterns. Invite children to make patterns with paint. Fill an old jelly roll pan with water. Children can drip small amounts of oil-based paint onto the water. Consider using a small set of enamel paints for painting models. Swirl the paint around with a toothpick. Lay a piece of finger paint paper on top of the water. Tap it lightly to make sure the paint touches the paper. Lift the paper off the water and set it out on newspapers to dry. This activity uses toxic art materials and needs constant adult supervision, but it's worth it.

Night and Day Pictures. Help children draw a representation of the concept of nighttime and daytime. Tell the children that when they are experiencing daytime, other people are experiencing nighttime, and while they sleep during the night, other people are experiencing daytime. Draw a line down the middle of a large sheet of construction paper. Encourage the children to draw a picture of themselves, their friends, or people they know on one side of the line. Then encourage the children to draw a picture of people from the other side of the world, where it's nighttime, on the other side of the line. Give the children very thin (wash) black tempera and a paintbrush. They can paint a night sky over their picture of people who are doing something this minute on the other side of the world.

Paint with Your Feet. Roll out a 5-foot length of butcher paper. Set out shallow trays of skin-colored paint at one end of the paper and dish tubs of water at the other end. Invite children to take off their shoes and socks, step into the pan of paint that is most like their skin color, walk across the paper, step into the pans of water, and then wipe off their feet with a towel. You can display the foot mural in the classroom or hallway.

Playing with Clay. Help children experience the sensation of working with natural clay. Cover a table with oilcloth or plastic, or set out plywood boards for children to work on. Set out potter's clay, a small bowl of water, plastic knives, and toothpicks. Encourage the children to work with the clay. They can add water if the clay begins to dry out, wet their hands to smooth the clay, and make decorations in the clay with the knives and toothpicks.

Sand Drawings. Use powdered tempera to color fine, clean sand or cornmeal. Set out the bowls of colored sand or cornmeal, glue bottles, and construction paper. Invite the children to create a design with glue and spoon colored sand or cornmeal over the glue. Gently lift the construction paper and tilt it so that the excess sand or cornmeal falls back into the bowl. Repeat the process until the design is complete. Let dry.

Soap Sculptures. With a hand beater, mix 2 cups soap flakes and ½ cup water. Mold and sculpt the mixture into different shapes.

Sunlight Pictures. Encourage children to punch holes in dark-colored construction paper. Then glue pieces of tissue paper onto the construction paper, covering the holes. Brush a light coating of watered down glue over the entire picture. Let dry and display on the windows so that children can see the sun coming through.

Texture Design. Set out construction paper, glue bottles, and pans of colored sand or cornmeal. Invite the children to squirt a glue design onto the paper. Then spoon on one color of sand or cornmeal and pour off the extra. Spoon on other colors and pour off one at a time.

Critical Thinking

Double Sense. Give children a chance to explore ways we use two or more senses together to get information or to complete a task. Ask the children the following questions:

> When do we use our eyes and ears together?
>
> When do we use our eyes and nose together?

When do we use our eyes and mouth together?

When do we use our eyes and hands together?

When do we use our mouth and nose together?

No Sense. To help children explore the limitations of our senses, bring to group time actual objects that don't have a smell, taste, or sound. Ask the children questions that encourage them to think about things that can't be identified by using our senses:

What are some things you can't see?

What are some things you can't hear?

What are some things you can't smell?

What are some things you can't taste?

What are some things you can't touch?

Emotional Development

Feeling Sense. Show the children pictures of people expressing a variety of feelings. Tell them we can use our senses to recognize feelings. For example, we can tell how other people are feeling by looking at their faces. Show the pictures to the children and ask them to name the feelings they see. Then tell them we can also tell how other people are feeling by using our ears to listen to their voices. Speak in an angry, scared, sad, happy, excited, and frustrated voice. After each example, ask the children to guess how you are feeling.

Gentle Touch. We can use our sense of touch to give someone a kind touch, like a hug, a pat on the back, a handshake, or a high five. Ask the children to turn to the person on their left and touch them in one of these gentle ways. Then have the children turn to the person on their right and touch them gently in a different way.

How Do You Feel About It? Use visualization to encourage the children to explore their senses. Ask the children to close their eyes and imagine the different smells in the situations you describe. Tell the children to use a facial expression to show you how they feel about each smell. Choose situations that are relevant to your children. Here are a few examples: We are walking by a flower garden with lots of roses…. Someone in the building is popping popcorn…. We walk down the hall past the kitchen and someone just burned some food in the oven…. We are on the street corner and a city bus goes by and we smell the exhaust…."

Too Much of a Good Thing. Ask the children if they ever get frightened by loud noises. Explain that when sounds are too loud they scare us and they might make our ears or head hurt. Ask the children the following questions:

What noises scare you?

Does the fire alarm scare you?

Do fireworks scare you?

Does a siren scare you?

Does thunder scare you?

Ask the children to brainstorm solutions by asking them, "What can you do when sounds are too loud?"

What's This Feeling? Give children a chance to recognize how other people might be feeling by the combination of their words and the sound of their voices. Tape-record yourself expressing a variety of feelings that your children would likely recognize. For example, "Is it going to hurt?" (said with fear), "Yippee, we get ice cream. We get ice cream" (said with excitement), and "I don't want to go to bed and you can't make me" (said in an angry tone). Play one statement at a time. Stop the tape and ask the children how you were feeling. For younger children, you could set out a photograph to represent each of the feelings, and the children could point to the picture that goes with the sound of the voice on the cassette tape.

Health, Safety, and Nutrition

Color Candy Circles. In a pan, stir together 2 cups sugar, ½ cup light corn syrup, and ¼ cup water. Cook on medium heat and stir occasionally until it boils. Boil it for 5 minutes and check to see if it has reached the hard and brittle stage by placing a drop in cold water. If it is hard and brittle to the touch, remove the pan from the stove. Stir in food coloring. Pour on the shiny side of a piece of aluminum foil. While the candy circle is still soft, poke a piece of string into the circle so that you can hang it from the ceiling when it's dry. This recipe makes two 8-inch circles. Make one circle in each of the primary colors.

Sensations. Help the children learn to notice sensations inside their bodies. Ask them the following question:

What does it feel like inside of your body when you are thirsty?

How do you know when your body is thirsty?

How do you know when your body is hungry?

How do you know when your body is tired?

How does your body feel when it is tired?

How do you know when your body is sick?

How does your body feel when it is sick?

How do you know when you have to go to the bathroom?

How does your body feel when you have to go to the bathroom?

Talk to the children about how they can pay attention to the sensations inside their body.

Too Much. Young children often have difficulty coping with sensory overload. Give children a chance to experience, recall, and reflect on sensory overload. Tell children that sometimes our sensory body parts get overworked. On a sunny day, turn off the classroom lights. Once the children's eyes have adjusted to the darkness, take the class outside. Help the children notice how they react to the brightness (they may squint, cover or shut their eyes, look down). Some children will likely say it hurts. Ask the children questions like, "What happens when our sensory body parts are overworked? What happens to your eyes when the light is too bright and there's a lot of glare?" Try a similar experiment by blowing a loud whistle or alarm, or by dipping a cotton ball in ammonia or another strong-smelling substance and inviting children to smell it. Ask them questions like, "What happens when a noise is too loud? What happens when there's an odor that's very strong?" You can extend their thinking to their other senses by asking questions like, "What happens when you put something in your mouth that is very bitter or sour? What happens if you pick up something that is sharp?"

Language Development

Home Language. *Learn the words for sensory organs and the senses in American Sign Language and the home languages of the children in your class. Consider learning the words and signs for* eyes, ears, nose, mouth, hands, fingers, see, smell, hear, taste, *and* touch.

Soft Things. Collect a variety of items that are soft: a powder puff, a cotton ball, a piece of velvet, a piece of fleece, a piece of sheepskin. Place them in a bag and invite each child to reach in and grab an object. Ask the child how it feels. What do the things have in common? Introduce the following verse:

> ### Touch
> I love soft things so very much
> Soft things to feel
> Soft things to touch
> A cushioned chair
> A furry muff
> A baby's cheek
> A powder puff
> A bedtime kiss
> A gentle breeze
> A puppy's ear
> I love all of these.

(*Busy Fingers Growing Minds: Finger Plays, Verses and Activities for Whole Language Learning*, Rhoda Redleaf. St. Paul: Redleaf Press, 1993; p. 116. Used with permission.)

Thankful for Our Senses. Ask the children to name all the things they're glad for and chart them in groups according to each of the five senses.

Five Senses Picture Cards. Use a commercial set of five senses teaching pictures or your own made by cutting out large magazine pictures of people using their senses (remember to include people with sensory impairments) and gluing them onto construction paper. Hold up one picture at a time. Ask open-ended questions like the following:

> Who can tell me about this picture?
>
> What do you see?
>
> What is this person doing?
>
> Which of our five senses is this person using?
>
> What do you think this person sees, tastes, smells, hears, touches?
>
> What do you like about this picture?

My Voice. Tape the children's voices one at a time. With a small group of children, play the tape and see if they can identify whose voice they hear. Ask them how they know who it was.

Our Senses Book. Invite the children to work together to make a book about their senses. Include a page for sight, hearing, smell, taste, and touch. Include pictures of people who are Deaf or blind.

Read with Your Hands. Make a set of textured alphabet cards. Trace letters in pencil onto construction paper. Punch holes along the lines using a very sharp pencil, nail, or awl. Turn the cards over so that the bumpy side is up. Blindfold the children and invite them to feel the letters with their fingers. See if children can identify the letters by tracing them with their fingers. You can talk about how people who are blind read and write in Braille. You can also make textured shape and number cards.

Senses Picture Stories. Sit down with a small group of children and some pictures showing people using their senses. Include pictures of people who are Deaf or blind. Show the children one picture at a time. Ask the children what they see in the pictures. Encourage the children to make up a story about the people in the pictures. If possible, write down the children's stories, or invite older children to write their own stories.

Sounds I Know. Tape-record common sounds. You might want to make a tape of sounds around the house, outside, and at school. Play the cassette and see if children can identify the sound on the tape.

Math

Color Match. Make eight or more sets of color matching cards. Use paint samples, felt tip pens, or paint to create two matching cards for each color. Include skin colors and colors commonly used by the cultures of the children in your class. Write the name of the color on the back of each card. Place the cards in a basket and encourage the children to find the matching sets.

Counting Rope. Tie a knot in a piece of cotton clothesline, leaving 2 inches of rope on either side of the knot. Cut another piece a little longer and tie two knots, leaving a space between the knots on the rope. Cut another piece and tie three knots. Continue up to five or ten. Set out the ropes and a blindfold. Invite the children to cover their eyes and try to count the number of knots on each length of rope.

Faces. Make simple flannel board faces by cutting ovals out of skin-colored felt. Cut out a variety of eyes, ears, noses, and mouths. Set out the materials and encourage the children to place the felt body parts onto the felt faces.

Numbers on My Skin. Play a game by asking a child to close her eyes and put her palm up. Use your finger to draw a numeral on the child's hand and see if the child can recognize the numeral. Make the game simpler by tapping your finger on the child's back and have her identify the number of taps. You can also trace numbers on a child's back, which is a little more difficult, and see if the child can recognize the numeral.

Peeks and Holes. Collect a variety of sensory-related photographs. For instance, you could include pictures of a person tasting food, listening to music, petting an animal, looking at a bug, or smelling a flower. Cut peek holes in the outside of a manila file folder. Put one picture at a time inside the folder. Invite children to see if they can guess what the picture is by looking at parts of the photo through the peek holes. Tell them to open up the folder to check their answers.

Texture Match. Make a set of matching texture cards or circles. Select a variety of textures(burlap, cork, satin, fake fur, leather, heavy grit sand paper, steel wool, sponge, fake suede, velvet). Glue two samples of each texture to small squares of poster board. Write the name of the texture on the back of each card. Set them out and invite the children to match the textures. If you want, cut out the textures in the shape of a hand.

Texture Shapes. Set out a variety of shapes cut out of fabric of different textures. Also set out glue and construction paper. Encourage the children to make a design or pattern with the shapes and glue the shapes to the construction paper.

What's the Temperature? Bring in a weather thermometer and a few cooking thermometers. Fill a cup with hot water, another cup with warm water, and a third cup with cold water. Put a thermometer in each cup and watch the mercury rise and fall. Once the children have had a chance to see how a thermometer works, set the weather thermometer outside and check the temperature daily. Make a chart to record and graph the temperature for a month.

Music

The Five Senses Song. Here's a simple song about senses that is sung to a familiar tune.

FIVE SENSES

Tune: *Old MacDonald Had a Farm*

On my face I have two eyes;
Use them every day.
They are used to help me see
When I work and play.
With a look, look here,
And a look, look there,
Here a look, there a look,
Everywhere a look, look,
On my face I have two eyes;
Use them every day!

On my face I have a nose;
Use it all the time.
When I sniff it I can tell
Vinegar from lime.
With a sniff, sniff here,
And a sniff, sniff there,
Here a sniff, there a sniff,
Everywhere a sniff, sniff.
On my face I have a nose;
Use it all the time!

In my mouth I have a tongue;
Use it when I eat.
Tasting with it I can tell
Sour from the sweet.
With a lick, lick here,
And a lick, lick there,
Here a lick, there a lick,
Everywhere a lick, lick.
In my mouth I have a tongue;
Use it when I eat!

On my head I have two ears;
Listening all day long.
And if I didn't have them there,
I couldn't hear this song!
With a listen here,
And a listen there,
Here a listen, there a listen,
Everywhere a listen, listen.
On my head I have two ears;
Listening all day long!

On my body I have skin;
Feeling cold and heat.
It stretches from atop my head
Way down to my feet.
With a touch, touch here,
And a touch, touch there.
Here a touch, there a touch,
Everywhere a touch, touch.
On my body I have skin;
Feeling cold and heat!

(*Sing and Learn*, Carolyn Meyer and Kel Pickens. Carthage, IL: Good Apple, 1989; pp. 18 and 19. Used with permission.)

Water Music. Set out four to five glass jars or drinking glasses that are all the same. Fill each with varying amounts of water (one-quarter full, one-half full, three-quarters full, full to the top). Add a few drops of food coloring to the water to help children see the water in the glasses more easily. Use a spoon to tap the side of each jar and hear the different tones. Encourage children to make up a song. Mark the water lines on the jars or glasses so that children can easily fill them with water.

Physical Development

 Classroom Sounds. Blindfold one of the children in a large or small group and pick another to make a sound with any object in the classroom. The child who is blindfolded must try to guess what object is making the sound.

 Guess Who? Play a simple sensory guessing games. Blindfold children and see if they can identity their classmates by the sound of their voices. You could also blindfold children and see if they can identify children by touching and feeling them.

 Foot Ball. Divide the class into two teams. Have the children take off their shoes and socks and sit in two rows facing each other and just far enough apart from one another so that their toes barely touch. Place a lightweight ball on top of the feet of the pair of children at one end of the line and challenge them to work together to pass the ball up and down the row with their feet.

Freeze Tag. One child is "The Freezer" and chases the rest of the children around the room. If a child is tagged by "The Freezer," she is frozen solid and cannot move. The last person left unfrozen becomes "The Freezer" in the next round.

Goopy Cornstarch. Mix several tablespoons of cornstarch with water in a cup until it's pasty. Invite the children to pick up the goop. Surprisingly, it will begin to change from a solid to a liquid in their hands. Encourage the children to gather up the liquid again and let it ooze through their fingers.

Hide and Seek. Pick one child to cover her eyes and count to ten. The rest of the children run around and find a place to hide. On the count of ten, the child who is "it" begins looking for the children. The last child to be found is "it" in the next round of the game.

Hot and Cold. Invite children to play this guessing game. Pick one child to close her eyes while another child hides an object. Once the object is hidden, the first child looks for it. The rest of the group helps the child by shouting "Hot!" when she is in the vicinity of the object and "Cold!" when she is moving away from or nowhere near the object. Once the object is found, pick two other children and start the game over!

Hot Potato. Ask the children to form a circle. Use a real potato or a ball. Ask the children to pretend that the potato is very hot and that it will burn their hands if they hold onto it too long. The children pass the potato to the next person very quickly. At random intervals yell out, "Hot Potato!" The person who has the potato sits in the middle of the circle until the game is done.

Salt Drawing. Place a dark sheet of construction paper on the bottom of a tray. Cover the paper with a thin layer of salt. Encourage children to use their fingers to draw in the salt. The dark construction paper shows through and provides a high contrast, making it easier for the children to see their drawings. Show the children how to erase the drawing by gently shaking the tray back and forth.

Senses Express. Invite the children to express various sensations through creative movement. Ask the children to move their bodies in ways that show they are freezing, hot, outside in bright sunshine, in a very dark room, hearing a fire alarm, listening to music, smelling smoke, and smelling dinner cooking.

Sensory Body Part Games. Play body part identification games like "Head, Shoulders, Knees, and Toes." Sing the words while touching the appropriate body parts. Start slowly the first time through and repeat faster and faster each time. Emphasize the "eyes and ears and mouth and nose" portion of the song.

> Head, shoulders, knees and toes, knees and toes,
> Head, shoulders, knees and toes, knees and toes,
> Eyes and ears and mouth and nose,
> Head, shoulders, knees and toes.

Sensory Walks. Take a variety of sensory walks. On each walk, focus on learning through one of the senses. Take a "touch walk" and give the children bags to collect things they can touch. Take a "listening walk" and tape-record various sounds. Take a "seeing walk" and give each child a paper towel tube to look through. When you return to the room, make a class list of all the things the children noticed by using that particular sense.

Texture Box. Make a touch-and-feel box so that children can reach into a box to feel and grasp small objects without seeing the object. Fill the box with a variety of objects that represent different textures. You might include fake fur, coil, bark, shell, carpet scrap, yarn ball, cotton ball, feather, rope, cellophane, brush, pinecone, wood, Styrofoam, sandpaper, rubber, and metal. Invite the children to put their hands in the box, find an object, and identify it by using their sense of touch. Pull out the item to see if their guess is correct. For a different experience, have children put on a rubber glove before reaching into the touch-and-feel box. Can they identify the object with the glove on?

Texture Walk. Set out materials with a variety of textures, like carpet squares, a sheet of bubble pack, a piece of fake fur, a resealable bag of Jell-O, a tub of water, a rough door mat, and pieces of satin fabric. Invite the children to take off their shoes and socks and walk on the different textures.

Touch! Play a movement game where the children must touch whatever you tell them to touch. The fun is in giving touch commands quickly. Shout out the next command just as children are about to touch the first thing you asked them to touch. You could call out colors, people's names, gender, textures, age, or physical features.

Science

Can You Taste It? Help children increase their awareness of the sense of taste and how their tongue helps them recognize different tastes. Have a tasting experience with a variety of foods so that children can taste something salty, sweet, sour, and bitter. You might set out pickles, salty potato chips, lemon or lime wedges, and hard candy or chocolate chips. Introduce children to the words *salty, sweet, sour,* and *bitter* to describe tastes. See if the children can find the part of their tongue that is most sensitive to each type of taste and predict common reactions to each type of taste.

Feel the Heat. This activity gives children a chance to compare how different materials conduct heat and cold. Pour water and ice cubes into one bowl. Pour water into a second bowl and place it on an electric hot plate set on low. Ask the children if they know the meaning of the word *conduct.* Show the children a variety of objects (plastic knife, wooden spoon, metal utensil with a plastic handle, wooden craft stick, a "string" of paper clips), and ask them to predict what will happen when they set them in the bowls of water. Invite children to hold one utensil at a time in the cold water. What do they feel? Repeat with each of the utensils. Then try holding the utensils, one at a time, in the hot water. You might want to make a graph of the results.

Potpourri. Gather herbs and flowers from your garden, or purchase them at a local farmers' market. Remove the leaves from the flower stems, but leave the herbs intact. Tie the flowers and herbs in bunches. Hang them upside down in a dry dark place for two or more weeks. Break off the dried flowers and herb leaves into a bowl. Add a few drops of essential oil (rose or another floral scent). Add cloves, allspice, juniper berries, cinnamon sticks, or dried orange peel. Give each child a bag of potpourri to take home.

Smelling Jars. Help children develop their awareness of the sense of smell and introduce children to smells of other cultures. Gather a number of small containers, such as margarine tubs or film containers. Place one spice, incense, or essential oil in each container. Consider using ginger, coriander, anise, five-spice powder, sesame oil, cilantro, cardamom, sandalwood, patchouli, or nutmeg. Ask the children to close their eyes and smell the contents of each container. Encourage children to identify the fragrance in each container. Talk about how people all over the world use different spices to cook with and have different smells in their homes.

Water Magnifying Glass. Trace three circles around the sides of a clean plastic pail. Cut out the circles using a knife or scissors. Tear off a piece of plastic wrap or dry cleaning plastic a little larger than the top of the pail. Secure the plastic to the top of the pail with a large rubber band. Pour water onto the plastic wrap. The holes in the side of the pail will allow you to place objects in the bottom of the pail. The water acts as a magnifier and makes the objects look larger than they are.

Social Development

I Can't Hear You. Ask children if they know anyone who is Deaf. Ask them if they know how Deaf people communicate. Tell them that many people who are Deaf use sign language. Some Deaf people read lips, and some speak. Ask children if they would like to see what it might be like to be Deaf. Set out earmuffs, disposable earplugs, or other ear covers. Invite children to wear them for a period of time (15 minutes to an hour). At circle time, talk with the children about what it was like not being able to hear and what they did to try to understand what people were saying to them.

Stop and Help. Invite the children to form a circle. Ask for a volunteer to stand in the middle and be blindfolded. Ask the rest of the children to hold hands, walk around the circle, and say "Around, and around, and around we go. When (_child's name_) says stop, we'll stand still and touch gently, just so." When the blindfolded child says stop, the children quietly stand in their places. The blindfolded child walks toward the children and attempts to identify a child by touching her.

Taking a Stand Against Annoying Behavior. Help children develop assertiveness in the face of annoying behavior, such as someone screaming in their ear, kicking the back of their chair, or poking them at circle time. Ask the children, "Does it bother you when someone screams in your ear or pokes at you during circle time? What are other things that bother you?" Use a doll or puppet to role-play the experience of being bothered by others. Ask the children, "How do you think the puppet feels? What can the puppet do when others bother her?" Discuss the children's answers. Tell the children that you know a way to respond that is strong and doesn't hurt anyone. It's called standing up for yourself. You have to stand tall and proud, look at the other person, speak in your strong voice, and speak your truth (what you know, what you feel, and what you need). Use the puppet to model standing up for yourself. Reenact the bothering incident and have the puppet stand tall, look at the puppet who bothered her, and say in a strong voice, "Please stop screaming in my ear. I don't like it and it hurts."

ACTIVITIES: AFFIRMING OURSELVES AND ONE ANOTHER

Human Rights

People with disabilities have a right to equal access to places and to information.

BARRIER: Many buildings, public places, houses, and jobs are not accessible to people. Many public events are not interpreted into American Sign Language, and public information is not always available in alternative formats. Making places and information accessible is not always easy and is sometimes expensive.

People with disabilities have a right to independence and to make their own decisions.

BARRIER: Many houses and schools are not set up so that they work for people with specific disabilities. Some people are confused and think that people with disabilities are not able to make their own decisions.

DISCUSSION QUESTIONS: Help children think about people who are Deaf or blind. Ask them questions like, "What kinds of things would be different in your life if you couldn't see or couldn't hear? What do you think people who are Deaf or blind need from hearing and/or sighted people who work with them or are their friends? What do you think people who are Deaf or blind need to be able to have equal access to public places, education, or information? What kinds of things do you think they need to have in their homes to make their homes work well for them? Why do you think some people who are Deaf or blind don't get what they need? What can we do to make public places and jobs be more fair to people who are Deaf and blind?"

Cultural Identity

Fabric and Patterns. Introduce the children to types of fabric and design patterns. Invite parents to share examples of clothing and fabric from their home culture. Give the children an opportunity to study the patterns and feel the textures. Set out crayons or paints and encourage the children to draw or paint a pattern similar to what is on the fabric.

If I Were In.... Read a story to the children about the homeland of one of their classmates. Follow up the story by asking the children these questions:

> If you were in (*child's homeland*), what might you see?
>
> If you were in (*child's homeland*), what might you hear?
>
> If you were in (*child's homeland*), what might you smell?
>
> If you were in (*child's homeland*), what might you taste?
>
> If you were in (*child's homeland*), what might you touch?

Smells from My Home. Ask parents to share some spices, perfumes, oils, or other items that have a scent that is common in their culture. Give children an opportunity to explore the scents.

Diversity

Colorless World. Invite the children to explore the possibility and consequences of living without the sensory experiences that we take for granted. Ask the children these questions:

> What would the world be like if we didn't have different colors.
>
> What if everything in the world was the same color?
>
> What would the world be like if we only had one sound?
>
> What would the world be like if we had only one taste?

Different and Similar. Help children explore ways in which different objects can have similarities. For instance, a variety of balls can be very different from one another (color, size, weight), however they are also similar because they are all round. A variety of foods that appear to be very different from one another—like hard candy, a candy bar, and pudding—can be similar in that they all taste like chocolate. Collect objects that represent these concepts and add them to the discovery table. Examples of objects to collect include objects that sound similar (a collection of shakers, for example), objects that have similar textures (for example, three soft things), a cassette tape of people talking, and pictures of children who are the same age, gender, or culture.

Finger Paint Mix-Up. Help children explore shades of skin color through finger painting. Put a small amount of black, brown, red, yellow, and white powder tempera onto finger paint paper. Pour about 3 tablespoons of liquid starch on the paper. Invite the children to mix the powdered tempera and starch by finger painting. Encourage them to make skin colors. They could even try to make the color of their skin.

Glasses. Help children learn about people who have poor eyesight and need glasses to see. Give each child a chance to look through a piece of frosted glass or spray cleaner on a piece of glass to make it smeared and hard to see through. Ask the children, "What might happen if you couldn't see clearly? What might happen if everything looked blurry, like looking through this piece of glass?" Tell children that glasses improve the vision of people whose eyesight is blurry. Use a persona doll with glasses to tell a story about a child who couldn't see very well but improved her vision by getting glasses.

One and Many. Give children an opportunity to use their senses to notice similarities and differences. Explore basic concepts, like an object having more than one color, sound, smell, taste, and texture. Set up a discovery table with collections of objects that illustrate these concepts. Foods are another way to explore some of these concepts. For example, an apple has many different colors on and inside it. You can make an apple taste many different ways. Lots of foods have an apple taste.

Skin Color Match-Ups. Set out a collection of knee-high stockings in shades of tan, white, black, yellow, and red. Encourage children to put the stockings on their hand to find a color that matches their skin color. Explore lighter and darker shades. Talk about how we are all shades of brown and that nobody's skin color is really white, red, or yellow.

Some People are Blind. Give children an opportunity to learn about people who are visually impaired or blind. The best way to learn about a disability is through direct experience. Invite adults who are blind to visit the classroom and talk with the children about all the things that they can do and the things they do differently because of their blindness.

Some People are Deaf. Give children an opportunity to learn about people who are hearing impaired and need a hearing aid to hear or are Deaf. Invite an adult who is Deaf or hearing impaired to visit your classroom and talk with the children about all the things that they can do and the things they do differently because they are Deaf or hearing impaired.

Bias and Stereotypes

One Is Not All. Young children tend to overgeneralize and assume that if one body part is not working well, all body parts are not working well. Help the children learn about all the things that people who are Deaf or blind can do. Read stories about people with disabilities leading active and productive lives. (See the Gallaudet Bookstore catalog for great books about Deaf people.)

Peepholes Can't See the Whole Picture. Collect enough paper towel cardboard tubes for each child. Invite the children to look at one another through the tubes. Encourage them to get really close to each other and look through the tube again. Help them recognize that when they look through a small tube they can't see the whole person. It's peephole vision. Peephole vision is when you only see one part of a person and don't see the whole person. For instance, if you are looking at someone who is blind and all you see is their blindness, you have peephole vision. If you meet someone whose skin color is different than yours and that is all you can see, you have peephole vision.

Rewrite It. Help children challenge stereotypes about people who are blind or Deaf. Read a familiar fairy tale in which the main character is made fun of for behaving or doing things differently. You might want to read *Rumplestiltskin* and help the children identify all the negative labels and descriptions of this character.

Community Service

Helping Dogs. Raise money for organizations that provide and train helping dogs for people with disabilities, or sponsor a dog guide for someone who is Deaf or blind.

A Sight for Sore Eyes. Paint a mural on the side of your building or wash off graffiti from your building.

Social Action Suggestions

Barrier-Free. Work together to eliminate physical barriers in your school or community to children who are Deaf or blind.

Clean Water. Work together with children, parents, and teachers to get clean drinking water at your center and in your community.

ACTIVITIES: OPENING THE DOOR

Classroom Visitor

Invite people who are Deaf or blind to visit your classroom and show the children how they function fully without the use of their eyes or ears.

Field Trips

Take a trip to a local children's museum or science museum that has exhibits designed to stimulate the senses.

Visit an early childhood special education class and invite them to visit your class.

Parent Involvement

Invite parents who have a disability or have a child with a disability to talk with the children about all the things they can do.

Invite parents to share their hobbies with the children. Hobbies often involve the senses. For instance, pottery, woodworking, and sewing involve a lot of different textures. Photography, painting, and drawing are visual. Playing a musical instrument involves the sense of sound. Cake decorating, cooking, and vegetable gardening involve the senses of taste and smell.

Parent Education

Invite an ear, nose, and throat specialist to discuss ear infections and hearing loss in early childhood. Or ask an allergist to give a presentation on childhood asthma and allergies.

Invite an early childhood educator to talk about Dr. Howard Gardiner's work around multiple intelligences and learning styles.

CLASSROOM RESOURCES

Children's Books

Brown Bear, Brown Bear, What Do You See? Bill Martin Jr. (New York: Holt, 1983).

Bubble Trouble, Mary Packard (New York: Scholastic, 1995).

A Button In Her Ear, Ada B. Litchfield (Morton Grove, IL: Whitman, 1976).

A Cane In Her Hand, Ada B. Litchfield (Morton Grove, IL: Whitman, 1977).

Cinnamon, Mint, And Mothballs: A Visit To Grandmother's House, Ruth Tiller (San Diego: Harcourt, 1993).

City Sounds, Craig Brown (New York: Greenwillow, 1992).

Did You Hear Wind Sing Your Name? An Oneida Song Of Spring, Sandra De Coteau Orie (New York: Walker, 1996).

Don't Touch, Suzy Kline (New York: Puffin, 1988).

Feel And Touch, Julian Rowe (Danbury, CT: Children's Press, 1994).

Five Senses, Tracy West (New York: Scholastic, 1997).

The Handmade Alphabet, Laura Rankin (New York: Dial, 1991).

I Can Tell By Touching, Carolyn Otto (North Dighton: World, 1994).

I Have A Sister, My Sister Is Deaf, Jeanne Peterson (New York: Harper, 1977).

I See A Song, Eric Carle (New York: Scholastic, 1996).

Joe Joe, Mary Serfozo (New York: McElderry, 1993).

Listen To The Desert, Pat Mora (New York: Clarion, 1994).

The Listening Walk, Paul Showers (New York: Harper, 1991).

Look, Michael Gejniec (New York: North South, 1993).

Look Closer! Peter Ziebel (Boston: Houghton, 1993).

Look! Look! Look! Tana Hoban (New York: Greenwillow, 1988).

Look Once, Look Twice, Janet Marshall (New York: Ticknor, 1996).

Look Up, Look Down, Tana Hoban (New York: Greenwillow, 1992).

Lucy's Picture, Nicola Moon (New York: Viking, 1997).

My Aunt Otilia's Spirits, Richard Garcia (Danbury, CT: Children's Press, 1986).

My First Look At Touch, Stephen Oliver (New York: Random, 1990).

My Five Senses, Aliki (New York: Harper, 1991).

My Five Senses, Margaret Miller (New York: Simon, 1994).

Nana's Place, Akimi Gibson

Of Colors And Things, Tana Hoban (New York: Morrow, 1996).

Polar Bear, Polar Bear What Do You Hear? Bill Martin Jr. (New York: Holt, 1993).

Quiet Please, Eve Merriam (New York: Simon, 1993).

Sense Suspense, Bruce McMillan (New York: Scholastic, 1994).

Touch…What Do You Feel? Nicholas Wood (Mahwah, NJ: Troll, 1997).

Welcome Back Sun, Michael Emberley (Boston: Little Brown, 1993).

A Whisper Is Quiet, Carolyn Lunn (Danbury, CT: Children's Press, 1988).

You Can't Smell A Flower With Your Ear! All About Your Five Senses, Joanna Cole (New York: Putnam, 1994).

Music

Complete Sound Effects Library (Educational Record Center, 1992).

Fink, Cathy, and Marcy Marxer. *Nobody Else Like Me* (A&M, 1994).

"Harry's Glasses"

"I See With My Hands"

Lefranc, Barbara. *I Can Be Anything I Want To Be* (Doubar, 1990).

"Senses"

"Touch A Rainbow"

Hartmann, Jack. *One Voice For Children* (Educational Activities, 1993).

"Listen, Really Listen"

Grammer, Red. *Teaching Peace* (Smilin' Atcha, 1986).

"Listen"

Hunter, Tom. *Bits and Pieces* (Song Growing, 1990).

"Listen With Our Hearts"

"Somos El Barco"

Tune Into Kids. *Color The World* (Endeavor, 1992).

"Listen"

Visual Displays

ABC School Supply
Five Senses Chart

Videos

Eye and Ear Care (Educational Associates).

Sign Me A Story by Linda Bove (Educational Record Center).

Sign Songs by Kevin Lonquist (Educational Record Center).

Sing 'N Sign For Fun (Educational Record Center).

Sounds Around (Bo Peep Productions).

Teaching Kits

Five Senses Discovery Kit, Lakeshore

The Five Senses Kit, ABC School Supply

Chef Combo's Fantastic Adventures
National Dairy Council
10255 W. Higgins Road, Suite 900
Rosemont, IL 60018-5616
(800) 426-8271
Fax (800) 974-6455

WORK

"I don't want you to go to work. I want to stay home." "I don't want to put my toys away. I don't want to clean up my room." "Stop! You can't feed the fish. It's my job. I'm the fish feeder today." "Let's go play restaurant. I'll be the cook and you be the order taker, okay?" Young children are becoming aware of the world of work. They may have parents or other family members who work. At home they may be taking on household responsibilities such as cleaning up their rooms, putting away their toys, or feeding the cat. At school they may be expected to clean up when play time is over and may be assigned classroom duties such as watering plants, feeding animals, or setting the table for snack.

Children enjoy taking on new responsibilities, being helpful, and feeling like they are needed. We want children to develop positive attitudes toward work. This unit allows everyone to learn about all the ways people work. Children can find out what work is and who they know who works. They can learn about different types of work, such as housework, classroom jobs, schoolwork, and work in the community. As a result, children will begin to value different kinds of work and recognize that we need people to do different kinds of work.

UNIT 8:

Work

BIG AS LIFE

WORK

Look for this symbol
to find activities you
can use for circle time.

Web

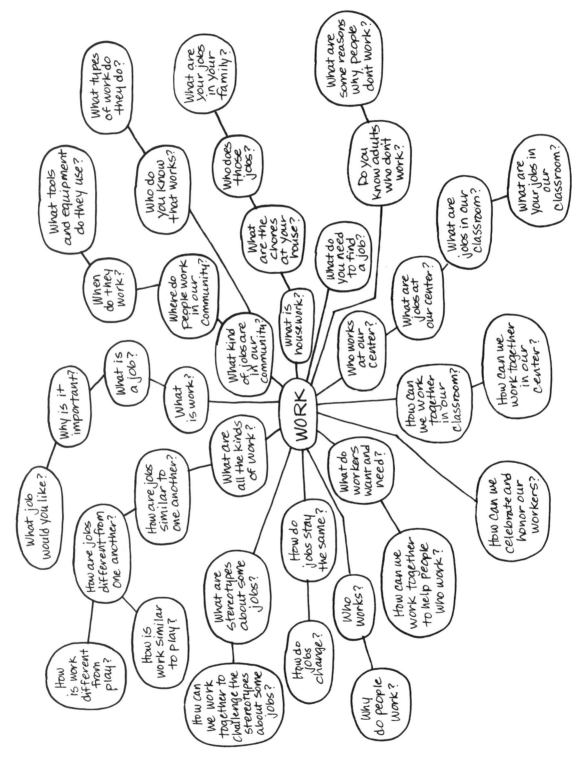

BIG AS LIFE

Outline

I. Who do you know that works?
    A. What types of work do they do?
    B. What is work?
    C. What is a job?
        1. Why is it important?
        2. What job would you like?
    D. Who works?
    E. Why do people work?

II. What is housework?
    A. What are the chores at your house?
    B. Who does these jobs?
    C. What are your jobs in your family?

III. Who works at our center?
    A. What are the jobs at our center?
    B. What are the jobs in our classroom?
    C. What are your jobs in our classroom?
    D. How can we work together in our classroom?
    E. How can we work together in our center?

IV. What kind of jobs are in our community?
    A. Where do people work in our community?
    B. When do they work?
    C. What tools and equipment do they use?

V. What do you need to find a job?
    A. Do you know adults who don't work?
    B. What are some reasons why people don't work?

VI. What are all the kinds of work?
    A. How are jobs similar to one another?
    B. How are jobs different from one another?
    C. How is work similar to play?
    D. How is work different from play?
    E. How do jobs stay the same?
    F. How do jobs change?
    G. What are stereotypes about some jobs?
    H. How can we work together to challenge the stereotypes about some jobs?

VII. What do workers want and need?

VIII. How can we work together to help people who work?

IX. How can we celebrate and honor workers?

Materials List

ART

skin-colored paints, markers, crayons, and craft paper

butcher paper roll

tool-shaped sponges (for example, Tool Sponges, *Kaplan*)

woodworking materials

clay and clay tools

magazines with pictures of various kinds of workers

BLOCKS

a variety of multicultural people figures, including figures of people with disabilities

career people figures (for example, Community Career Figures, Community Workers Bendables, *Constructive Playthings*; Firefighter Play Set, *Beckley-Cardy*; Inclusive Play People, *Educational Equity Concepts*; Our Helpers Play People, *Nasco*)

a variety of transportation vehicles (for example, Air Fleet, Jumbo Tuf Crane, Dump, and Bulldozer, Over-the-Road Set, *Constructive Playthings*; Classic Train Set, Real-Action Construction Fleet, *Lakeshore*; Ertl John Deere 5020 Diesel Tractor, Ertl John Deere Skid-Steer Loader, Jumbo Bulldozer, Toddle Tots Ferryboat, Tottle Tots Garbage Truck, *Nasco*; Mack Cement Mixer, Mack Construction Set, Mack Heavy-Duty Dump Truck, Mack Heavy-Duty Wrecker, Police Set, *Beckley-Cardy*)

transportation accessories (for example, Construction Rug, *Community Playthings*; International Sign Set, Super Garage/Service Station, *Constructive Playthings*)

building sets (for example, Brio Mec Tool Box, *Beckley-Cardy*; Nuts and Bolts Building Set, *Lakeshore*)

farm animal sets (for example, Classic Farm Animal Collection, *Lakeshore*)

DRAMATIC PLAY

career and worker dress-ups and props (for example, Construction Engineer, Firefighter's Uniform, Ironing Board and Iron, Laundry Center, Mail Carrier Uniform, Medical Cart, Medical Kit, Medical Team Uniforms, Police Officer's Uniform, *Constructive Playthings*; Dramatic Play Costumes, *J. L. Hammett*; Deluxe Housecleaning Set, Play Vacuum, *Constructive Playthings*, *Nasco*; Construction Prop Box, Career Costume Set, *Lakeshore*)

community signs (for example, Emerging Literacy Community Signs Kit, *Lakeshore*)

preschooler dolls and career dolls (for example, Career Character Dress-Up Dolls, Multi-Ethnic School Dolls, *Lakeshore*)

prop boxes for a variety of workers

construction worker: carpenter's apron, hammer, saw, T square, measuring tape, pencil, safety goggles, project plans

plumber: plastic pipe sections, wrench, old faucet parts, lunch bucket

office worker: briefcase, computer keyboard, steno pad, pencil, telephone

chef: chef's hat, apron, cooking utensils, cookie sheet, cooking pot, recipe book

store clerk: cash register, pretend money, receipt book, pencil

LARGE MOTOR

equipment to encourage worker play (for example, Carry-All Trike, *Constructive Playthings*; Mailbox, *Beckley-Cardy*; Gas Pump, Traffic Signs, *Beckley-Cardy*, *Constructive Playthings*)

LITERACY

children's books: fiction, nonfiction, and bilingual books about work (see resource list at the end of the unit)

cassette player and theme-related storybook cassettes

work-related flannel board sets (for example, Giant-Size Felt Community Helpers, *Constructive Playthings*; We Dress for Work Flannel Board Concept Kits, *Lakeshore*)

career puppets (for example, Career Groups Hand Puppets, *Edvantage*, *Lakeshore*)

work-related matching cards (for example, People and Places Cards, *Kaplan*)

MANIPULATIVES

multiethnic career puzzles (for example, Farm Giant Floor Puzzle, *Constructive Playthings*; Career Puzzle Set, *Lakeshore*; Non-Sexist Multiethnic Career Puzzles, *Constructive Playthings*, *Lakeshore*)

career-related board and matching games (for example, Community Careers Match-Up Lotto, *Lakeshore*)

pipe construction sets and bolt boards (for example, Bolt Board, Bolt Builder, Gears! Gears! Gears! Pipe Construction Set, *Constructive Playthings*; Junior Erector Set, *Lakeshore*)

work-related theme boxes (for example, Community and Careers, Tools and Machines Theme Boxes, *Lakeshore*)

SCIENCE

earthworm or ant farm (for example, Giant Ant Farm, *Lakeshore*)

clear plastic pipes and connectors

pendulums and pulleys (for example, Simple Machines, *ABC School Supply*)

SENSORY

water pumps and water wheels (for example, Water Maze, *Kaplan*; Water Play Pumps, Water System, *Constructive Playthings*)

dirt, sand, or potting soil and small construction tools or vehicles

Teaching Through the Interest Areas

Art

Add woodworking materials, clay, magazines with pictures of workers, and a variety of clay tools.

Blocks

Add figures of career people and transportation vehicles like buses, taxis, and cars to the block area to encourage work-related play.

Set out various trucks and road signs in the block area. Mark off a road that winds around and through the block area to encourage truck driver play.

Dramatic Play

Add prop boxes for a variety of different workers, such as a construction worker (carpenter's apron, hammer, saw, T square, measuring tape, pencil, safety goggles, blueprints), plumber (plastic pipe sections, wrench, old faucet parts, lunch bucket), office worker (brief case, computer keyboard, steno pad, pencil, telephone), chef (chef's hat, apron, cooking utensils, cookie sheet, cooking pot, recipe book), and store clerk (cash register, pretend money, receipt book, pencil).

Add gas pumps, traffic signs, mailboxes, and trikes to encourage worker play.

Literacy

Set out a collection of fiction, nonfiction, and bilingual books on work. Include a tape player and work-related storybook cassettes, career puppets, dress-for-work flannel board sets, and materials for keeping journals and making books.

Manipulatives

Add pipe construction sets, bolt boards, multi-ethnic career puzzles, matching games, and career board games.

Music

Set out cassette tapes that contain work-related songs.

Science

Set out an earthworm farm or ant farm to observe how they work, clear plastic pipes and connectors to learn about the flow of water, or pulleys and pendulums for exploring simple physics concepts.

Sensory

Add water pumps, waterwheels, and water to the sensory table.

Add a few inches of dirt, sand, or potting soil and small construction tools or construction vehicles to the sensory table.

ACTIVITIES: INVESTIGATING THE THEME

Creative Development

Woodworking. Set out woodworking materials and encourage the children to build something as a construction worker or woodworker might do.

Worker Badge. Set out construction paper, poster board, foil, marking pens, scissors, glitter, and glue. You could cut some poster board into the shape of badges ahead of time. Talk with the children about workers they know who wear badges or name tags. Invite children to make a badge or name tag that a worker might wear on the job.

Worker Hats. Give each child two large pieces of coated easel paper. Have the children cover the entire side of one piece of paper with watered down glue. Put the two pieces of paper together and press down. While wet, place the two layers of paper on top of the child's head and tie around the crown with a string. Let it dry a few minutes. As it dries, the child can fold the brim into any shape. When it is dry, the brim can be cut and the hat decorated. Encourage children to make hats that are similar to ones worn by workers that they like.

Worker Portraits. Set up the easels and take out the tempera paints. Invite children to paint a picture of their favorite worker.

Critical Thinking

Adult Workers. Ask various workers to share their careers with your class. Ask them to talk to the children about their jobs. Encourage each worker to bring their uniforms, tools, or equipment they use on the job. Be sure not to perpetuate gender stereotypes by the people you invite. Older children could prepare questions to ask the workers before they arrive. Consider asking questions like

> How did you choose your job?
>
> What do you need to know to do your job?
>
> How did you learn to be a _____?
>
> Did you have a different job before this one?
>
> What do you like about your job?
>
> What don't you like about your job?

Do you have a family?

Are you a mommy or a daddy?

Where do you sleep?

Emotional Development

Look at My Work. Foster children's pride in their accomplishments. Tell them that working often makes people feel good about themselves. They feel a sense of pride and accomplishment—a sense inside their body of a job well done. Give the children a chance to do their best work and to feel a sense of pride and accomplishment. Invite them to paint or draw the best pictures they can. Take their finished work and iron out the wrinkles, crop the pictures, and frame them to make them look professional and very attractive. Have an art show and display the children's artwork for all to see.

Power Hats. This activity helps children foster their internal sense of power. Talk about how some workers wear hats. Sometimes we can tell what kind of work a person does by looking at their hat. Set out a box of career hats. Hold them up one at a time and talk about the qualities of the workers who wear that hat. For example, firefighters wearing their helmets are considered brave and strong and helpful. Ask children what quality they would like to have. For instance, would they like to be smart, brave, caring, strong, friendly? Invite children to make a hat that would help them feel that way. Help the children think about what a smart hat or a brave hat would look like. Set out a variety of art materials, and help the children make their power hats.

Practice Makes Perfect. Help children recognize that workers practiced a long time to learn how to do their jobs. Ask the children to think of something that they can do that took a lot of practice to learn. Remind them that it takes a lot of practice to learn how to cut with scissors, learn a new song, recite a finger play, or write your name. Teach children a new song. On the bulletin board, keep a count of how many times you practice it before everyone knows all the words.

We Do Our Best. Encourage children to try to do their best. Talk about how workers try to be the best at their jobs. Ask the children, "Do you think a firefighter tries to be a bad firefighter? No, she tries to be the best firefighter she can be. Do you think a nurse tries to be a bad nurse? No, he tries to be the best nurse he can be. Do you think a cook tries to be a bad cook? No, he tries to be the best cook he can be." Ask each child to name one thing he does really well. Invite the children to show their talents to the class. Make a badge for each child that says, "I'm the best…"

What Is Work? Begin the unit with an introductory discussion on work. To generate discussion, ask the following questions:

What is work? Who works?

What are jobs people do?

What else do you know about work and workers?

What would you like to know about work?

What would you like to know about workers?

When I Grow Up. Children are beginning to form gender-related ideas related to work. Ask the children what kind of work their mothers or other women they know do. Ask them what kind of work their dads or other men they know do. Continue the discussion with questions like:

What are jobs women can do?

What are jobs men can do?

What would you like to do when you grow up and are a woman?

What would you like to do when you grow up and are a man?

What would happen if a woman really wanted a job that men usually do?

What would happen if a man really wanted a job that women usually do?

Work Can Make You Tired. Help children recognize that some types of work are very physically or mentally draining and make people very tired. Ask the children questions like these:

Do your parents ever come home from work tired?

What kind of work makes people's bodies tired?

What kind of work makes people's heads tired?

What things do you do at school that make you tired?

Set up a relay game where children have to walk from one side of the room to the other, pick up a small object like a clothespin, carry it back, and put it in a bowl. Encourage the children to see how many they can do until they get tired. They'll be tired in five minutes. Help them recognize that they worked hard for a few minutes and that some people work like that all day long. Ask the children, "How can you help your parents when they are tired after a long day of work?"

Health, Safety, and Nutrition

Safety on the Job. Remind children of safety rules. Talk with them about how workers need to follow safety rules on the job. Workers who repair the streets wear vests that help us see them. Construction workers wear hard hats to keep their heads safe. Dentists and doctors wear gloves to protect them from germs. Welders and carpenters wear goggles to protect their eyes. Ask the children, "What are things we can do to keep us safe when we are working in our classroom?" As a group, brainstorm a list of classroom safety rules.

Language Development

Home Language. *Learn the words for work and the job titles of the children's parents in American Sign Language and the home languages spoken by the children in your classroom.*

Worker Finger Plays and Rhymes. Here are three finger plays and rhymes that celebrate the work of farmers, carpenters, and firefighters.

FARM CHORES

Five little farmers woke up with the sun. *(hold up hand, palm forward)*
It was early morning and the chores must be done.
The first little farmer went out to milk the cow. *(hold up hand, point to thumb)*
The second little farmer thought he'd better plow. *(hold up hand, point to index finger)*
The third little farmer cultivated weeds. *(point to middle finger)*
The fourth little farmer planted more seeds. *(point to fourth finger)*
The fifth little farmer drove his tractor round. *(point to last finger)*
Five little farmers, the best that can be found. *(hold up hand)*

(*Creative Resources for the Early Childhood Classroom*, second edition, Judy Herr and Libby Yvonne. Albany, NY: Delmar Publishers, 1995; p. 423. Used with permission.)

CARPENTER

The carpenter's hammer goes tap, tap, tap
And her saw goes seesaw, seesaw
And she planes and she measures
And she saws
While she builds a big house for me.

(*Finger Frolics*, Liz Cromwell and Dixie Hibner. Livonia, MI: Partner Press, 1976; p. 64. Used with permission.)

TEN BRAVE FIREFIGHTERS

Ten brave firefighters sleeping in a row
Dingdong, goes the bell
And down the pole they go.
Off on the engine oh, oh, oh.
Using the big hose, so, so, so.
When all the fire's out, home so-o-slow.
Back to bed, all in a row.

(*Finger Frolics*, Liz Cromwell and Dixie Hibner. Livonia, MI: Partner Press, 1976; p. 65. Used with permission.)

Career Workers Picture Cards. Glue large magazine pictures of people working onto construction paper, or use a commercial set of career teaching pictures. Hold up one picture at a time and ask open-ended questions like these:

Who can tell me about this picture?

What do you see?

Who's in this picture?

What are they doing?

Where are they?

What do you think their job is? How do you know?

What do you like about the work this person does?

Name That Worker. Bring pictures of a variety of workers or a variety of tools that workers use to circle time. Give the children one clue at a time about one of the pictures of tools. Describe the work, where it is done, and who the worker helps or what the worker makes. If you are using a tool, describe its color, shape, and size, as well as the work it is used for. Let the children guess after each clue, and keep giving clues until the type of work is named by one of the children. When a child guesses the worker or type of work, give him the picture or tool to hold while you continue to play the game.

Our Work Book. Make a class book about work. Encourage the children to include people they know who work and the types of work children would like to do when they get big. You could include information like the type of work the person does, where they work, and when they work.

What Do You Want to Be? Ask each child, "What kind of work would you like to do when you grow up?" Write the child's answer on a large piece of paper. Give it to the child and encourage him to draw or paint a picture of himself in that role.

Worker Picture Stories. Sit down with a small group of children and some teaching pictures of adults working. Show the children one picture at a time. Ask the children what they see in the pictures. Encourage the children to make up stories about the workers in the pictures. If possible, write down the children's stories.

Math

Career Match. Make eight or more sets of career matching cards. Find duplicate photos in magazines, use a color photocopier to duplicate the photos of people working, or use a photocopier to duplicate the wooden figures of people working that are used in the block area. Glue the pictures of people in various careers to index cards. Write the name of the career on the back of the card. Place the cards in a basket and encourage the children to find the matching sets.

Career Tools. Collect a variety of tools that workers use. Trace the objects on a large sheet of poster board. Set out the poster board and tools. Invite children to match each tool to the corresponding outline.

Community Worker Sort. Collect photos of a variety of community workers. Make sure that your collection is nonsexist, multicultural, and includes people with disabilities. Glue the pictures to index cards and write the name of the career or job title on the back of the card. Set out the pictures in a basket along with a sorting tray. Invite the children to sort the pictures of community workers any way they like.

Counting Keys. Collect a variety of old keys and key chains. Ask hardware stores, parents, and coworkers for extra keys. Place one key on one chain, two keys on another chain, three keys on the third chain. Continue up to ten keys on a chain. Invite the children to count the number of keys on a chain. To make the activity more difficult, simply set out a bowl of keys and key chains and the children can count the keys and place them on the key chains.

Counting Tiles. Collect a variety of scrap ceramic tiles. Set them out in a basket with number cards and lengths of yarn. Invite the children to count the tiles to match the numeral cards, separating the groups with the yarn.

Matching Keys and Locks. Collect a variety of padlocks. Set out the locks and keys in a basket. Invite the children to see if they can find the key that will open each lock.

Nuts and Bolts. Collect different sized bolts and corresponding nuts. Set out the nuts and bolts in a basket and invite the children to find the matching nut for each bolt.

Workers and Tools Match. Make four or more sets of matching cards that are related to workers and the tools they use. Find photos of workers and tools in magazines, or draw your own. Write the name of the career or tool on the back of each card. For example, you could have cards that show a doctor and a stethoscope, a mechanic and a tow truck, a secretary and a desk, and a waiter and an order pad and pencil. Be sure to avoid gender and racial stereotypes when you create the cards. Place the cards in a basket and encourage the children to find the matching sets.

Music

Working Songs. Here are simple songs with familiar tunes to teach the children.

FAMILIES WORKING

Tune: *Frère Jacques*

Families working, families working,
At home and away, at home and away.
Busy, busy families,
Busy, busy families,
Work all day, work all day.

(*Make It Multicultural—Musical Activities for Early Childhood Education*, Paul Fralick. Hamilton, Ontario, Canada: Mohawk College, 1989; p. 50. Used with permission.)

COMMUNITY WORKERS

Tune: *Did You Ever See a Lassie?*

Do you know the friendly workers
The workers, the workers?
Do you know the friendly workers
Who work in our town?

There's doctors and dentists
And bakers and firefighters.
Yes, I know the friendly workers
Who work in our town.

Do you know the friendly workers
The workers, the workers?
Do you know the friendly workers
Who work in our town?
There's grocers and mail carriers
And bankers and police officers.
Yes, I know the friendly workers
Who work in our town.

Do you know the friendly workers
The workers, the workers?
Do you know the friendly workers
Who work in our town?

There's carpenters and plumbers
And nurses and pilots.
Yes, I know the friendly workers
Who work in our town.

*(You can modify this song by inserting the titles of workers who are
familiar to your children.)*

(*Sing a Song All Year Long*, Connie Walters and Dianne Totten. Minneapolis: T. S.
Denison & Company, 1991; p. 195. Used with permission.)

Physical Development

Automobile Factory. Ask the children if they can figure out how to move their
bodies to pretend to be a factory that makes automobiles. Invite the children to be
another kind of factory that is relevant to your community.

I Am a Can Crusher. Make a simple can crusher that young children can use suc-
cessfully. Take two lengths of 2-by-4-inch wood studs and lay one on top of the other.
Attach the two together by screwing a hinge into them. Now you can open and close
the can crusher. Make a simple holder for the cans by taking the lid of a one-quart jar
and placing it upside down on the bottom board. Nail the lid to the board so that the
cans can fit inside the lid. Show children how to crush food and beverage cans. Put
the cans in your recycling bin and set them out for curbside recycling or take them to
your local recycling center.

I Am a Sculptor. Ask children to find partners. One child is the sculptor and the other is the clay. The sculptor gets to "mold" or "sculpt" the other child into a position. Have the children switch places. Then combine pairs and have one sculptor make a body sculpture using three children.

Let's Build a Machine. Invite the children to work together in small groups to build a human machine with their bodies. Encourage the children to think about what kind of machine they want to build, the parts of the machine, the sounds the machine makes when it's working, and how to include everybody in the group. Invite each group to demonstrate their machine for the rest of the class.

Simon Says. Play a different version of this traditional game. Use the format to invite children to role-play being a worker. For instance, "Simon says be a garbage collector. Simon says be a tow truck operator. Simon says be an office worker. Simon says be a school teacher." Invite children to think of a worker they could be.

Upset the Workers. Make a set of cards that have pictures of different community workers on them. You will need one card for each child in the group, and two to four duplicates of each picture you include. Ask children to sit in a circle and give each child a card. When you call out a worker, all the children who have that card jump up and exchange places. To make the game more complex, the teacher can take a seat after calling the first worker, which leaves one of the children without a place to sit. That child becomes the next caller.

What's My Job? Invite children to take turns role-playing an occupation while the rest of the children guess what worker he is trying to be.

Wheelbarrow Race. Invite children to participate in a game that takes cooperation. Ask the children to find partners. One child lies on his stomach and the other child stands between his partner's legs. To make a wheelbarrow, the standing child picks up his partner's feet and pushes while the other child walks on his hands. Set a traffic cone or a chair 12 feet away and challenge the children to move like wheelbarrows to the cone and back.

Worker Walk. Take a walk through the neighborhood and look for all the different types of workers.

Science

Build a Water Fountain. Collect four plastic jars like those used for tempera paint. Punch a hole in the bottom of each jar. Punch two holes directly across from one another near the bottom on the sides of one of the jars. Punch three holes in another jar and four holes in the third jar. Fill the last jar with water. Place it in the sensory table. Place the jar with two holes on top of it, the jar with three holes on top of that, and the jar with the four holes on the very top. Pour water into the top jar and watch what happens.

Earthworms. Raise earthworms so the children can observe how the earthworms make compost. You can purchase a worm composter from a garden center or a garden supply catalog, or you could make one from a plastic storage container with a lid. Choose one the size of a small ice chest or file box (approximately 12 inches by 10 inches by 10 inches). Use a screwdriver or a drill to poke drainage holes in the bottom of the box. Place the box on blocks that raise it off the ground and provide circulation. Set the box on a large cafeteria tray or jelly roll pan. Fill the container half full with some damp organic material—you can use grass clippings, shredded leaves, straw, or shredded newspaper. Moisten the material so that it is like a damp and wrung-out sponge. Purchase 180 red worms at a bait shop or garden supply store. The worms need to be kept at a moderate and consistent temperature (40 to 50 degrees). Feed the worms kitchen scraps like egg shells, old bread, vegetable peels, apple cores, and coffee grounds. They'll eat the same type of scraps usually thrown into a compost bin. You can also toss in leaves. The worms will eat about a pint of scraps a week. The children can pour in the scraps and turn them into the bedding material. Check the temperature and moisture level regularly and watch for compost to come out the holes in the bottom.

Elevator Please. Make a very simple pulley with a nail and a wooden spool. Hammer a large nail into the railing on the upper level of the loft, if you have one in your room or play yard, so that it is perpendicular to the floor. Put the wooden spool over the nail. It should spin freely around the nail. Cut a piece of yarn or heavy string twice the length between the floor and the nail. Attach a basket to one end of the string. Put various objects in the basket and raise it up to the top of the loft by pulling on the other end of the string. Let out the string to bring the basket back down.

Heavier, Harder, Faster. Give children a chance to experiment with weight and force by setting out three to four different sizes of real hammers, nails, and scrap wood (preferably pine). Ask the children questions like these:

> Which hammer is the lightest?
>
> Which hammer is the heaviest?
>
> Which hammer is the easiest for you to use?
>
> Which hammer is the hardest for you to use?
>
> Which one hammers nails into the wood the fastest?

Plumbing. Help children explore gravity and the flow of water. Set out a variety of plastic PVC pipes and joints. Include elbow, T joints, and caps. Invite the children to put the pipes together. If you are working outside, you can use Velcro strips to connect the pipes to a chain link fence. Place a funnel in an opening. Pour water into the pipes. Listen and watch the water flow, and see where it comes out.

Rivers and Reservoirs. Hook up a garden hose to an outside spigot and run the hose to the sandbox. Set out scoops, shovels, pails, and plastic drop cloths. Invite the children to dig out rivers and reservoirs. Help them figure out how to cut the plastic drop cloth so that it will cover the hole for the reservoir and riverbeds. Use sand to hold the plastic in place. Put the end of the hose in the riverbed and observe the flow of the water. Children may want to add boards for bridges, construction vehicles, plastic boats, and boxes for buildings.

Take Aparts. Set out a variety of work-related objects that children can take apart, explore, and put back together. Encourage the children to see if they can figure out how the objects work. For example, you might set out a flashlight, a telephone, lamp, vacuum cleaner, transistor radio, clock, or record player.

What's Serrated? Set out nonserrated knives (butter or dinner knives), serrated knives (steak or bread knives), and slices of bread. Invite the children to try to cut the bread using each of the knives. Which one works better? Show the children other serrated cutting surfaces, like the edges of aluminum foil and plastic wrap boxes.

Worker Ants. Give the children an opportunity to learn about ants. Take a quart jar and fill it near to the top with earth. Put a small lid filled with water on top of the soil. Sprinkle crumbs and a little sugar on top of the soil. Cover the outside of the glass jar with black construction paper. Carefully dig up ants from an anthill and put them into the jar. Cover the top of the jar with a piece of netting and secure it with a rubber band.

Wrecking Ball. Children may be familiar with wrecking balls used to demolish buildings. Wrecking balls are a type of pendulum. Give the children an opportunity to experiment with a pendulum. Use a piece of string to hang a tennis ball from the ceiling. Suspend the ball so that it hangs at thigh level for most of the children in your class. Build a tower with blocks. Encourage the children to knock down the tower by grabbing the tennis ball, taking a few steps back, and then releasing the ball to make the pendulum swing.

Social Development

Classroom Work. Review the helping jobs in your classroom. Talk about the importance of helping and doing our share to make the classroom operate smoothly.

Housework. Help children learn about housework. Brainstorm all the types of work at home. The list could include cooking, cleaning, shopping, caring for people, caring for pets, fixing things, and yard work. Ask the children questions like

> What would happen if these jobs weren't done?
>
> What would happen if no one in a family did housework?
>
> What are your jobs in your family?
>
> How do you help your family with housework?

You might follow up by having the children make a coupon book for their parents. Each coupon is good for help with a job around the house.

I Have Permission. Show children your driver's license, day care license, teaching certificate, and so on. Talk about how some workers need to get permission to do their jobs. Talk about how a license means that the worker has learned how to do his job. Ask the children, when do you need to ask an adult for permission? Talk about the importance of asking adults for permission. Make pretend licenses for jobs about the classroom. Children could earn a license to feed the fish, handle the guinea pig, serve snacks, or drive a tricycle.

Interview Workers. We can also ask people questions to learn more. Tell the children that they can learn about work by talking with workers. Tell the children that asking workers questions about their work is called an interview. As a class, brainstorm questions that the children could ask workers. Write the questions on a piece of paper for the whole class to see. Help the children practice asking their questions by role-playing interviews. Grab the tape recorder, a blank tape, and your group's questions and interview some workers!

Take Turns. Here's a fun activity to reinforce the importance of taking turns in order to get a job done. Collect enough clothespins for each child in your class. Tie a 12-inch piece of yarn to each clothespin. Place the clothespins inside a plastic container with a narrow neck, like a laundry detergent bottle or a gallon juice bottle. Make sure that the yarn hangs outside the bottle. Invite each child to take a piece of yarn and try to pull out the clothespin. When everyone does this at once the clothespins get stuck in the opening of the bottle. If you pass the bottle around and each child takes a turn, they will be able to pull the clothespins out of the bottle.

What Workers Need. Introduce children to the concept that workers need things to do their jobs. Help children recognize that workers need knowledge, skills, tools and equipment, transportation (so that they can get to work and get back home again), a safe place to work, a salary, sick pay (so they can stay home when they are sick), and vacations (so that they can relax and spend time with their family and friends). Set up the dramatic play area like an office, construction site, or restaurant. Emphasize all the things the children do when they take on worker roles. Facilitate a discussion immediately following the dramatic play session. Ask questions like these:

What did you need to know to do your job?

What tools and equipment did you need?

How did you get to work?

How did you get home again?

What would happen if you worked all day and didn't get paid? How would you pay your bills, buy food, or buy gas for your car?

What if you got sick and couldn't go to work, and then you didn't get paid?

Who Doesn't Work? Invite the children to explore reasons why some people don't work. Ask them questions like, "Do you know any adults who don't work? What are some reasons people don't work?" Children may have limited experience with this subject and you may need to provide them with simple and accurate information. For instance, children can understand that some people don't work because they have retired, they go to school, or they have an illness or an injury that prevents them from working. Children can also understand that some people don't work because they want or need to stay home and take care of their children, and some people don't work because they don't want to, they can't find work, or they got laid off or fired.

Work Crews. Invite children to explore how people can work on a task together. Ask the children, "How can we share work? How do you share the work at home? How do we share the work in our classroom? How do workers share the work on their jobs?" Introduce the concept of a work crew and divide the class into work crews. Give each work crew a different assignment in the classroom.

Work Together. Ask the children to find partners. Give each pair a set of rhythm sticks. Ask the children to stand across from one another, each holding on to the ends of the rhythm sticks. Set some balloons on the floor and ask the children to work together to pick up the balloon with their sticks and carry them to a basket. If children can easily pick up and carry the balloons, use foam balls or tennis balls.

Work at School. Introduce children to the different types of work involved in running a child care center or elementary school. Take a walk through the building to find the answers to these questions: Who works here? What do workers at our school do? How can we help the people who work at our school?

ACTIVITIES: AFFIRMING OURSELVES AND ONE ANOTHER

Human Rights

People have a right to work and to choose the work they want to do.

BARRIER: Many people can't find work, and many people don't have a choice about the kind of work they do.

People have a right to good working conditions.

BARRIER: In some places, people have to work at dangerous jobs without enough protection to keep them safe. Some people have to work for too many hours every day, or have to do too much work in too short a time. Some people have to work at jobs where they are not treated well by other workers.

People have a right to equal pay for equal work.

BARRIER: Some kinds of jobs pay less than others, even though they are equally hard work. Sometimes women or people of color earn less for doing the same work that men or white people do, because of sexism and racism.

People have a right to earn enough money to support their families and to have the things they need to live and be healthy.

BARRIER: Many people work very hard at jobs that don't pay enough for them to buy the things that they need.

Children have a right not to have to work while they are growing up.

BARRIER: In many places around the world, children have to work to help their families survive, or to get enough food to eat or a place to sleep.

DISCUSSION QUESTIONS: Help children think about work. Ask them questions like, "How do you think people decide what work to do? What kind of work do you think women can do? What kind of work do you think men can do? Are the two different? Why? What do you think 'good working conditions' means? What do workers need from the place where they are working? Why do you think they don't always get those things? Why do you think people don't always get the same pay for the same job? Why do you think some jobs pay less than others? Why do you think some jobs don't pay enough for people to support themselves? What could we do to make work more fair?"

Cultural Identity

A Better World. Introduce children to famous workers and inventors and their inventions from the cultures represented in your classroom and community.

Parents Are Workers. Explore the different types of work that the children's parents are involved in. Invite all of the parents to share their work, whether they are homemakers, or students, or any other kind of worker. Ask them to visit your class and talk to the children about their work.

Work

BIAS AND STEREOTYPES

People Work to Keep Our Culture Alive. Introduce children to people in the community who work to keep their cultures strong. You might include someone who works at a culturally specific community agency, a cultural center, a cultural museum, or a culturally specific school.

Diversity

Work and Play. Give the children an opportunity to explore the similarities and difference between work and play. Make a simple file folder game. Designate one side of the folder "Work" and the other side "Play." Also paste or draw a picture on each side of the folder to designate work and play. Glue a number of small pictures of people engaged in a variety of work and play activities to index cards. Set out the cards and file folder and invite the children to sort the pictures.

Work Is Similar and Different. Help children explore the similarities and differences among various types of work. Show the children pictures of four different workers that they are already familiar with. Ask the children, "Who is this? What kind of work do they do?" Set the pictures out side by side. Ask the children, "How are these jobs similar to one another? How are these jobs different from one another?" Repeat the process with another set of four pictures.

Bias and Stereotypes

Everyone Can Work. Children may have racial or disability-related stereotypes about workers. They may falsely believe that people with disabilities can't be teachers or a person of color can't be a doctor. They may also overgeneralize due to their limited experience. For instance, they might falsely believe that all Chinese Americans work in restaurants or all African American males are athletes. Provide children with exposure to people and books that expand their view of workers.

Job Titles That Include All of Us. Young children may have gender stereotypes related to work. They may think that some jobs are only for women and some jobs are only for men. Help children understand that jobs are not restricted by gender and everyone can choose the type of work they want to do. Model inclusive language to the children and talk about what inclusive language means and why it's important. We can use titles for workers that include both girls and boys. For instance, use the job title "mail carrier" rather than "postman," "police officer" rather than "policeman," and "firefighter" rather than "fireman." Make a chart that shows limiting job titles and inclusive job titles.

Nontraditional Jobs. Use pictures, books, and classroom visitors to show children examples of men and women in nontraditional work roles. This will also promote the children's belief that they can be anything they want to be.

Community Service

Computer Users. Share the classroom computer with parents who are out of work. Invite them to use the computer one morning or afternoon a week to prepare their resumes and cover letters.

Coupon Books. Have children make coupon books to give to their parent. Each coupon is good for help with a job around the house.

Social Action Suggestions

Family Leave. Work together for parental leave, family medical leave, or child care subsidy for working parents.

Worthy Wages. Work together with teachers and parents to advocate for worthy wages for child care workers.

ACTIVITIES: OPENING THE DOOR

Classroom Visitors

Invite local workers that help the children on a daily basis to visit the classroom. For instance, invite the sanitation workers who collect the center's garbage, the truck driver who delivers the center's food, the mail carrier who delivers the mail, or the salesperson who takes the center's order for classroom supplies.

Field Trips

Take a trip somewhere in your community where there are many workers doing a variety of jobs and all doing their part to make something work. Possible locations include a local factory, processing plant, or airport.

Parent Involvement

Invite parents and grandparents to visit the classroom and talk about their jobs with the children.

Encourage parents to participate in a take-your-child-to-work day.

Parent Education

Invite a parent educator to talk with parents about teaching children responsibility, instilling a work ethic and good work habits in children, and skills children will need for the workforce of the future.

CLASSROOM RESOURCES

Children's Books

A. J.'s Mom Gets A New Job, Lawrence Balter (Hauppauge, NY: Barron's, 1990).

Abuela's Weave, Omar S. Castañeda (New York: Lee, 1995).

All About Things People Do, Melanie and Chris Rice (New York: Doubleday, 1990).

All The Places To Love, Patricia MacLachlan (New York: Harper, 1994).

Amelia's Road, Linda Jacobs Altman (New York: Lee, 1995).

Apple Valley Year, Ann Turner (New York: Macmillan, 1993).

By The Dawn's Early Light, Karen Ackerman (New York: Atheneum, 1994).

Calling The Doves, Juan Felipe Herrera (Danbury, CT: Children's Press, 1995).

The Daddies Boat, Lucia Monfried (New York: Puffin, 1990).

Daddies At Work, Eve Merriam (New York: Simon, 1989).

A Day's Work, Eve Bunting (New York: Clarion, 1994).

Emergency! Gail Gibbons (New York: Holiday, 1995).

Finding A Job For Daddy, Evelyn Hughes Maslàc (Morton Grove, IL: Whitman, 1996).

Firehouse Dog, Amy and Richard Huthings (New York: Scholastic, 1993).

Fly Away Home, Eve Bunting (New York: Clarion, 1991).

The Goat In The Rug, C. Blood and M. Link (New York: Macmillan, 1980).

Good Morning, Monday, Dsheila Keenan.

The Heart Of The Wood, Marni McGee (New York: Atheneum, 1991).

I'm Going To Be A Farmer, Edith Kunhardt (New York: Scholastic, 1996).

I'm Going To Be A Firefighter, Edith Kunhardt Davis (New York: Scholastic, 1995).

I'm Going To Be A Police Officer, Edith Kunhardt Davis (New York: Scholastic, 1995).

I'm Going To Be A Vet, Edith Kunhardt (New York: Scholastic, 1996).

AfroBets Kids I'm Gonna Be! Wade Hudson (East Orange, NJ: Just Us, 1992).

Jamal's Busy Day, Wade Hudson (East Orange, NJ: Just Us, 1991).

Josefina, Jeanette Winter (San Diego: Harcourt, 1991).

Little Ninos Pizzeria, Karen Barbour (San Diego: Harcourt, 1991).

Mel's Diner, Marissa Moss (Mahwah, NJ: BridgeWater, 1996).

Mom Goes To Work, Libby Gleeson (New York: Scholastic, 1995).

Mommies At Work, Eve Merriam (New York: Simon, 1989).

My Apron, Eric Carle (New York: Putnam, 1994).

My Dad Takes Care Of Me, Patricia Quinlan (Buffalo, NY: Firefly, 1987).

The Night Ones, Patricia Grossman (San Diego: Harcourt, 1997).

No-Job Dad, James Hiram Malone (Monterey, CA: Victory, 1997).

A Painter, Douglas Florian (New York: Greenwillow, 1993).

Painter Man, Dianne Johnson-Feelings (Atlanta: Humanics, 1993).

The Piñata Maker, George Ancona (San Diego: Harcourt, 1994).

Red Light, Green Light, Mama and Me, Cari Best (New York: Orchard, 1995).

Road Builders, B. G. Hennessy (New York: Viking, 1994).

Saturday At The New You, Barbara E. Barber (New York: Lee, 1994).

Shoe Shine Shirley, Leah Komaiko (New York: Doubleday, 1993).

The Terrible Thing That Happened At Our House, Marge Blaine (New York: Scholastic, 1991).

Through My Window, Tony Bradman (Parsippany: Silver Burdett, 1986).

Tools, Ann Morris (New York: Lothrop, 1992).

Uncle Jed's Barbershop, Margaree K. Mitchell (Boston: Houghton, 1995).

We Keep A Store, Anne Shelby (New York: Orchard, 1990).

What Are Scientists? What Do They Do? Let's Find Out, Rita Golden Gelman (New York: Scholastic, 1991).

What I Want To Be, P. Mignon Hinds (New York: Western, 1996).

When I Grow Up, P. K. Hallinan (Nashville: Hambleton, 1995).

Who Uses This? Margaret Miller (New York: Greenwillow, 1990).

Working Cotton, Sherley Anne Williams (San Diego: Harcourt, 1992).

Music

Hartmann, Jack. *Make a Friend, Be a Friend* (Educational Activities, 1990).

"What Would It Be Like"

Lefranc, Barbara. *I Can Be Anything I Want To Be* (Doubar, 1990).

"I Can Be Anything I Want To Be"

Rogers, Sally. *Peace By Peace* (Western, 1988).

"I Can Be Anything I Want To Be"

Ronno. *People In Our Neighborhood* (Educational Record Center, 1996).

Visual Displays

Constructive Playthings
Home and Community Helpers Picture Packet

Organization for Equal Education of the Sexes
Women at Work Posters

Videos

Moving Machines (Bo Peep Productions, 1989).

Road Construction Ahead, Focus Video (Educational Record Center, 1991).

Teaching Kits

Community Awareness Resource Chest, Lakeshore

PART 2

Designing Your Own Transformative Curriculum

Curriculum: A Process and A Product

Good curriculum doesn't just happen; it's carefully planned. Early childhood curriculum is both a process and a product. Developing curriculum involves following specific steps or using a process. The curriculum plans you produce and implement (the product) are always changing (or "in process") because you incorporate what happens in the classroom on a daily basis and the interests and questions of the children. As early childhood teachers often say, "The process is as important as the product." In other words, *how* you plan curriculum is as important as the curriculum plans you come up with, because the plans themselves are fluid and always changing. If you follow the process step-by-step, you'll likely end up with a developmentally appropriate curriculum that fosters your goals and objectives and is consistent with your philosophy.

You'll need a lot of thought and creativity to plan curriculum—that's why many refer to curriculum planning as both a science and an art. The science is following the steps, making sure that there is a logical progression to the curriculum. For learning to take place, you'll need to recognize children's skills and interests and design the curriculum so it flows from simple to complex and familiar to unfamiliar. You'll need to make sure that you include learning experiences that foster the development of the whole child.

Curriculum planning is also an art. It is an opportunity for you as a teacher to express yourself. You use your creativity to revise and adapt activities, figure out new ways of using existing materials, and write new verses to familiar songs. Through the process of planning curriculum you individualize it, put your own unique perspective on it, and make it your own.

You'll get good results—and good curriculum—if you follow a specific planning process. I use a nine-step process that is the result of trial and error. It's a process I've been using for the past five years and teaching to others for the past year, with great results. In this section, you'll find a description of each step using a curriculum unit on the theme of "food" as an example.

Transformative Curriculum Planning Process

1. Create a collaborative climate
2. Learn about the context
3. Identify the themes
4. Web the unit
5. Outline the web
6. Identify materials to add to the learning environment
7. Select and plan learning experiences
8. Identify curriculum resources
9. Transfer the information to lesson plans

STEP 1 CREATE A COLLABORATIVE CLIMATE

Every early childhood program has its own climate. Climate includes the roles, duties, norms, and decision-making style of an organization. In a climate characterized by mistrust, the program's administration may hand the teachers a "canned curriculum" to implement. A climate of competition might lead to teachers planning their own curriculum and rarely sharing their ideas with one another. A climate of teamwork would be reflected through members of a teaching team meeting together to plan their curriculum.

A transformative curriculum requires a climate that is collaborative, creative, and family-oriented. In a collaborative environment, everyone shares their ideas. Administrators, teachers, assistants and aides, and parents come together to identify key issues affecting the children, families, and community. A creative environment means that people put their energy into generating new ideas and new ways to reach children. A family-oriented environment seeks to reflect the lives of the children and families. Collaboration among staff and parents means that a variety of experiences and perspectives are heard. It means creating a community in which everyone has something to teach and something to learn from everyone else.

To create a climate that fosters collaboration and creativity, identify other teachers and parents who are interested in transforming the curriculum. Agree to work together for a year. Try to meet at least once a month. Identify your goals and set ground rules so that the group can create a safe working environment.

STEP 2 LEARN ABOUT THE CONTEXT

Planning a transformative curriculum requires a working knowledge of child development, prejudice, racism, and culture. You use this knowledge to understand the individual children, families, and communities you serve. A developmentally appropriate curriculum is no longer enough. Curriculum must also be individually and contextually appropriate. In order to design a curriculum that is meaningful to children and takes into account their lives and their communities, you must observe and learn about the children, families, and the local community. Once you learn about the qualities, strengths, and needs of the people you work among, you will be ready to plan and implement a transformative curriculum that is multicultural and anti-bias.

> "...a good curriculum must be individually appropriate to the needs and interests of the children in a program. In addition, it must be culturally salient and locally relevant and meaningful in the context of a specific community."
>
> *Reaching Potentials: Appropriate Curriculum and Assessment for Young Children* by Sue Bredekamp and Teresa Rosegrant

GET TO KNOW THE COMMUNITY

A multicultural curriculum must reflect the social context and the children's development. The social context refers to the geographic region, type of community, history, and current social issues that surround the children and families. Each of these elements is reflected in the children's and families' lives. The same curriculum cannot reflect and be relevant to every classroom. A curriculum that is meaningful to a Head Start classroom on a reservation in South Dakota may be totally irrelevant to the lives of the families and children at a Jewish community center nursery school in Houston, Texas. In other words, I'd expect a curriculum that reflects the community to look unique to that community. A cookie-cutter approach doesn't work—obviously, one multicultural curriculum can't reflect all the possible situations of children and families. An African American prekindergarten in New Orleans, a bilingual African American and Latino program in Seattle, a small rural child care center in a town of 500 in Vermont, and a Baptist child care center in a midwestern suburb will each create a culturally relevant/anti-bias curriculum that reflects the lives, language, values, and dreams of the families and children involved in the program.

Identify the social context by talking to parents and community leaders, reading neighborhood newspapers, and learning about the community's history. Chances are you know a lot more about your community than you might think. As you identify the social context, try to answer these questions:

>Where is our community located?
>
>What type of community is it? How would I describe our community to an outsider?
>
>What is the history of our community?
>
>How is our community changing?
>
>How is our community portrayed in the media?
>
>What are the natural resources in our community?
>
>How do people make a living in our community?
>
>What do people do for recreation in our community?
>
>What community issues are parents and children concerned about?
>
>What are the threats to people's health in our community?
>
>What are the prevailing stereotypes in our community?
>
>What are the conflicts, controversies, or ongoing tensions in our community?

GET TO KNOW THE FAMILIES

The first goal of a multicultural/anti-bias curriculum is the development of a positive, knowledgeable, self-identity within a cultural context (see the introduction). Culture is defined as values, beliefs, and behavior. Culture is also language, customs, and traditions. Much of family life and child-rearing is influenced by culture. Sonia Nieto, in her book *Affirming Diversity: The Sociopolitical Context of Multicultural Education*, shows that children who maintain their home language and culture experience greater academic achievement. She challenges schools to "do everything in their power to use, affirm, and maintain" children's culture and language as a foundation for school policies, curriculum, and teaching practice (p. 236).

Curriculum must therefore be culturally relevant, in order to support children in developing a positive, knowledgeable self-identity. According to Bredekamp and Rosegrant, in their book *Reaching Potentials: Appropriate Curriculum and Assessment for Young Children*:

> Curriculum decisions always occur in cultural contexts; cultural values are one of the many sources of curriculum. In the model of transformational curriculum, culture is not viewed as a separate source of curriculum but rather as the context within which all curriculum decisions are made...for example, the culture of the children and the community affects the selection of conceptual organizers for curriculum because what is meaningful to children and of value to the community is influenced by diverse cultural experiences. Culture certainly influences decisions about which discipline-based knowledge is included and how it is interpreted.... The inclusion or exclusions of specific curriculum content often reflects the cultural values of a region, state, or community. (p. 71)

For example, a unit titled "I'm Me, I'm Special" is often very popular among European American teachers. This unit reflects the cultural values of individuality, pride in oneself, individual uniqueness, and the belief that individual attention and recognition foster self-esteem. These values are very different from the values of other cultural groups in the United States that include group identity, group pride, and the belief that calling attention to oneself is inappropriate and arrogant.

Young children reflect their culture. They behave in culturally appropriate ways, but they do not have the self-awareness and communication skills to teach you about their culture. You have to look to families to give you the information that can help you understand their children as cultural beings. Then, in partnership with parents, you can create a curriculum that fosters children's identities and strengthens their connections to their families and home cultures. You might want to create a family and cultural information form that parents fill out during the enrollment process. Or you might use the first parent conference, home visit, or parent meeting to gather cultural information from the families in your program. As you learn more about the children's cultural context, you might want to ask the following questions:

What is most important for your family?

What are the obstacles and challenges facing your family?

What values do you want your child to learn?

How do you maintain closeness within your family?

What are your expectations of your child?

What are ways you support and encourage your child?

How do you show pride in your child's accomplishments?

What do you want from our program for your child?

What changes do you want to make in your child's life?

What are the ethnic origins of your family?

What language(s) are spoken in your home?

If you speak a language other than English, how do you plan to maintain your home language?

What are some activities your family does together?

What are important rites and rituals in your family?

What other cultural traditions does your family practice?

GET TO KNOW THE CHILDREN

Just as a transformative curriculum must reflect the social and cultural context, it must also be appropriate to the developmental level of the children. Therefore, a curriculum for three to five year olds will differ from a curriculum for seven to eight year olds. You can learn about children's development of cultural identity, their developing awareness of diversity, the development of bias and prejudice by

Watching children play

Listening to their conversations

Asking them open-ended questions

Conducting diagnostic activities

When you watch children play, listen to their conversations, and ask them honest questions, you find that indeed they are aware of human diversity. Children have questions about skin color or hair texture; they may want to know why somebody did something. Children are trying to understand who they are and where they fit in. They are constructing their own beliefs about why people are different and the meaning of human diversity.

You can learn a lot about children by simply watching them play, listening to their conversations, and asking them open-ended questions. Observation helps you understand how children process information and construct their knowledge.

A few years ago, teachers involved in the Culturally Relevant/Anti-Bias Leadership Project listed the comments and questions they had heard that indicate young children are struggling with race (skin color and physical features), ethnicity, culture, class, physical ability, age, and sexual orientation (see table on next page).

Clearly, children are trying to understand the social and political context in their own way, constructing their own social beliefs about human diversity. Many young children have already acquired stereotypic information, formed negative attitudes and feelings, and adopted self-protective or hostile behavior in the face of diversity.

Gender	Ethnicity	Class	Physical Ability	Age	Sexual Orientation
Am I a girl?	What's my color? (skin)	Is my dress pretty?	What's that? (pointing to a person in a wheelchair)	How old am I?	Are we gay?
Am I a boy?	What color are my eyes?	Is my shirt new?	Am I a handicapped?	How old are you?	What is he?
How do I know if I'm a girl?	Look at that muddy guy.	Can I be your friend? (said to a child with a new toy)	Are my eyes going to get broken?	I'm three. (said as child introduces self)	What is she?
How do I know if I'm a boy?	When I get big, I'm going to have skin like yours.	She can't be my friend. She's got ugly clothes.	Deaf people can't work.	You're a baby.	She likes girls.
When I grow up I'm going to be a daddy.	You talk funny.	He can't be my friend He's got dirty clothes.	Blind people can't have babies.	When I grow up, I'm gonna do that.	He likes mommy.
You cut your hair. Now you got boy hair.	Where do you come from?		She's weird.	That's a baby toy.	Do you have two moms?
He's not a boy. He's got an earring.	You eat that?		He's not right.	No little kids allowed.	Do you have two dads?
That's a girl toy. That's a boy toy.	I'm glad I don't have to eat that yucky stuff.		I'm not sitting next to him. He can't talk.		You can't have two moms.
You can't do that, you're a girl.	You're not an Indian. Where's your horse?		I'll help her. She can't do it.		You can't have two dads.
You can't do that, you're a boy.	You can't play. You got brown skin.		We hate handicaps.		Well then, I have three moms.
Go away. No girls allowed.	White girls go first.				Well then, I have three dads.
Get out of here. No boys allowed.	You Chink! Get out of my way.				Girls don't marry girls.
We don't like boys.					Boys don't marry boys.
We don't like girls.					I'm going to marry Cindy and there's nothing you can do about it.
					Boys can get married if they love each other.
					You fag.
					You queer.

For more information about this project, contact The Culturally Relevant/Anti-Bias Leadership Project, Pacific Oaks College, 65 South Grand Avenue, Pasadena, CA 91105; (818) 397-1306; fax (818) 397-1304.

STEP 3   **IDENTIFY THE THEMES**

By identifying the context, you create a situation in which the families and children become the subjects of the curriculum. The educational process has begun with parents naming the reality of their lives. The next step is to identify the important or key issues in the children's lives. Ask yourself these questions:

> What are the children interested in?
>
> What are they curious about?
>
> What are they passionate about?
>
> What do the parents want their children to know about?
>
> What do you want children to know about?
>
> What topics do children need to be introduced to so they can be competent?
>
> What topics lend themselves to creating strong ties between families and school?
>
> What topics would strengthen children's connection to their home culture?

In this step, you take everyone's concerns and experiences and group them into themes. Combine or group together similar items. Use careful consideration to translate the social context and the children's developmental levels into curriculum themes.

> Keep in mind that an appropriate theme
>
> Starts where the children are
>
> Is based on children's questions and real-life experiences
>
> Draws on the knowledge of the children, parents, community members, and teachers
>
> Places learning within the social-cultural context of the children
>
> Is broad enough to provide in-depth learning and exploration
>
> Models organizing learning through classifying and categorizing
>
> Encourages children to identify what they know, what they don't know, and what they want to know
>
> Integrates the content/subject areas across the curriculum

A NOTE ABOUT UNIT THEMES

There are many ways to plan curriculum. Some programs plan curriculum around the environment, some around key experiences, and others around unit themes. *Thematic curriculum planning* is probably the most widely used method and is perhaps the easiest. As a new teacher who felt overwhelmed by curriculum planning, I found unit themes to be particularly helpful. They helped me focus and provided structure. Themes also helped me identify, select, and organize learning experiences.

Thematic curriculum planning has come under a lot of criticism lately—mainly because so many teachers misuse themes. Here are some examples of the inappropriate use of unit themes.

Developmentally Inappropriate. A good unit theme is concrete. Some teachers, however, make the mistake of selecting themes that are too abstract or don't lend themselves to hands-on learning experiences. Themes such as "dreams," "journeys," and "peace" are too vague.

Irrelevant. A good unit theme is relevant to the children's daily lives. Unit themes such as "circus" and "Olympics" are examples of themes that are not part of children's daily experience. Many children have never experienced these events.

Superficial. Many programs make the mistake of planning curriculum around daily or weekly unit themes. Over the course of the year, the children are exposed to a wide variety of topics, but the curriculum lacks depth and intellectual integrity. There is a saying: "You can cover a mile and go an inch deep or you can cover an inch and go a mile deep." Superficial curriculum planning deprives children of in-depth learning and meaningful experiences.

Teacher-Centered. Another mistake that teachers make in using unit themes is to plan a year's worth of curriculum without ever meeting the children or families who will make up the class.

Tourist Themes. Avoid themes such as "Children Around the World" or "Let's Visit Hawaii." They encourage activities that focus on countries, artifacts, traditional clothing, and ceremonies. They teach children to be tourists (outsiders visiting an unknown culture that is totally irrelevant to their daily life). This method of curriculum planning teaches children trivia, ignores that people of other cultures really exist today and live normal everyday lives, and does nothing to build a foundation for living in a diverse multicultural world. Children learn about the culture for a week, two weeks, or a month and then they move on to unit themes like "circus" or "dinosaurs." And the culture they just studied may not be talked about for the rest of the year.

Eurocentric. Traditionally, thematic units have been used to teach a Eurocentric perspective of the world and perpetuate the status quo. For example, a week-long unit on family often included concepts such as

> A family is a mother, father, and children.
> Families live in homes.
> Some family members go to work and some family members stay home.
> Families buy food at the grocery store.
> Families buy clothes.
> Families drive cars.
> Families do fun things together.

Ask yourself the following questions: To what extent does this unit reflect the lives of the children in my classroom? Who is included in this unit? Whose life is left out of this unit? Will it help my students develop positive feelings about their family?

Given the diversity in most classrooms today, this type of unit excludes a lot of children. For example, in a family unit, questions to ask include the following: What other people might be included in a family (and what are the cultural connections to that structure)? Where else might families live? Where else might families buy food? How else might families get around?

As you select themes, ask yourself: How will I be able to incorporate human diversity into this theme? Topics that relate to people and social conditions lend themselves to incorporating multicultural education across the curriculum.

WEB THE UNIT

Once you've chosen a theme, brainstorm possible concepts for study within the unit theme. The brainstorming process known as *cognitive webbing* or *mind mapping* is particularly effective in fleshing out a unit theme.

I'm so excited about this process. Over and over, I've experienced great results by webbing out curriculum units. When a teaching team gets together to web a unit, a synergy is created. Within minutes, the collective creative juices flow and great content emerges. The team laughs, smiles, has fun. And when the team is done, the members stand back and look at the web and pat themselves on the back for a job well done.

Following are the eight basic steps to webbing a unit theme.

1. Set out a large chalkboard or tape a large piece of butcher paper to the wall. Choose one person to be the recorder. Write the name of the theme in the middle of the chalkboard or paper and draw a circle around it (see figure 1).

figure 1

2. Take the children's perspective. In other words, put yourself in their shoes. Given this theme, what questions would the children ask? Fill in the web by writing down these questions. Creating a unit of questions makes the curriculum inquiry-based and shifts the expertise from the teacher to the children, families, community, and then the teacher.

Webbing questions based on children's interests and real lives naturally brings the diversity of the class into the curriculum. This helps you meet the first goal of a multicultural curriculum—to help children construct a positive self-identity. Write out the questions you think the children would ask about this topic (see figure 2).

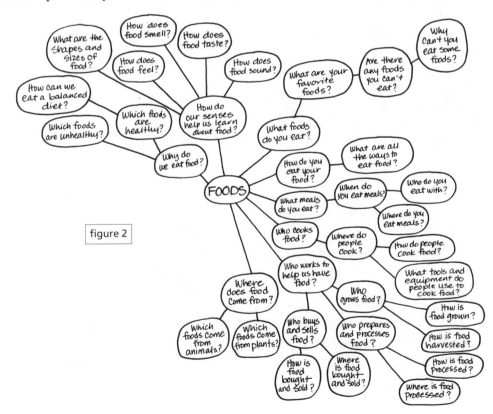

figure 2

THE EVERYDAY INCLUSIVE CURRICULUM

3.   In order to achieve the second goal of a multicultural/anti-bias curriculum—fostering comfortable and empathetic interaction with diversity among people—you need to make a conscious effort to incorporate the range of human diversity. Look through the web and identify where you can add human diversity. Add a question that helps you think about all the different types of possibilities.

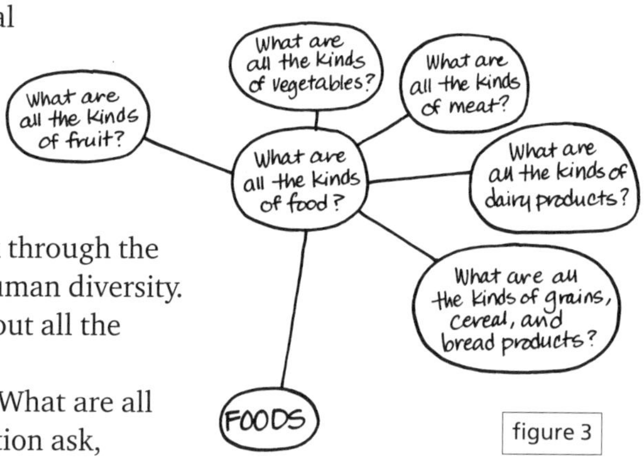

For example, for a food unit ask, "What are all the kinds of food?" And from that question ask, "What are all the kinds of fruits?" "What are all the kinds of vegetables?" "What are all the kinds of meats?" "What are all of the kinds of dairy products?" and "What are all the kinds of grains, cereal, and bread products?" (see figure 3).

What are all the kinds of fruit?

What are all the kinds of vegetables?

What are all the kinds of meat?

What are all the kinds of food?

What are all the kinds of dairy products?

What are all the kinds of grains, cereal, and bread products?

FOODS

figure 3

4.   You also achieve the second goal of a multicultural/anti-bias curriculum by adding two other sets of key questions to the web. The first set is "How is it similar?" and "How is it different?" Exploring similarities and differences in each unit helps children become comfortable with differences as a natural part of life. This questions addresses the cognitive tasks of attending to detail, describing characteristic, sorting, and classifying.

For example, in the unit on foods ask, "How are foods similar to one another?" and "How are they different from one another?" You could explore different varieties of the same food, different ways to prepare the same food, and different foods that taste the same.

The second set of questions is, "How does it stay the same?" and "How does it change?" Change is a part of our modern world. Children need to be able to embrace change. This question gets at the issues of transformation and conservation, which are important cognitive concepts for young children.

For the food unit ask, "How does food stay the same?" and "How does food change?" (see figure 4). You could examine growing food, the ripening and molding process, observe the change in physical states that occurs through cooking food, and changes in food by adding spices and flavorings.

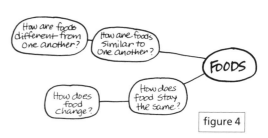

How are foods different from one another?

How are foods similar to one another?

FOODS

How does food change?

How does food stay the same?

figure 4

5.   The third goal of a multicultural/anti-bias curriculum is to help children recognize bias. You can add two other sets of questions to the web to address this goal.

The first set is, "What is real?" and "What is pretend?" Children between the ages of four and nine struggle to differentiate reality from fantasy. Inability to tell the difference between real and pretend leaves children vulnerable to believing stereotypes about people. This is a first step toward recognizing biases. For the food unit, you could ask "What are real foods?" and "What are pretend foods?" You could explore the difference between real and artificial flavors in a food unit and compare real and artificial fruit.

The second set of questions to ask is, "What are the stereotypes?" and "How can we challenge the stereotypes?" With the food unit, think about the stereotypes around food. Ask, "What are stereotypes about food?" and "How can we work together to challenge the stereotypes about food?" (see figure 5). Children may have stereotypic notions about what is girl food and boy food, baby food and adult food, stereotypes about foods that people from other cultures eat, stereotypes about what people with disabilities eat. Draw out the stereotypes through class discussion and activities. Then challenge them through field trips, visitors, books, pictures, and class discussion.

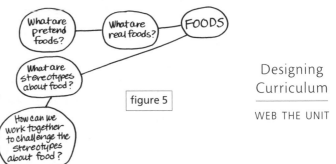

figure 5

6. The last goal of a multicultural/anti-bias curriculum is to help children stand up for themselves and others in the face of bias or discrimination. Sometimes the questions about stereotypes also provide an avenue for fostering this goal. But I also like to include the questions "What are our human rights?" and "How can we work together to achieve our human rights?" A simpler way of posing these questions are "What do people want and need?" and "Who doesn't have what they need?" These questions help children develop their growing sense of fairness and justice. They provide a way for class members to identify action that they can take together to challenge unfair and hurtful situation in their lives.

figure 6

Two basic human rights regarding food are that everyone deserves to have enough to eat and safe water to drink. You could ask, "What are people's food wants and needs?" and "What is hunger?" (see figure 6). From explorations of human rights around food, children may choose to advocate on behalf of classmates who don't have enough food, on behalf of themselves for safe drinking water in their school building, or on behalf of themselves for culturally relevant school lunches.

7. Community service or service learning can also be incorporated into each unit by adding the question "How can we work together to help people?" In the food unit, you might ask, "How can we work together to help people who don't have enough food to eat?" (see figure 7). Children may decide to conduct a canned food drive for a local food bank.

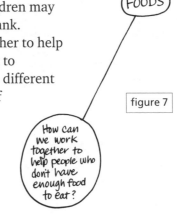

figure 7

Service learning is a way for children to work together to help their local neighborhood and community. It is important to remember that volunteerism and community service are different from activism and advocacy. Children need both types of experiences on a regular basis to develop citizenship skills and learn how to be participating members of a democratic society.

8. When planning a unit, address the question of how to handle holidays. Holidays and celebrations should never drive the curriculum. In other words, a holiday or celebration should not be the unit theme. Rather, holidays and celebrations should occur within the context of the unit. Add the question "How can we celebrate...?" to the web.

If the unit is food, you could add the questions "When does your family eat special foods?" "What special foods does your family eat?" and "How can we celebrate food?" (see figure 8). A celebration is a wonderful way to build a sense of community within the classroom and an appropriate culmination to a unit of study.

A complete web on food could look something like the one in figure 9.

Designing
Curriculum

WEB THE UNIT

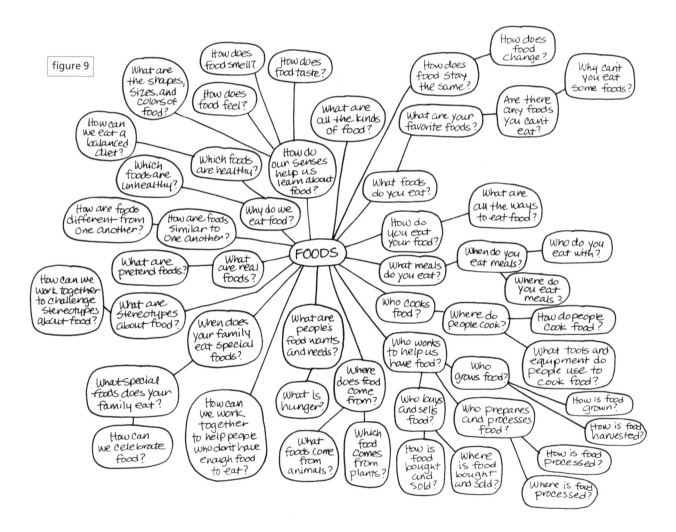

figure 8

figure 9

What Is "Webbing"?

Webbing is a brainstorming method many people use to quickly generate ideas. The term *webbing* refers to the final result, which resembles a spider web.

Webbing is different from traditional brainstorming, which results in a list of ideas. This listing, which has been described as a linear form of thinking, is a style of processing information most often used by European American males. Women and people from other cultures, on the other hand, are more likely to use a circular style of thinking. Webbing depicts this circular style of thinking and shows the connections and relationships between ideas.

Webbing allows you to branch many ideas from one idea. It helps you see all the directions in which you could go—that's why some people call it *mind mapping*. Webbing also provides you with a one-page record of all your ideas, which is very helpful for people who are visual learners or like to see the whole picture at a glance.

STEP 5   OUTLINE THE WEB

Organizing and sequencing the content of the web is the next step in the curriculum planning process. Now it is time to practice your classifying and sequencing skills. Look over the web and ask yourself, "Are there strands of questions that seem related?" Cluster this information into categories or subthemes. You might want to think about the length of time the class will spend studying the unit. For example, you could organize a month-long unit into four weekly subthemes.

Another effective curriculum planning strategy is to sequence the subthemes. To do this, review the web and subthemes. Do you see a logical progression? Try to sequence the content from the child's point of view. What is the most familiar? What is the least familiar? What are the basic concepts? What are the most complex? Organizing and sequencing the web results in a unit outline that ensures curriculum is presented in a logical, orderly fashion.

Organizing and Sequencing a Web

Identify subthemes

Sequence topics from familiar to unfamiliar, simple to complex

Order concepts to foster building skills

Here's an example of the food web organized into weekly subthemes.

WEEK 1: FOODS I KNOW AND EAT

Designing
Curriculum

OUTLINE THE WEB

    I. What foods do you eat?
       A. What are your favorite foods?
       B. Are there any foods that you can't eat?
       C. Why can't you eat some foods?
   II. How do you eat your food? What are all the ways to eat food?
  III. What meals do you eat?
       A. When do you eat meals?
       B. Where do you eat meals?
       C. Who do you eat with?

WEEK 2: PEOPLE HELP US HAVE FOOD TO EAT

   IV. Who cooks food?
       A. Where do people cook?
       B. How do people cook food?
       C. What tools and equipment do people use to cook food?
    V. Who works to help us have food?
       A. Who grows food?
          1. How is food grown?
          2. How is food harvested?
       B. Who prepares and processes food?
          1. How is food processed?
          2. Where is food processed?
       C. Who buys and sells food?
          1. Where is food bought and sold?
          2. How is food bought and sold?
   VI. Where does food come from?
       A. Which food comes from animals?
       B. Which food comes from plants?

WEEK 3: LET'S EXPLORE ALL KINDS OF FOOD

   VII. How do our senses help us learn about food?
       A. How does food taste?
       B. How does food smell?
       C. How does food feel?
       D. How does food sound?
       E. What are the shapes, sizes, and colors of food?
 VIII. Why do we eat food?
       A. Which foods are healthy? Which foods are unhealthy?
       B. How can we eat a balanced diet?

WEEK 4: FOODS ARE ALIKE AND DIFFERENT

IX. What are all the kinds of food?
   A. What are all the kinds of fruit?
      1. What are all the kinds of vegetables?
      2. What are all the kinds of meat?
      3. What are all the kinds of dairy products?
      4. What are all the kinds of grains, cereal, and bread products?
   B. How are foods similar to one another? How are foods different from one another?
   C. What are real foods? What are pretend foods?
   D. How does food stay the same? How does food change?
   E. What are stereotypes about food?
   F. How can we work together to challenge the stereotypes about food?

WEEK 5: EVERYBODY NEEDS FOOD TO EAT

X. What are people's food wants and needs?
   A. What is hunger?
   B. How can we work together to help people who don't have enough food to eat?

WEEK 6: LET'S CELEBRATE FOOD

XI. When does your family eat special foods?
   A. What special foods does your family eat?
   B. How can we celebrate food?

STEP 6   IDENTIFY MATERIALS TO ADD TO THE LEARNING ENVIRONMENT

A well-designed classroom is the foundation of any early childhood curriculum. It is standard practice to arrange the classroom into interest areas. An early childhood classroom often includes an art area, sensory table, block area, book area, manipulative area, science area, dramatic play area, music area, and an open area for circle time.

Free-choice play or work time is the largest component of the daily schedule in an early childhood classroom. During this time, children freely choose which interest areas they wish to play in and which materials they wish to play with. As teachers we strive to set out a variety of open-ended materials that are easily combined to foster increasingly more complex levels of play and exploration.

For this step, review the curriculum web and outline. Identify materials, props, and supplies that you could add to the interest areas to enhance children's play and invite children to engage in theme-related learning through play. Ask yourself questions such as, "What accessories could I add to the block area that would support this theme?" "What art materials could I set out that would support this theme?" and "What props could I add to the dramatic play area to support this theme?"

Be creative. Make materials. Gather materials from garage sales, tag sales, and thrift stores. Each unit includes a list of materials and their sources. You can find the list of commercial educational suppliers in the Resources and References section.

Here is a sample of materials you could add to classroom interest areas to support the food unit.

DRAMATIC PLAY

Set up the dramatic play area as a restaurant, pizza parlor, bakery, or ice cream shop.

Set out a cash register, pretend money, paper sacks, empty food containers, and grocery carts to encourage pretend play around going to the grocery store and purchasing food.

BLOCKS

Set out plastic or wooden farm animals, people figures, play farm implements and vehicles, fencing, and a pretend barn and silo to encourage farm-related play.

SENSORY

Fill the sensory table with field corn for a different dry sensory experience.

Make a fishing game. Set small, plastic fish in the sensory table and make fishing rods; encourage the children to try to hook the fish.

MUSIC

Set out a variety of cassettes with food-related songs.

Set out materials such as plastic containers, cardboard tubes, masking tape, baby bottles, plastic juice bottles, dried beans, and rice for making simple shakers.

SCIENCE

Set out jars with a variety of grains and flours. Talk about the fact that people eat bread that they make from the grains that they grow. People living in different places grow different grains and make different kinds of bread.

Set out collections of dried beans. Fill small jars with different types of dried beans.

STEP 7 SELECT AND PLAN LEARNING EXPERIENCES

Learning experiences are planned, intentional opportunities for children to gain new information, develop their abilities, and acquire new skills. You can offer learning experiences or activities as a child-choice during free play, as a teacher-directed small group experience, or as a teacher-directed large group experience (also known as circle time).

You can easily foster the multicultural goals and objectives through learning experiences. Planned activities are thought out in advance. Materials are gathered, preparations made, and a time and place are set. Planned activities allow you to go beyond routine events. They provide children with first-hand experiences that are beyond what children are likely to come up with on their own, or what might happen just by chance. Planned activities are especially helpful when you are trying to teach something new or a specific concept or skill.

Developmentally appropriate activities have some of the following characteristics:
Based on children's interests
Match the children's abilities and skills
Provide hands-on experiences
Encourage children to interact with one another
Encourage children to interact with adults
Expose children to new experiences, ideas, and materials
Allow children to work at their own pace
Offer children freedom to make choices and do it their own way
Provide enough space, time, and materials for children to actively explore experience
Allow children to work alone, in small groups, or in informal groups
Allow children to be active learners

Learning experiences give you a chance to foster children's skills in all areas of development. The curriculum in part 1 includes twenty-two different types of activities:

Creative Development	Human Rights
Critical Thinking	Cultural Identity
Emotional Development	Diversity
Health, Safety, and Nutrition	Bias and Stereotypes
Language Development	Community Service
Home Language	Social Action Suggestions
Math	Classroom Visitors
Music	Field Trips
Physical Development	Parent Involvement
Science	Parent Education
Social Development	Sensory

My attitude toward planning activities is that there is no use reinventing the wheel. Begin identifying activities by reviewing the curriculum web and outline. Go through your activity card file and favorite curriculum activity books to collect ideas.

Chances are, however, you won't be able to find activity ideas for all of the curriculum areas or ones that foster all of the goals. In that case, look for activity ideas you can adapt, revise, or expand to foster your curriculum goals. As a last resort (only because it is so time consuming) create new, original activities. Here are two examples of food activities.

Family Foods. Explore some of the traditional ethnic foods of the children in your class. Ask the parents to help you select a food that is specific to the cultures in your class and relatively simple to prepare. With the children, cook a dish from each child's culture and serve it for snack.

Breads. Help children experience different types of bread. Plan a bread-tasting party for snack time. Include a variety of breads (cornbread, tortillas, Mexican sweet bread, matzo, rusk, lefse, pita bread, steamed buns, chapatis, scones, black bread, fry bread, piki bread). Talk with the children about how people from different cultures eat different kinds of bread. Introduce the different breads. Ask the children if they have ever eaten any of them before. Give each child a sample of the breads. Talk about the name of the bread and where the bread comes from. Follow up with books about bread, or bake bread for another snack.

LEARNING EXPERIENCES FOR PARENTS

Since parents are an integral part of a transformative curriculum, each unit contains at least three different types of learning experiences for them.

Parent involvement activities are those that bring parents into the classroom. These experiences place parents in the role of expert and teacher. They are an important way to honor children and families' lives and strengthen children's connection to their family and home culture. Parent education experiences provide an opportunity for parents to gain information, share their experience with and learn from other parents, reflect on their children and families, and try new behaviors. Celebrations provide an opportunity for teachers, parents, extended family members, and children to come together as a community to celebrate children's interests and accomplishments.

STEP 8 IDENTIFY CURRICULUM RESOURCES

There may be special materials that you want to add to the classroom or use in planned activities. Resources can be purchased commercially, borrowed from the library, or made by hand. It is helpful to identify any bulletin board or posters; materials for interest areas; children's books, songs, or videos; finger plays and chants; teaching kits; and sources of related information or free materials. All of these materials enhance curriculum and children's learning. Including resources with your curriculum plans can save you time organizing and setting up the curriculum unit.

Here are some examples of resources for the food unit:

MANIPULATIVES

food and farm life puzzles (for example, Didacta Shopping Puzzle, Market Puzzle, *Sandy and Son*; Eating An Apple Puzzle, Food Groups Puzzle, *Nasco*; Farm Giant Floor Puzzle, Fruit Puzzle, Giant Stand-Up Farm Puzzle, Good Habits Puzzles, Vegetables Puzzle, *Constructive Playthings*; Our Teeth Puzzle, *J. L. Hammett*; Farmer Puzzle, *Lakeshore*; The Farm Giant Floor Puzzle, *Beckley-Cardy*; Make-a-Meal Puzzles, *Constructive Playthings*, *Edvantage*)

card, board, lotto, and sorting games about food (for example, Harvest Time Board Game, *Childswork/Childsplay*; Fruit Count Matching Game, *J. L. Hammett*; Nutrition

Lotto, *Lakeshore*; Orchard Game, *Sandy and Son*; The Very Hungry Caterpillar Game, *Constructive Playthings*)

food-related counting and sorting materials (for example, Half Dozen Eggs Shape Sorters, One Dozen Eggs, *Nasco*; Count 'n Sort Produce, Food Blocks, Orange Grove Abacus, Fruits and Vegetables Sorting/Counting Materials, *Constructive Playthings*; Fractional Fruit Plate, *Sandy and Son*)

other food-related manipulatives (for example, Food and Nutrition Theme Box, Food Group Pyramid Mats, What Comes From What? Discovery Kit, *Lakeshore*)

STEP 9   TRANSFER THE INFORMATION TO LESSON PLANS

The final step in planning curriculum is to transfer your plans onto a lesson planning form. Some teachers use daily lesson plans and others use weekly planning forms. Many school districts and programs have their own lesson planning forms. You may have a form that you prefer to use. The trick with lesson plans is to write enough detail so that you can understand what you had in mind and not so much detail that the process becomes overwhelming and time consuming.

The following pages show the food unit written out onto lesson plan forms.

Curriculum Planning Form

Theme __FOOD__   Week __1 - FOODS I KNOW AND EAT__

	Monday	Tuesday	Wednesday	Thursday	Friday
Large Group	Group Discussion What is food? What foods do you eat?	Introduce fruits and vegetables	Introduce breads and cereals	Introduce dairy products	Introduce meats and legumes
Free Choice	Food collage What is it?	Plants from food Prepare snack veggies and dip	Paint with wheat sheaths Grow wheat	Egg shell collage Prepare snack milkshakes	Plant bean seeds Bean bag toss
Small Group	Foods I know and don't know	Food picture cards	Food match	Persona Doll Story	"Try it, you'll like it"
Large Group	Parent volunteer to share a family food	Play "Hot Potato"	Parent volunteer to share a family food	"Egg Roll"	Parent volunteer to share a family food

Art Area
Magazines with food pictures
Egg shells
Wheat sheaths

Dramatic Play Area
Empty food containers, cooking utensils, pots and pans, cookbooks, shopping lists

Manipulatives
Food puzzles

Block Area
Farm set

Sensory Table
Water and cooking utensils

Science
Plants from food
Plant bean seeds
Food reference books

Curriculum Planning Form

Theme **FOOD**

Week **2- PEOPLE HELP US HAVE FOOD TO EAT**

	Monday	Tuesday	Wednesday	Thursday	Friday
Large Group	Group Discussion Who cooks food?	Women and men who cook	Introduce Farms and farmers	Farm Flannel	Introduce restaurant Read stories about restaurant
Free Choice	Make chef hats Play dough and Cookie Cutters	Kitchen gadget prints Cooking tools	Food from seeds Make a barn	Milk the cow Animal and food product match	Restaurant play Spatter paint—Place settings
Small Group	Visit kitchen and interview cook	Prepare snack	Our garden	Our garden	Field trip to local restaurant
Large Group	Read books about cooks	Parent volunteer to share a family food	Sing farm songs	Parent volunteer to share a family food	Eat lunch at restaurant

Art Area
Magazines with people cooking
Cooking catalogs, seed catalogs

Block Area
Farm set

Dramatic Play Area
Restaurant
Foods, dishes, cash register, menus, check pads, pencils

Sensory Table
Soil and miniature farm set

Manipulatives
Food puzzles
Farm Puzzles

Science
Samples of seeds

Curriculum Planning Form

Theme ___FOOD___   Week __3 – LET'S EXPLORE ALL KINDS OF FOODS__

	Monday	Tuesday	Wednesday	Thursday	Friday
Large Group	Introduce grocery store Read books about grocery stores	Persona Doll Story	Read "Bread, Bread"	Introduce food books	Review with food picture cards
Free Choice	Explore different fruits set up grocery store	Explore different vegetables Sweet Potato vines	Explore different breads Make bread	Explore different dairy products Make food books	Explore different meats and legumes Make food books
Small Group	Explore food smells	Explore food textures	Explore the shape and size of food	Explore the colors of food	Foods from Native Americans
Large Group	Names of fruits in other languages Sing fruit songs	Names of vegies in other languages "Upset the Vegetable basket"	Names for bread in other languages Sing bread songs	Names for dairy products in other languages	Names for meat in other languages "Hot Potato" with bean bags

Art Area
Food stencils

Dramatic Play Area
Grocery store, bags, shopping baskets, cash register, food containers, grocery carts, shopping lists, newspaper ads

Manipulatives
Counting eggs
Food Count and match

Block Area
Farm Set

Sensory Table
Plastic eggs and Easter grass

Science
Collection of grains and flours

Curriculum Planning Form

Theme **FOOD**   Week **4 - FOODS ARE ALIKE AND DIFFERENT**

	Monday	Tuesday	Wednesday	Thursday	Friday
Large Group	Discussion How are foods similar? How are foods different?	Name that food	Who eats this?	Persona Doll Story about child who is teased for using chopsticks	Discussion about Field Trip What will we see?
Free Choice	Make food shape pancakes / Food shapes	Big and small, short and tall / How much does it weigh?	Food sort / Food Pyramid	Chopsticks Different ways of eating food	FIELD TRIP to an Ethnic Restaurant or Bakery
Small Group	Explore tongues, taste buds, tastes	Food changes What will happen if we leave out bread or fruit?	Are all changes alike?	Play bagels and chopsticks	
Large Group	Read books about foods	Play "Balance it"	Sing food songs	Read "Cleversticks" and "How My Parents Learned to Eat"	Write a group story about the trip to the restaurant

Art Area
Food Containers, food packing, Building sculptures

Block Area
Farm set

Dramatic Play Area
Farmer's Market - Bushel baskets, Strawberry baskets, plastic fruit, vegetables, signs, aprons

Sensory Table
Fishing Game

Manipulatives
Food Classifying Food board games

Science
Collection of food smelling jars Balance scale

Curriculum Planning Form

Theme **FOOD**   Week **5 - EVERYBODY NEEDS FOOD**

	Monday	Tuesday	Wednesday	Thursday	Friday
Large Group	Healthy and unhealthy foods	Dental health	How can we eat a balanced diet?	Discussion What is hunger?	Discussion How can we work together to help those who are hungry?
Free Choice	Make a collage of healthy food Pizza fractions	Homemade toothpaste Paint with toothbrushes	Food Pyramid Make a class cookbook	Collage of what we are thankful for Make a cookbook	Make a class recipe for fruit salad Make cooperative fruit salad
Small Group	Prepare a healthy snack	Food guessing game	Class graph of what we ate today	No seconds	The Great Divide
Large Group	Persona Doll story about a child who won't eat	Visit from a dietician	Sing food songs	Not everyone gets enough	Read stories about children who share food
Art Area Toothbrushes Food stencils Magazines with food pictures		Dramatic Play Area Cooking - food containers, Pots and Pans, utensils, Cookbooks		Manipulatives Food puzzles, farm puzzles, food matching games, food board games	
Block Area Farm set		Sensory Table Water and cooking utensils		Science Balance Scale Collections Growing plants from previous weeks	

When Curriculum Gets Off Track

Sometimes curriculum planning gets off track—often it is underdeveloped. I know one child care center that distributes weekly lesson plan forms to all of the teachers. During naptime, the teachers write in the name of an activity for each day of the week. For example, during one week, the preschool curriculum consists of playground day, water day, balloon day, video day, and kickball day. Very little thought, effort, or creativity goes into the design of this curriculum. We have to ask ourselves: What is the educational value of this curriculum? What goals and objectives are fostered through the curriculum?

In another program, the teachers met during naptime and planned the curriculum. I visited during farm animal week. The lesson plan forms posted in the hallway told me that the children would learn about a different farm animal each day. But as I observed through the morning, I saw no evidence that the teachers were implementing the curriculum plan. There weren't any farm animals in the block area, and there weren't any books about farms in the book area. And to top it off, one teacher led a circle time on pets. Here was a minimal planning process, and the curriculum plan was not even carried out.

Designing
Curriculum

THE ADDITIONAL
BURDEN OF
EDUCATIONAL
INITIATIVES

The Additional Burden of Educational Initiatives

There's another difficulty faced with curriculum planning that often occurs in public schools and Head Start programs. Many school districts try to update the curriculum and address societal pressures on their students through educational initiatives. Teachers in these programs have been asked or required to incorporate one or more of the following learning initiatives into their daily curriculum:

Whole Language	Democracy Education
Project Approach	Media Literacy
Service Learning	Violence Prevention
Creative Thinking	Gender-Fair Curriculum
Critical Thinking	Multicultural Education
Character Education	Disability Awareness

Often these important educational initiatives are presented as a separate entity to be added to the regular curriculum. Teachers often feel as though these initiatives are nothing more than an additional burden—when I look at the list I feel overwhelmed. Each can feel like just one more thing to add to a plate that is already overflowing. Each of the current initiatives listed above, however, are important and can enhance the curriculum and improve the outcomes of children.

The exciting thing is that they are interrelated and complement one another. Whole language learning and the project approach complement one another. Whole language and multicultural education complement one another. Peace education and multicultural education complement one another. Basically, each of these educational initiatives have much in common, and their purposes are very similar. Unfortunately, when they are presented to teachers as separate things to add to the basic curriculum, teachers are left to struggle with how to integrate them into the daily life of their class.

Evaluate the Curriculum

Evaluation is a much-avoided exercise in education. It is often left to the last minute and given little thought and even fewer resources. Many programs see evaluation as a necessary evil in order to secure grants and financial aid. Ironically, it is often the first thing to be cut by foundations unwilling to fund educational programs fully.

Evaluation needn't be so offensive and unnerving to teachers and administrators. Evaluation is simply an attempt to increase our effectiveness by asking some basic questions: What was the children's experience? What was the parents' experience? What was the teachers' experience? What were the strengths and weaknesses of the curriculum? Did we accomplish what we set out to do? What should we do differently next time? How can we make the curriculum better? When well done, evaluation is incredibly useful. Evaluation helps us gather information so that we can make informed decisions about the curriculum. It helps us learn what works and what doesn't.

We evaluate the curriculum so that we can revise it and improve it. The whole purpose of *Big As Life* is to create communities of learning that help children reach their full potential and make the world a better place. So choose evaluation methods that match the curriculum. I'd suggest an informal, qualitative approach that is very personal. Use evaluation to get a sense of what the children and parents experienced and what it meant to them. You can also use evaluation to see if the curriculum met its goals.

Use evaluation methods already common to early childhood practice. Observe the children and collect anecdotal records. Talk with the parents face to face. Interview them or facilitate a parent focus group. Evaluate the curriculum using the approach popularized by current methods like authentic assessment, student portfolios, Sam Meisel's work sampling system, or the High/Scope Foundation's Child Observation Record. Consider collecting the following types of data:

- direct quotes from parents, community members, teachers, and administrators

- direct quotes from children

- samples of children's writing or your dictation of their spoken words

- children's artwork

- photographs of children involved in activities and interacting with one another and with others (teachers, parents, classroom visitors)

- audiotapes of classroom discussions

- videotapes of classroom visitors, parent involvement, and field trips

- copies of agendas and notes from curriculum planning meetings

- anecdotal records from the classroom

Consider evaluating the curriculum development process as well as the curriculum itself. Evaluate the process by asking: Who made the curriculum decisions? Who participated in preparing the curriculum materials and activities? Who presented the curriculum? Who evaluated the curriculum? Who revised the curriculum? In asking these questions, look for instances in which individuals or groups of people were overrepresented, underrepresented, or excluded entirely.

Evaluate the curriculum by asking questions like, How well did the curriculum meet children where they were? How well did the curriculum reflect and honor children's home culture and language? How well did the curriculum help children get along with others who are different from them? How well did the curriculum help children recognize and think critically about bias? How well did the curriculum help children stand up for themselves and others? How well did the curriculum foster children's physical, cognitive, language, social, and emotional development? How well did the curriculum involve children's parents and families? How well did the curriculum involve the community?

One way to answer these questions is to look at outcomes. In other words, look to see if children behave differently after experiencing the curriculum. Ask questions like, Do children use their home language at school more than they did? Do children talk freely about their home culture and family traditions? Are children more accepting of one another? Do children have a wider variety of friends? Have incidents of prejudice or bias decreased? Do children recognize and challenge stereotypes? Do children stand up for themselves in the face of bias? Collect anecdotal records that support your answers to these questions.

Whatever you do, take time out to reflect on the families, children, and your classroom. Make notes to yourself and review them. Think of ways to revise the activities presented in *Big As Life* so that they work better for you and the children. Design your own activities and teaching materials. Make your curriculum the best it can be. Make it your own.

RESOURCES AND REFERENCES

Educational Supply Companies

Early childhood educational supply companies began making multicultural materials in the mid- to late eighties. Today most suppliers carry very similar materials, but there are a few standouts that are worth mentioning.

Lakeshore Learning Materials carries the most complete selection of multicultural teaching materials and seems to put the most effort into the development of new products. Lakeshore recently came out with children puppets that are exceptional, and they are the only major supplier to have developed their own skin-colored art materials. Their people-colors paints, crayons, and papers are the most realistic and include the greatest number of colors. Lakeshore also has decent anatomically correct multiethnic baby dolls and school dolls. Their block play people figures are by far the best. They are three dimensional, plastic, and include people of all colors, abilities, and ages, all with natural facial expressions. And to top it off, some of the women are wearing pants.

Other companies also offer fine materials and excel in certain areas. Look to Scholastic to produce some of the best photographs in the industry. The bright, clear faces of children are available in posters, children's books, and classroom magazines like *Let's Find Out*, *Parent and Child*, and *Early Childhood Today*. Constructive Playthings offers the widest array of multiethnic pretend food. Sandy and Son has the best multiethnic puzzles. Kaplan has wonderful puzzles of children with disabilities. Environments carries the best animal figures and environmental teaching materials. They also have some very interesting multicultural clothes that are cultural without being stereotypic. If you are interested in using persona dolls, check out People of Every Stripe. Their cloth dolls are perfect for storytelling, and they'll custom make a doll to fit your specific need. They're also the friendliest folks around.

ABC School Supply Inc.
3312 North Berkeley Lake Road
Duluth, GA 30136-9419
(800) 669-4222
Fax: (800) 933-2987
A good resource for multiethnic people cutouts, posters, Spanish/English ABC charts, and posters.

African American Images
1909 West 95th Street, Dept. A-Am
Chicago, IL 60643
(800) 552-1991
A large selection of posters, Kwanzaa materials, and books on African American culture for both children and adults.

American Academic Supplies
P.O. Box 339
Cary, IL 60013-0339
(800) 325-9118
Fax: (800) 437-8028
E-mail: amacad@aol.com

American Guidance Service (AGS)
4201 Woodland Road
P.O. Box 99
Circle Pines, MN 55014-1796
(800) 328-2560
Fax: (612) 786-9077
E-mail: ags@skypoint.com
Web site: www.agsnet.com
A great resource for teaching kits that support social and emotional development.

Animal Town
P.O. Box 757
Greenland, NH 03840
(800) 445-8642
Specializes in games and books on cooperative family activities.

Arab World and Islamic Resources and School Services
2095 Rose Street, Suite 4
Berkeley, CA 94709
(510) 704-0517
A collection of books, posters, and curriculum materials that relate to Arabic cultures.

Asian American Curriculum Project
234 Main Street
San Mateo, CA 94401
(800) 874-2242
Fax: (415) 343-5711
E-mail: aacp@best.com
A nice selection of books on Asian American culture for both adults and children. They also carry Asian American dolls.

Beckley-Cardy Group
1 East First Street
Duluth, MN 55802
(800) 227-1178
Fax: (888) 454-1417
A general school supply company that offers a wide selection of science materials, posters, computer software, Playmobil sets, and the Dinkytown Day Care kids play set.

Bo Peep Productions
P.O. Box 982
Eureka, MT 59917
(800) 532-0420
A producer and distributor of fine early childhood educational videos.

Childswork/Childsplay
c/o Genesis Direct, Inc.
100 Plaza Drive
Secaucus, NJ 07094-3613
(800) 962-1141
A distributor of board games, children's books, posters, and resource materials that help children manage their feelings, learn nonviolent problem solving, and improve their social skills.

Constructive Playthings
1227 East 119th Street
Grandview, MO 64030-1117
(800) 448-4115
Fax: (816) 761-9295
A school supply company that includes a variety of multicultural materials. They offer posters, videos, art stencils, paint sponges, wooden figures of special needs children, flannel board sets, food sets, puzzles, and computer software.

Educational Activities Inc.
P.O. Box 87
Baldwin, NY 11510
(800) 645-3739
Fax: (516) 623-9282
A good source for a wide selection of
children's music and videos.

Educational Equity Concepts, Inc.
114 East 32 Street, Suite 701
New York, NY 10016
(212) 725-1803
Develops and distributes materials that
support nonsexist, gender-fair, and disability-
aware curriculum materials.

Educational Record Center
3233 Burnt Mill Drive, Suite 100
Wilmington, NC 28403
(800) 438-1637

Edvantage
5806 West 36th Street
St. Louis Park, MN 55416
(800) 966-1561
A school supply company that carries a wide
range of materials, including a set of feelings
puppets and flannel board sets.

Environments Inc.
P.O. Box 1348
Beaufort Industrial Park
Beaufort, SC 29901-1348
(800) EI CHILD
Fax: (800) EI Fax Us
The most beautiful school supply catalog.
Carries the best collections of animals and
environmental teaching materials. Also
carries great dress up clothes and fabric
banners for the classroom.

Gryphon House Inc.
P.O. Box 207
Beltsville, MD 20704-0207
(800) 638-0928
Fax: (301) 595-0051
E-mail: leah@ghbooks.com
Web site: www.ghbooks.com
A publisher and distributor of children's
books and curriculum books for teachers.
Staff carefully selects children's books for
both diversity and literary value.

J. L. Hammett Company
Hoovers Brothers
2050 Postal Way
Dallas, TX 75212
(800) 333-4600

Kaplan School Supply
Box 609
Lewisville, NC 27023
(800) 334-2014
A school supply catalog that includes a
number of multicultural materials, including
holiday videos, puzzles, and painting
sponges. Great puzzle sets of children with
special needs and wooden barns and silos.
Some of their multicultural kits tend to be
stereotypic.

Kimbo Educational
P.O. Box 477
Long Branch, NJ 07740-0477
(800) 631-2187
Fax: (732) 870-3340
A wide selection of children's music and videos.

Knowledge Unlimited
P.O. Box 52
Madison, WI 53701-0052
(800) 356-2303
Fax: (608) 831-1570
A good source for educational resource mate-
rials such as books and posters. They carry an
Arabic alphabet poster that I haven't seen
anywhere else.

Lakeshore Learning Materials
P.O. Box 6261
2695 East Dominguez Street
Carson, CA 90749
(800) 421-5354
Fax: (310) 537-5403
A school supply catalog that has one of the
best collections of multicultural materials
available. Actively seeks teachers' ideas and
consistently develops new materials. Look for
poster packs, anatomically correct baby dolls,
multiethnic school dolls, Children of America
doll puppets, block play people, multiethnic
cooking sets, flannel board sets, and skin-
colored art materials.

Lee & Low Books
95 Madison Avenue, Room 606
New York, New York 10016
(212) 779-4400
Fax: (212) 683-1894
A small publisher of outstanding multi-cultural children's books featuring authors and illustrators of color.

mpi School and Instructional Supplies
P.O. Box 24155/1200 Keystone Avenue
Lansing, MI 48909-4155
(800) 444-1773
Fax: (517) 393-8884
Web site: www.mpi-ts.com

Nasco
901 Janesville Avenue
Fort Atkinson, WI 53538-0901
(800) 558-9595
Fax: (920) 563-8296
E-mail: info@nascofa.com
Web site: www.nascofa.com
A school supply company that carries a wide assortment of materials. Good science resources, pretend food for dramatic play, teaching charts, and career block play people.

National Association for the Education of Young Children (NAEYC)
1509 16th Street NW
Washington, DC 20036-1426
(800) 424-2460, ext. 633
Fax: (202) 328-1846
E-mail: naeychq@naeyc.org
Web site: www.naeyc.org/naeyc
The largest professional organization for early childhood educators. Their catalog contains excellent posters, a car safety teaching kit, and Week of the Young Child resources. Shipping is slow so order early.

National Black Child Development Institute
1023 15th Street NW, Suite 600
Washington, DC 20005
(800) 556-2234
Fax: (202) 234-1738
E-mail: moreinfo@nbcdi.org
Web site: www.nbcdi.org
A professional organization promoting the well-being of Black children in America. Some lovely posters are available through their catalog.

New Moon
P.O. Box 3620
Duluth, MN 55803-3620
(218) 728-5507
Fax: (218) 728-0314
Web site: www.newmoon.org
A magazine for preadolescent girls started and published by girls. Also offers colorful posters for the early childhood classroom.

Northern Sun Merchandising
2916 East Lake Street
Minneapolis, MN 55406-2065
(800) 258-8579
Fax: (612) 729-0149
Web site: www.northernsun.com
A supplier of posters, buttons, and T shirts that support social causes. They always carry a few posters and materials for early child-hood classrooms.

Northland Poster Collective
P.O. Box 7096
Minneapolis, MN 55407
(800) 627-3082
Web site: www.northlandposter.com
A good source for worker and labor move-ment posters.

The Olive Press
5727 Dunmore
West Bloomfield, MI 48322
(248) 855-6063
(800) 797-5002
A catalog of wonderful multicultural chil-dren's books hand-picked by an early child-hood educator.

Organization for Equal Education of the Sexes Inc.
P.O. Box 438
Blue Hill, ME 04614-0438
(207) 374-2489
Fax: (207) 374-5350
Posters and resource materials that promote nonsexist education.

Parent's Choice
Box 185
Waban, MA 02168
A newsletter that reviews all types of early childhood materials. A great way to stay abreast of the newest and brightest in toys, books, and music.

People of Every Stripe!
P.O. Box 12505
Portland, OR 97212
(800) 282-0612
Fax: (503) 282-0615
E-mail: people@teleport.com
Web site: www.teleport.com/~people
One of my favorite companies. This small, family-owned business makes cloth dolls with hand-painted faces and lifelike hair. The collection includes dolls with visual, hearing, and mobility impairments, as well as dolls representing friends and elders. Send them a photograph of somebody and they'll make a special doll to match the person.

The People's Publishing Group Inc.
230 West Passaic Street
Maywood, NJ 07607
(800) 822-1080
Fax: (201) 712-0045
A resource for multicultural children's books and resource books for teachers.

Pueblo To People
2105 Silber Road, Suite 101-80
Houston, TX 77055
(800) 843-5257
A catalog company that sells crafts, fabric, toys, and clothing made by the indigenous peoples of Central America.

Roots and Wings
P.O. Box 19678
Boulder, CO 80308-2678
(800) 833-1787
Fax: (303) 776-6090
A good catalog of multicultural children's books.

Sandy and Son Educational Supplies
1360 Cambridge Street
Cambridge, MA 02139
(800) 841-7529
Fax: (617) 491-6821
A supply company that carries quality resources that are multicultural and inclusive. They have multicultural growth charts, posters, classroom pet puppets, and wooden puzzle sets.

Scholastic Inc.
P.O. Box 7502
Jefferson City, MO 65102
(800) 724-6527
Fax: (573) 635-5881

Scott Foresman/Addison-Wesley Publishing Company
School Services
One Jacob Way
Reading, MA 01867
(800) 552-2259
Fax: (800) 333-3328
Web site: www.sf.aw.com

SRA
220 East Danieldale Road
Desoto, TX 75115
(888) 772-4543

The Story Teller Inc.
P.O. Box 921
Salem, UT 84653
(800) 801-6860
A producer and distributor of flannel board sets.

Syracuse Cultural Workers
P.O. Box 6367
Syracuse, NY 13217
(315) 474-1132

Time Life Education
P.O. Box 85026
Richmond, VA 23285-5026
(800) 449-2010
Fax: (800) 449-2011
Web site: www.timelifeedu.com

UNICEF
United Nations Children's Fund
P.O. Box 182233
Chattanooga, TN 37422
(800) 553-1200

West Music
P.O. Box 5521
Coralville, IA 52241
(800) 397-9378
Fax: (888) 470-3942
A source for music-related materials. Carries a wide selection of classroom instruments, drums, and recordings of children's music.

Resource Books

* — Multicultural/Anti-Bias Curriculum Books

Adcock, D., and M. Segal. *Play Together, Grow Together: A Cooperative Curriculum for Teachers of Young Children* (White Plains, NY: The Mailman Family, 1983).

Althouse, Rosemary, and Cecil Main. *Science Experiences for Young Children* (New York: Teachers College, 1975).

*Baily, Cindy. *Start-Up Multiculturalism: Integrate the Canadian Cultural Reality in Your Classroom* (Markham, Ontario, Canada: Pembroke, 1991).

*Baker, Gwendolyn C. *Planning and Organizing for Multicultural Instruction* (Reading, MA: Addison-Wesley, 1983).

*Banks, James A. *An Introduction to Multicultural Education* (Boston: Allyn, 1994).

*Banks, James A., and Cherry A. McGee Banks. *Multicultural Education: Issues and Perspectives* (Boston: Allyn, 1989).

*Banks, James A. *Multiethnic Education: Theory and Practice*, 2nd ed. (Boston: Allyn, 1988).

Baratta-Lorton, Mary. *Workjobs* (Reading, MA: Addison-Wesley, 1992).

*Berman, Sheldon, and Phyllis La Farge, eds. *Promising Practices in Teaching for Social Responsibility* (Albany, NY: SUNY Press, 1993).

*Bisson, Julie. *Celebrate! An Anti-Bias Guide to Enjoying Holidays in Early Childhood Programs* (St. Paul: Redleaf, 1997).

Bittinger, Gayle. *Learning and Caring About Our World* (Everett, WA: Totline, 1990).

Brick, Peggy, et al. *Bodies, Birth, and Babies: Sexuality Education in Early Childhood Programs* (Hackensack, NJ: The Center for Family Life Education Planned Parenthood of Bergen County, 1989).

*Byrnes, Deborah A., and Gary Kiger, eds. *Common Bonds: Anti-Bias Teaching in a Diverse Society* (Wheaton, MD: Association for Childhood Education International, 1992).

*Byrnes, Deborah A. "Teacher, They Called Me a _____!" *Prejudice and Discrimination in the Classroom* (New York: Anti-Defamation League of B'nai B'rith, 1987).

Carlson, Laurie. *Kids Create!* (Charlotte, VT: Williamson, 1990).

*Carroll, Jeri A., and Dennis J. Kear. *A Multicultural Guide to Thematic Units for Young Children* (Carthage, IL: Good Apple, 1993).

*Chandler, P. A. *A Place for Me: Including Children with Special Needs in Early Care and Education Settings* (Washington, DC: NAEYC, 1994).

*Chang, Heddy Nai-Lin. *Affirming Children's Roots: Cultural and Linguistic Diversity in Early Care and Education* (San Francisco: California Tomorrow, 1993).

Charlesworth, Rosalind. *Experiences in Math for Young Children*, 3rd ed. (Albany, NY: Delmar, 1996).

Charner, Kathy, ed. *The Giant Encyclopedia of Circle Time and Group Activities for Children 3 to 6* (Beltsville, MD: Gryphon, 1996).

*Chech, Maureen. *Globalchild: Multicultural Resources for Young Children* (Reading, MA: Addison-Wesley, 1991).

*Chud, Gyda, and Ruth Fahlman. *Early Childhood Education for a Multicultural Society* (British Columbia: Pacific Educational, 1985).

Colwell, Lida C. *Jump to Learn: Teaching Motor Skills for Self-Esteem* (San Diego: Pennant, 1975).

*Crawford, Susan Hoy. *Beyond Dolls and Guns: 101 Ways to Help Children Avoid Gender Bias* (Portsmouth, NH: Heinemann, 1996).

Cromwell, Liz, and Dixie Hibner. *Finger Frolics* (Livonia, MI: Partner, 1976).

Curtis, Sandra R. *The Joy of Movement in Early Childhood* (New York: Teachers College, 1982).

Cutting, Beth J., and Ann Lovrien. *Parenting with a Global Perspective* (St. Paul: Vocational Consumer and Family Education Network, Minnesota State Board of Vocational Technical Education, 1986).

*Derman-Sparks, Louise, and the ABC Task Force. *Anti-Bias Curriculum: Tools for Empowering Young Children* (Washington, DC: NAEYC, 1989).

*Derman-Sparks, Louise, and Dorothy Granger. *Deepening Our Understanding of Anti-Bias Education for Children: An Anthology of Readings* (Pasadena: Pacific Oaks College, n.d.).

*Derman-Sparks, Louise. "Reaching Potentials Through Anti-Bias, Multicultural Curriculum." *Reaching Potentials: Appropriate Curriculum and Assessment for Young Children*. Eds. Sue Bredekamp and Teresa Rosegrant, vol. 1. (Washington, DC: NAEYC, 1992).

Edwards, Carolyn Pope. *Social and Moral Development in Young Children* (New York: Teachers College, 1986).

*Fleisher, P. *Changing Our World: A Handbook for Young Activists* (Tucson, AZ: Zephyr, 1992).

*Fralick, Paul. *Make It Multicultural—Musical Activities for Early Childhood Education* (Hamilton, Ontario, Canada: Mohawk College, 1989).

*Froschl, M., et al. *Including All of Us: An Early Childhood Curriculum About Disability* (New York: Educational Equity Concepts, 1984).

*Gaeme, J., and R. Falham. *Hand in Hand: Multicultural Experiences for Young Children* (Reading, MA: Addison-Wesley, 1990).

Gikow, Louise. *For Every Child, A Better World*. by Kermit the Frog, in cooperation with the United Nations, as told to Louise Gikow and Ellen Weiss (New York: Golden Books, Western Publishing, 1993).

*Grant, Carl A., and Christine E. Sleeter. *Turning on Learning: Five Approaches for Multicultural Teaching Plans for Race, Class, Gender, and Disability* (Columbus, OH: Merrill, 1989).

Green, Moira D. *474 Science Activities for Young Children* (Albany, NY: Delmar, 1996).

*Guillean, A., ed. *A World of Difference: A Preschool Activity Guide to Celebrate Diversity and Combat Prejudice* (New York: Anti-Defamation League of B'nai B'rith, 1991).

*Hall, Nadia Saderman, and Valerie Rhomberg. *The Affective Curriculum Teaching: The Anti-Bias Approach to Young Children* (Toronto: Nelson Canada, 1995).

Harrison, Marta. *For the Fun of It! Selected Cooperative Games for Children and Adults* (Philadelphia: Philadelphia Yearly Meeting of the Religious Society of Friends—Peace Committee, 1975).

*Hernández, Hilda. *Multicultural Education: A Teacher's Guide to Content and Process* (Columbus, OH: Merrill, 1989).

Herr, Judy, and Yvonne Libby. *Creative Resources for the Early Childhood Classroom*, 2nd ed. (Albany, NY: Delmar, 1995).

*Hoose, Phillip. *It's Our World Too! Stories of Young People Who Are Making a Difference* (Boston: Little Brown, 1993).

*Hopkins, Susan, and Jeffry Winters. *Discover the World: Empowering Children to Value Themselves, Others and the Earth* (Gabriola Island, Canada: New Society, 1990).

*The Human Rights for Children Committee. *Human Rights for Children: A Curriculum for Teaching Human Rights to Children Ages 3–12* (Alameda, CA: Hunter, 1992).

Janke, Rebecca Ann, and Julie Penshorn Peterson. *Peacemaker's A, B, Cs for Young Children: A Guide for Teaching Conflict Resolution with a Peace Table* (Marine-on-St. Croix, MN: Growing Communities for Peace, 1995).

Jenkins, Peggy. *The Joyful Child: A Sourcebook of Activities and Ideas for Releasing Children's Natural Joy* (Tucson, AZ: Harbinger, 1989).

Judson, Stephanie, ed. *A Manual on Non-violence and Children* (Gabriola Island, Canada: New Society, 1977).

*Kendall, Frances E. *Diversity in the Classroom* (New York: Teachers College, 1983).

*King, Edith W., Marilyn Chipman, and Marta Cruz-Janzen. *Educating Young Children in a Diverse Society* (Boston: Allyn, 1994).

Kissinger, Katie. *All the Colors We Are* (St. Paul: Redleaf, 1994).

Kohl, MaryAnn, and Cindy Gainer. *Good Earth Art: Environmental Art for Kids* (Bellingham, WA: Bright Ring, 1991).

Kohl, MaryAnn, and Jean Potter. *Science Arts: Discovering Science Through Art Experiences* (Bellingham, WA: Bright Ring, 1993).

Kohl, MaryAnn. *Scribble Cookies* (Bellingham, WA: Bright Ring, 1985).

Koskie, Beth, and Jacqui Schafer. *Anti-Biased Curriculum: Teaching Young Children About Native Americans* (Minneapolis: Greater Minneapolis Day Care Association, 1987).

*Kubat, Patricia, et al. *Teaching Young Children About African-Americans* (Minneapolis: Greater Minneapolis Day Care Association, 1990).

*Lewis, Barbara A. *The Kid's Guide to Service Projects* (Minneapolis: Free Spirit, 1995).

*———. *The Kid's Guide to Social Action* (Minneapolis: Free Spirit, 1991).

*Mallory, Bruce, and Rebecca S. New. *Diversity and Developmentally Appropriate Practices: Challenges for Early Childhood Education* (New York: Teachers College, 1994).

Marotz, Lynn R., et al. *Health, Safety, and Nutrition for Young Children*, 4th ed. (Albany, NY: Delmar, 1997).

*Mattiella, Ana Consuela. *The Multicultural Caterpillar: Children's Activities in Cultural Awareness* (Santa Cruz: Network, 1990).

*———. *Positively Different: Creating a Bias-Free Environment for Young Children* (Santa Cruz: Network, 1991).

*McCaleb, Sudia Paloma. *Building Communities of Learners: A Collaboration Among Teachers, Students, Families, and Community* (New York: St. Martin's, 1994).

*McCracken, Janet Brown, ed. *Helping Children Love Themselves and Others: A Professional Handbook for Family Day Care* (Washington, DC: The Children's Foundation, 1990).

*McCracken, Janet Brown. *Valuing Diversity: The Primary Years* (Washington, DC: NAEYC, 1993).

McGinnis, Kathleen, and Barbara Oehlberg. *Starting Out Right: Nurturing Young Children as Peacemakers* (Oak Park, IL: Meyer Stone, 1988).

Meyer, Carolyn, and Kel Pickens. *Sing and Learn* (Carthage, IL: Good Apple, 1989).

*Miller, Darla Ferris. *First Steps Toward Cultural Difference* (Washington, DC: Child Welfare League of America, 1989).

*Moll, Patricia Buerke. *Children and Books I: African American Story Books and Activities for All Children* (Tampa: Hampton Mae Institute, 1991).

*Neugebauer, Bonnie, ed. *Alike and Different: Exploring Our Humanity with Young Children* (Washington, DC: NAEYC, 1992).

Neuman, Susan B., and Renee P. Panoff. *Exploring Feelings: Activities for Young Children* (Atlanta: Humanics Limited, 1983).

Nichols, Wendy, and Kim Nichols. *Wonderscience: A Developmentally Appropriate Guide to Hands On Science for Young Children* (Albuquerque: Learning Expo, 1990).

Nickelsburg, Janet. *Nature Activities for Early Childhood* (Reading, MA: Addison-Wesley, 1976).

*Nieto, Sonia. *Affirming Diversity: The Sociopolitical Context of Multicultural Education* (New York: Longman, 1992).

Oehlberg, Barbara. *Making It Better: Activities for Children Living in a Stressful World* (St. Paul: Redleaf, 1996).

Oppenheim, Carol. *Science Is Fun! For Families and Classroom Groups* (St. Louis: Cracom, 1993).

Orlick, Terry. *The Cooperative Sports & Games Book* (New York: Pantheon, 1978).

———. *The Second Cooperative Sports & Games Book* (New York: Pantheon, 1982).

Park, Mary Joan. *Peacemaking for Little Friends* (St. Paul: Little Friends For Peace, 1985).

*Parker, Carol Johnson. "Multicultural Awareness Activities." *Dimensions* 10 (1982).

*Perry, Theresa, and James W. Fraser. *Freedom's Plow: Teaching in the Multicultural Classroom* (New York: Routledge, 1993).

*Peterson, Bob. "Columbus in the Elementary Classroom." *Rethinking Columbus: Teaching About the 500th Anniversary of Columbus's Arrival in America* (Milwaukee: Rethinking Schools, 1991).

*Prutzman, Priscilla, et al. *The Friendly Classroom for a Small Planet* (Gabriola Island, Canada: New Society, 1988).

*———. *The Friendly Classroom for a Small Planet: A Handbook on Creative Approaches to Living and Problem Solving for Children* (Gabriola Island, Canada: New Society, 1987).

*Ramsey, Patricia G. "Social Studies That Is Multicultural." *Multicultural Education in Early Childhood Classrooms* (Washington, DC: National Education Association of the United States, 1992).

*————. *Teaching and Learning in a Diverse World* (New York: Teachers College, 1987).

Redleaf, Rhoda. *Busy Finger Growing Minds: Finger Plays, Verses and Activities for Whole Language Learning* (St. Paul: Redleaf, 1993).

Rice, Judith Anne. *The Kindness Curriculum: Introducing Young Children to Loving Values* (St. Paul: Redleaf, 1995).

Rocha, Ruth, and Otavio Roth. *The Universal Declaration of Human Rights: An Adaptation for Children* (New York: United Nations Publications, 1989).

Rockwell, Robert E., et al. *Everybody Has a Body* (Beltsville, MD: Gryphon, 1992).

*Saracho, Olivia N., and Bernard Spodek. *Understanding the Multicultural Experience in Early Childhood Education* (Washington, DC: NAEYC, 1983).

Slaby, Ronald G., et al. *Early Violence Prevention Tools for Teachers of Young Children* (Washington, DC: NAEYC, 1995).

*Sleeter, Christine E., ed. *Empowerment through Multicultural Education* (Albany: State U of New York, 1991).

*Sleeter, Christine E., and Carl A. Grant. *Making Choices for Multicultural Education: Five Approaches to Race, Class, and Gender* (Columbus, OH: Merrill, 1988).

Smith, Charles A. *The Peaceful Classroom* (Beltsville, MD: Gryphon, 1993).

————. *Promoting the Social Development of Young Children: Strategies and Activities* (Palo Alto, CA: Mayfield, 1982).

*Sprung, B. *Non-Sexist Education for Young Children: A Practical Guide* (New York: Citation, 1975).

Sunal, Cynthia. *Early Childhood Social Studies* (Columbus, OH: Merrill, 1990).

*Turney, Monica. *One World Many Children: A Multicultural Program for Early Childhood Education* (Compton, CA: Santillana/Smithsonian, 1994).

*United Nations Association of Minnesota. *WE: Lessons on Equal Worth and Dignity, the United Nations, and Human Rights.*

(Minneapolis: United Nations Association of Minnesota, n.d.).

*Vold, Edwina Battle, ed. *Multicultural Education in Early Childhood Classrooms* (Washington, DC: National Education Association of the United States, 1992).

Wade, Rahima Carol. *Joining Hands: From Personal to Planetary Friendship in the Primary Classroom* (Tucson, AZ: Zephyr, 1991).

Walters, Connie, and Diane Totten. *Sing a Song All Year Long* (Minneapolis: Denison, 1991).

Warren, Jean. *Piggyback Songs for School* (Everett, WA: Warren, 1991).

*Wichert, S. *Keeping the Peace: Practicing Cooperation and Conflict Resolution with Preschoolers* (Gabriola Island, Canada: New Society, 1989).

*Williams, Leslie R., and Yvonne DeGaetano. *ALERTA: A Multicultural, Bilingual Approach to Teaching Young Children* (Reading, MA: Addison-Wesley, 1985).

Williams, Robert A., et al. *Mudpies to Magnets: A Preschool Science Curriculum* (Beltsville, MD: Gryphon, 1987).

*York, Stacey. *Developing Roots and Wings: A Trainer's Guide to Affirming Culture in Early Childhood Programs* (St. Paul: Redleaf, 1992).

*————. *Roots and Wings: Affirming Culture in Early Childhood Programs* (St. Paul: Redleaf, 1991).

Magazines

Early Childhood Today
Scholastic Incorporated
P.O. Box 54813
Boulder, CO 80323-4813
(800) 544-2917

Multicultural Education
Caddo Gap Press
3145 Geary Boulevard, Suite 275
San Francisco, CA 94118
(415) 750-9978

Rethinking Schools
1001 East Keefe Avenue
Milwaukee, WI 53212
(414) 964-9646

Teaching Tolerance
400 Washington Avenue
Montgomery, AL 36104

Young Children
National Association for the Education of
Young Children (NAEYC)
1509 16th Street NW
Washington, DC 20036-1426
(800) 424-2460
Fax: (202) 328-1846
E-mail: naeychq@naeyc.org
Web site: www.naeyc.org/naeyc

Organizations

Anti-Defamation League
823 United Nations Plaza
New York, NY 10017
(212) 490-2525

**Association for Childhood Education
International**
17904 Georgia Avenue, Suite 215
Olney, MD 20832
(800) 423-3563

**Council for Exceptional Children,
Division for Early Childhood**
1920 Association Drive
Reston, VA 22901-1589
(703) 620-3660

**Culturally Relevant/Anti-Bias Education
Leadership Project**
Pacific Oaks College
5 Westmoreland Place
Pasadena, CA 91103

Educational Equity Concepts
114 E. 32nd Street
3rd Floor, Room 306
New York, NY 10016

National Association for Family Day Care
725 15th Street NW, Suite 505
Washington, DC 20005

**National Association for Multicultural
Education (NAME)**
1511 K Street NW, Suite 430
Washington, DC 20005

**National Association for the Education of
Young Children (NAEYC)**
1509 16th Street NW
Washington, DC 20036-1426
(800) 424-2460, ext. 633
Fax: (202) 328-1846
E-mail: naeychq@naeyc.org
Web site: www.naeyc.org/naeyc

**National Black Child Development
Institute**
1023 15th Street NW, Suite 600
Washington, DC 20005
(800) 556-2234
Fax: (202) 234-1738
E-mail: moreinfo@nbcdi.org
Web site: www.nbcdi.org

**National Information Center for Children
and Youth with Disabilities**
1233 20th Street NW
Washington, DC 20036

**Southern Poverty Law Center/Teaching
Tolerance Magazine**
400 Washington Avenue
Montgomery, AL 36104

Women's Action Alliance Inc.
370 Lexington Avenue
New York, NY 10017

Children's Music

Allen, Lillian. *Nothing But A Hero* (Redwood, 1991).

Bonkrude, Sally. *Celebrating Differences With Sally B* (Musical Imaginings, 1992).

The Children of Selma. *Who Will Speak For The Children?* (Rounder, 1987).

Fiesta Musical, with Emilio Delgado (Music For Little People, 1994).

Fink, Cathy, and Marcy Marxer. *Nobody Else Like Me* (A&M, 1994).

Grammer, Red. *Hello World!* (Smilin' Atcha, 1995).

————. *Teaching Peace* (Smilin' Atcha, 1986).

Harley, Bill. *I'm Gonna Let It Shine* (Rounder, 1990).

Hartmann, Jack. *Let's Read Together and Other Songs for Sharing and Caring* (Educational Activities, 1991).

———. *Make a Friend, Be a Friend* (Educational Activities, 1990).

———. *One Voice For Children* (Educational Activities, 1990).

Hunter, Tom. *Bits and Pieces* (Song Growing Company, 1990).

———. *Connections* (Song Growing, 1994).

Lefranc, Barbara. *I Can Be Anything I Want To Be* (Doubar, 1990).

Music For Little People. *Peace Is The World Smiling* (Music for Little People, 1989).

Pirtle, Sarah. *Two Hands Hold The Earth* (Gentle Wind, 1984).

Positively Reggae (Sony, 1994).

Raffi. *Baby Beluga* (Troubadour, 1980).

———. *Corner Grocery Store* (Troubadour, 1979).

———. *Everything Grows* (Troubadour, 1987).

———. *More Singable Songs* (Troubadour, 1977).

———. *One Light, One Sun* (Troubadour, 1983).

———. *Rise and Shine* (Troubadour, 1982).

———. *Singable Songs for the Very Young* (Troubadour, 1976).

Rogers, Sally. *Peace By Peace* (Western, 1988).

Seeger, Pete. *Abiyoyo and Other Story Songs for Children* (Folkways, 1958).

Sweet Honey In The Rock. *All For Freedom* (Music For Little People, 1989).

Sweet Honey In The Rock. *I Got Shoes* (Music For Little People, 1994).

Thomas, Marlo, and Friends. *Free To Be…A Family* (A&M Records, 1988).

Tune Into Kids. *Color the World* (Endeavor Music, 1992).

Turney, Monica. *One World Many Children: A Multicultural Program for Early Childhood Education.* (Santillana/Smithsonian, 1994).

Vitamin L. *Walk A Mile* (Lovable Creature, 1989).

Appendix A:

CURRICULUM GOALS AND OBJECTIVES

The four goals of a multicultural/anti-bias education are made more concrete through the use of objectives. On the following pages are listed the goals and objectives of a transformative curriculum.

GOAL 1

Foster each child's positive, knowledgeable, and confident self-identity within a cultural context.

OBJECTIVES

- recognize and celebrate own physical features
- recognize and celebrate own home language
- recognize and celebrate own dress
- recognize and celebrate own diet and style of eating
- recognize and celebrate own family
- recognize and celebrate own name
- identify the meaning of one's name
- identify own culture
- identify own cultural traditions and customs
- appreciate own cultural heritage
- recognize the concept of homelands
- recognize and use one's home language
- experience self-worth
- believe in one's strengths and abilities
- recognize one's beauty
- experience dignity and pride
- set high expectations for oneself
- feel special and unique
- accept one's cultural identity
- use positive, descriptive language to describe one's physical features
- identify with one's culture
- recognize own family's celebrations
- share own family's celebrations with others
- share own cultural experiences with others
- learn about role models within one's culture
- believe in oneself
- feel valued
- experience an opportunity to contribute to classroom life

GOAL 2

Foster each child's comfortable, empathetic interaction with diversity among people.

OBJECTIVES

- appreciate the beauty and value of others
- accept others
- appreciate physical characteristics of others
- learn about similarities and differences
- appreciate people who are different
- experience positive, respectful interactions with people who are different from oneself
- recognize that people have the same basic needs
- recognize that people have different lifestyles
- develop positive attitudes toward human differences
- understand that all people are similar to and different from one another
- recognize that people do things in different ways
- recognize that human differences make people unique and special
- recognize that our community is made up of many different types of people
- name some of the cultural groups that make up the United States
- recognize own culture within the United States
- understand that all people deserve respect
- show respect to all people
- feel empathy for others
- learn about the cultures of the other children in the class
- notice another's point of view
- recognize ways people grow and change
- increase ability to cope with change
- develop an open, flexible attitude toward change
- develop openness to new experiences
- learn the names of their classmates
- pronounce the names of their classmates correctly
- experience human diversity
- increase comfort with human diversity
- learn about leaders from diverse cultural groups
- recognize the contributions from all cultural groups

Goal 3

Foster each child's critical thinking about bias.

Objectives

- learn about stereotypes
- begin to recognize stereotypes
- compare real and pretend
- learn about the concept of prejudice
- recognize that some people are afraid of others
- recognize that some people have misconceptions about others
- recognize that some people treat others unfairly because of differences
- understand that unfair treatment because of differences is wrong
- compare respectful and disrespectful behavior
- learn about the concept of fair and unfair behavior
- recognize unfair behavior when it occurs
- compare fair and unfair
- recognize that name-calling hurts others
- resist name-calling
- recognize that teasing others hurts
- resist teasing
- recognize who is left out and who is included
- recognize that rejecting others hurts
- explore why people are discriminated against
- think of ways to respond to discrimination
- resist rejecting others
- put self in other person's situation
- learn to think before acting
- learn about human rights
- show a concern about people's well-being
- show concern for people in our community
- learn about the importance of doing something about discrimination
- recognize one's misconceptions about human diversity
- learn simple, truthful information about human diversity
- recognize importance of not making judgments based on appearance
- recognize that people within a group are not all alike
- think for oneself
- practice distinguishing right from wrong

GOAL 4

Foster each child's ability to stand up for himself or herself and others in the face of bias.

OBJECTIVES

- stand up for self
- stand up for another person
- positively contribute to the classroom
- positively contribute to the community
- recognize that people can work together to help one another
- develop conflict resolution skills
- develop a sense of personal social responsibility
- cooperate with others
- relate values and principles to action
- develop a sense of responsibility to oneself
- develop a sense of responsibility to one's family
- develop a sense of responsibility to one's culture
- develop a sense of responsibility to one's community
- seek protection from harm
- seek adult assistance in case of mistreatment
- take action against bias
- participate as a group member
- participate in group decision making
- generate solutions to problems
- experience nonviolent conflict resolution
- experience working cooperatively with others
- coordinate actions with others to accomplish a shared goal
- recognize human rights

GOAL 5

Foster each child's healthy social and emotional development.

OBJECTIVES

- recognize emotions
- describe own emotions
- express emotions appropriately
- show sensitivity to the emotions of others
- initiate friendships
- maintain friendship
- attract and hold the attention of others
- lead and follow peers
- cooperate with others
- offer, accept, and request generosity
- offer, accept, and request help
- offer, accept, and request sharing
- offer, accept, and request affirmation
- differentiate between an accident and "on purpose"
- differentiate between right and wrong
- respect authority
- recognize rules
- respect rules
- know appropriate ways to protest rules
- participate as a group member
- set high expectations for oneself
- try new things
- believe in oneself
- demonstrate trust
- demonstrate initiative
- demonstrate honesty
- experience joy
- take turns
- identify classmates by name
- greet and welcome others
- invite others into play
- cope with frustration and disappointment
- share with others

GOAL 6

Foster children's cognitive development.

OBJECTIVES

- be aware of numbers
- count by rote
- count logically
- measure people and objects
- match
- classify
- sequence and order objects and events
- recognize shapes
- describe spatial relationships
- observe changes over time
- estimate
- use graphs
- participate in problem solving
- use all one's senses to learn about the world
- experience situations from different points of view
- observe changes and transformations
- recognize cause and effect
- evaluate the result of cause and effect
- predict possible outcomes
- examine alternatives
- think about consequences
- make choices
- use all senses to learn about the world
- observe natural materials
- describe the property of objects
- explore the natural world
- relate to animals
- care for animals
- care for plants
- care for the environment

GOAL 7

Foster children's language development.

- listen to others
- experience being listened to
- recognize voices
- notice differences in language
- learn new words
- label people, objects, and feelings
- use words to describe similarities and differences
- use words to acknowledge unfairness
- express self through words
- give and receive information
- participate in a conversation
- ask who, what, where, when, how, why, and how much questions
- answer questions with words
- explore printed materials
- listen to a story
- follow the sequence of a story
- retell a story
- recognize one's written name
- explore writing materials
- see one's words in writing

GOAL 8

Foster children's creative development.

OBJECTIVES

- express and develop creativity
- express self through art
- express self through music
- listen to instrumental music
- listen to songs
- sing songs
- create songs
- move body to music
- respond to rhythm with body
- recognize rhythmic patterns
- create rhythmic patterns
- explore simple instruments
- express self through movement
- express self through drama
- use imagination
- appreciate beauty
- explore and experiment with art media
- dance to music
- participate in pretend play

GOAL 9

Foster children's physical development.

- be aware of body in space
- develop kinesthetic awareness
- identify body parts
- discriminate left from right
- balance body
- develop and improve coordination
- move body in a variety of ways
- walk up and down steps
- climb on equipment
- run
- jump
- hop on one foot
- gallop/skip
- catch a ball
- throw a ball
- kick a ball
- pedal a tricycle
- put things together and take things apart
- manipulate objects and tools
- eye-hand coordination
- understand need for healthy bodies
- develop skill in caring for one's body
- identify health helpers
- learn how to keep oneself safe
- use tools and equipment safely
- practice safety procedures

Appendix B:

WORKSHEETS FOR DESIGNING YOUR OWN TRANSFORMATIVE CURRICULUM

Design Your Own Transformative Curriculum

STEP 1: CREATE A COLLABORATIVE CLIMATE

Ask yourself these questions:

1. Who is involved with the children at school?

2. Who is involved with the children at home?

3. Who is interested in working together over time to transform our curriculum?

4. How can we involve people who can't make a long-term commitment?

5. How do we involve people from outside the school?

6. What do we have in common as a working group? What are our differences?

7. What are our goals for the curriculum? How would we like it to change? What would be the end result if it did? What would that look like, feel like, sound like, smell like?

Design Your Own Transformative Curriculum

STEP 2: LEARN ABOUT THE CONTEXT

Get to Know the Community

Here are questions to help you start your investigation. Take the time to answer them thoroughly, and include the perspectives of all the different segments of your community.

1. Where is our community located?

2. What type of community is it? How would I describe our community to an outsider?

3. What is the history of our community?

4. How is our community changing?

5. How is our community portrayed in the media?

6. What are the natural resources in our community?

7. How do people make a living in our community?

8. What do people do for recreation in our community?

9. What community issues are parents and children concerned about?

10. What are the threats to people's health in our community?

11. What are the prevailing stereotypes in our community?

12. What are the conflicts, controversies, or ongoing tensions in our community?

Get to Know the Families

Use these questions to explore the lives of the families in your program. You might use these as the basis for interviewing each family, or make them into a questionnaire.

1. What is most important for your family?

2. What are the obstacles and challenges facing your family?

3. What values do you want your child to learn?

4. How do you maintain closeness within your family?

5. What are your expectations of your child?

6. What are ways you support and encourage your child?

7. How do you show pride in your child's accomplishments?

8. What do you want from our program for your child?

9. What changes do you want to make in your child's life?

10. What are the ethnic origins of your family?

11. What language(s) are spoken in your home?

12. If you speak a language other than English, how do you plan to maintain your home language?

13. What are some activities your family does together?

14. What are important rites and rituals in your family?

15. What other cultural traditions does your family practice?

Get to Know the Children

1. Watch children play.

2. Listen to their conversations.

3. Ask them open-ended questions.

4. Conduct diagnostic activities.

Design Your Own Transformative Curriculum

STEP 3: IDENTIFY THE THEMES

1. What are the children interested in?

2. What are they curious about?

3. What are they passionate about?

4. What do the parents want their children to know about?

5. What do you want children to know about?

6. What topics need to be introduced so children can be competent?

7. What topics lend themselves to creating strong ties between families and school?

8. What topics would strengthen children's connection to their home culture?

Design Your Own Transformative Curriculum

STEP 4: WEBBING THE UNIT

Questions to achieve the first goal of a multicultural/anti-bias education (positive and knowledgeable self-identity within a cultural context). See figure 2 in part 2 for an example of how to use these questions.

1. Who?

2. What?

3. Where?

4. When?

5. Why?

6. How?

7. How much? How many?

Questions to achieve the second goal of a multicultural/anti-bias education (comfortable empathetic interaction with diversity among people).

1. What are all the different kinds of…?

2. How are they similar to one another? How are they different from one another?

3. How do they stay the same? Who do they change?

Questions to achieve the third goal of a multicultural/anti-bias education (critical thinking about bias).

1. What is real? What is pretend?

2. What are stereotypes about…?

3. How can we work together to challenge the stereotypes?

Questions to achieve the fourth goal of a multicultural/anti-bias education (the ability to stand up for oneself or others in the face of bias).

1. What are people's wants and needs?

2. Who doesn't have what they need?

3. How can we work together to help people?

If you want to incorporate holidays or celebrations add the question "How can we celebrate…?"

Design Your Own Transformative Curriculum

STEP 6: IDENTIFY MATERIALS TO ADD TO THE ENVIRONMENT

Art

Blocks

Dramatic Play

Large Motor

Literacy

Manipulatives

Music

Science

Sensory

Design Your Own Transformative Curriculum

STEP 7: SELECT AND PLAN LEARNING EXPERIENCES

Investigating the Theme

Creative Development

Critical Thinking

Emotional Development

Health, Safety, and Nutrition

Language Development

Home Language

Math

Music

Physical Development

Science

Social Development

Affirming Ourselves and One Another

Human Rights

Cultural Identity

Diversity

Bias and Stereotypes

Community Service

Social Action Suggestions

Opening the Door

Classroom Visitors

Field Trips

Parent Involvement

Parent Education

Design Your Own Transformative Curriculum

STEP 8: IDENTIFY CURRICULUM RESOURCES

Children's Books

Music

Visual Displays

Videos

Computer Software

Teaching Kits

Additional Resources

Appendix C:

CURRICULUM PLANNING FORM

Curriculum Planning Form

Theme _____

Week _____

	Monday	Tuesday	Wednesday	Thursday	Friday
Large Group					
Free Choice					
Small Group					
Large Group					

Art Area	Dramatic Play Area	Manipulatives
Block Area	Sensory Table	Science

INDEX

BIG AS LIFE

Also From Redleaf Press

All the Colors We Are: The Story of How We Get Our Skin Color - Outstanding full-color photographs showcase the beautiful diversity of human skin color and offers children a simple, accurate explanation of how we are the color we are.

Celebrate! An Anti-Bias Guide to Enjoying Holidays in Early Childhood Programs - Filled with strategies for implementing holidays that are exciting, not biased, and developmentally appropriate.

For the Love of Children: Daily Affirmations for People Who Care for Children - An empowering book filled with quotes, stories, and affirmations for each day of the year.

The Kindness Curriculum - Over 60 imaginative, exuberant activities that create opportunities for kids to practice kindness, empathy, conflict resolution, respect, and more.

Making It Better: Activities for Children Living in a Stressful World - This important book offers bold new information about the physical and emotional effects of stress, trauma, and violence on children today and gives teachers and caregivers the confidence to help children survive, thrive, and learn.

Reflecting Children's Lives: A Handbook for Planning Child-Centered Curriculum - A practical guide to help you put children and childhood at the center of your curriculum. Rethink and refresh your ideas about scheduling, observations, play, materials, space, and emergent themes.

Roots and Wings: Affirming Culture in Early Childhood Programs - A unique approach to multicultural education that helps shape positive attitudes toward cultural differences.

Developing Roots and Wings: A Trainer's Guide to Affirming Culture in Early Childhood Programs - Over 170 high-quality multicultural training activities and more than 50 handouts. Everything you need to offer excellent trainings.

Star Power for Preschoolers: Learning Life Skills Through Physical Play - More than 60 active games and movement activities that develop concentration, relaxation, cooperation, imagination, and self-esteem.

Training Teachers - Original strategies and training tools that bring a new approach to the how of teaching and also supports professional development.

Transition Magician - Over 200 original, fun activities that help you magically turn transition time into calm, smooth activity changes.

800-423-8309